CLAN, KING AND COVENANT

CLAN, KING AND COVENANT

History of the Highland Clans from the
Civil War to the Glencoe Massacre

John L. Roberts

EDINBURGH
University Press

© John L. Roberts, 2000

Edinburgh University Press
22 George Square, Edinburgh

Typeset in Bulmer
by Pioneer Associates, Perthshire, and
printed and bound in Great Britain by
Creative Print and Design, Ebbw Vale, Wales

A CIP record for this book is available from the
British Library

ISBN 0 7486 1393 5

The right of John L. Roberts to be identified as
author of this work has been asserted in accordance
with the Copyright, Designs and Patent Act (1988).

CONTENTS

ACKNOWLEDGEMENTS

I am grateful to the two referees whose comments on the original typescript I found very useful in revising the text. The book could not have been written without access to the libraries of the University of St Andrews, for which I am very grateful. I should like to thank Nicola Carr at Edinburgh University Press for her efficient and very supportive manner in seeing the book to press. I am also grateful to Clara Young for her help in finding a suitable picture for the cover. Finally, my thanks go to my wife Jessica. She not only made useful comments on the text, but was unfailing in her support and encouragement.

FOREWORD

Few events in the bloodstained history of the Highland clans have quite the dreadful resonance of the Glencoe Massacre, perpetrated in 1692 just two years after William of Orange had seized the throne of Great Britain from James VII of Scotland. As John Prebble comments in the introduction to his emotive account *Glencoe: The Story of the Massacre*, it was not just 'a bloody incident in a meaningless feud between Campbell and MacDonald . . . incidental to the political events of the time'. While other atrocities had occurred on a far greater scale during the course of Highland history without attracting such opprobrium, they had not been carried out so cynically as a matter of public policy by central government. Even at the time, the country was outraged by what was seen as the cold-blooded plotting of 'murder under trust'.

Chief among the King's ministers, and acting with his approval, was Sir John Dalrymple of Stair, Secretary of State for Scotland. It was his savage and vindictive orders that ended with the slaughter of nearly forty men, women, and children, in the early morning of 13 February 1692. How many others perished as they fled across the snow-covered passes into the surrounding glens remains unknown. But the circumstances were made far worse by the decision taken by the local commanders, whose regular troops of the standing army in Scotland carried out the massacre. By quartering their men upon their intended victims for almost a fortnight before the massacre itself, they ignored the elaborate code of military honour that still existed at the end of the seventeenth century, and by violating Highland traditions of hospitality, they were judged guilty of treacherous and utterly disreputable conduct.

Yet the Glencoe Massacre encapsulates in a microcosm the momentous events of the previous half-century. The seventeenth century in Scotland witnessed a bitter and protracted struggle between Church and Crown, which ended with the overthrow of a Catholic king in favour of the staunchly Protestant William of Orange, and the establishment of a national Church, governed by Presbyterian principles. The origins of such a struggle lay in the Scottish Reformation of 1560, which had rejected Papal authority over the established Church in favour of the Calvinist doctrines of John Knox. However, episcopacy was not abolished, and subsequently James VI succeeded in restoring the rule of bishops to the Reformed Church as a means of bolstering his own authority.

Once Charles I had succeeded James VI of Scotland on the throne of Great Britain in 1625, his autocratic rule almost inevitably brought about a crisis in the nation's affairs. It culminated in the signing of the National Covenant in 1638. Stubbornly refusing to abandon his belief in the Divine Right of Kings, Charles I by his own actions triggered a religious and political revolution. But many revolutions contain the seeds of their own destruction, and Scotland was no exception. Determined to establish God's kingdom on Earth, governed by the Elect, the more fanatical Presbyterians of the Kirk party pursued policies with a zealotry that would divide the country. Once the Civil War had broken out in England, the sense of divided loyalties became ever more acute, especially among the Scottish nobility, who still recognised their allegiance to the King. It was James Graham, fifth Earl and first Marquis of Montrose, who first broke with the Covenanters in rallying to the King's defence in 1643.

It was under Montrose's leadership that the Highland clans first emerged upon the national stage during the seventeenth century, driven by religious differences within the country. Before then, apart from the periodic forays made by the disaffected clans, especially against the lowlands of Moray and Ross, only the expedition of Donald, second Lord of the Isles, which ended at the battle of Harlaw in 1411, seriously threatened the stability of Scotland. Now, however, the group which later became known as the 'loyal clans' joined Montrose in a year of spectacular campaigning for Charles I, which only ended with his defeat at the battle of Philiphaugh in September 1645.

Yet while fighting under the Royalist standard, Montrose and the 'loyal clans' had a common enemy in Archibald Campbell, eighth Earl of Argyll, foremost among the leaders of the Kirk party in supporting the National Covenant. Indeed, the nucleus of Montrose's Highland army consisted of the MacDonalds of Antrim under the command of Alasdair MacDonald, who was arguably Montrose's equal as a military leader. Acting on behalf of Randal MacDonald, second Earl and first Marquis of Antrim, their chief objective in fighting for Charles I was the restoration of Clan Donald to their ancestral lands in Argyll, now held by the Campbells.

Once enlisted in the Royalist cause, nearly all the Highland clans who had fought for Montrose and Alasdair MacDonald remained loyal to the Stuarts. Except for the 'Engagement' of 1648, which ended in defeat at the battle of

Preston, the loyal clans took up arms once again during a whole series of Royalist campaigns over the next half-century – resisting Cromwell's occupation of Scotland during the 1650s, putting down Argyll's rebellion against James VII in 1685, and rising in arms under John Graham of Claverhouse, Viscount Dundee, after the overthrow of James VII in 1689 in what became known as the Highland War. The Glencoe Massacre marked the very end of the Highland War, but even so, the loyal clans still rallied to the Stuart cause after James VII had died in 1701, giving their armed support to the Jacobite rebellions of 1715, 1719, and 1745, fighting for the restoration of James Edward Stuart, the 'Old Pretender'.

Sites of battles fought during the seventeenth century involving the Highland clans

Chapter One

THE HIGHLANDS BEFORE 1625

The year 1625, when Charles I succeeded James VI of Scotland on to the throne of Great Britain, proved to be a turning-point in the history of the Highland clans. Provoked by his disastrous rule over the country, they were subsequently drawn into a century of nationwide conflict, and the Highlands were turned into a 'theatre of war'. Before the seventeenth century, the clans had rarely involved themselves in the national affairs of Scotland, except when they had answered the call to arms in defence of the kingdom. Even so, prior to 1625, they had been rather more likely to take advantage of the weakness of the Stewart dynasty (which became the Stuart dynasty in the 1500s) during its many periods of minority rule than to support it.

This was especially true of Clan Donald when it held the Lordship of the Isles in the fifteenth century. Acting almost as a kingdom within a kingdom, the Lords of the Isles were even prepared to side with Scotland's enemies, allying themselves with England. Indeed, they often acted with cynical expediency in pursuing what they saw as their own self-interest against the Scottish Crown. Such policies contained the seeds of their own destruction. It was the short-sighted alliance made in 1462 under the Treaty of Ardtornish by John MacDonald, fourth and last Lord of the Isles, with Edward IV of England that brought about his downfall. He first forfeited the earldom of Ross in 1475, when his act of treason was finally revealed to James III, and then in 1493 the Lordship of the Isles itself, when he could no longer control the warring factions within Clan Donald.

The Lordship of the Isles had brought peace and prosperity to the Highlands and Western Isles, despite repeated clashes with the Crown in the early fifteenth century. Its forfeiture ended what later came to be regarded as the golden age of Gaeldom with Clan Donald at its head, dating back to the twelfth century and the time of Somerled, King of the Isles. The 150 years after 1475 would be known instead as *Linn nan Creach*, or the Age of Feuds and Forays, as lawlessness became endemic throughout the Highlands and Western Isles.

Outbreak of Disorder

Indeed, Clan Donald struggled time and again after 1475 to regain first the earldom of Ross, and then the widespread lands of the Lordship itself. Already, it had split into several distinct septs or branches, whose chieftains traced their lineage back to successive Lords of the Isles, or to their more distant ancestors, so giving them a claim to the Lordship itself. Yet apart from the MacIains of Ardnamurchan, nearly all these septs rallied to Clan Donald in its repeated attempts to regain the Lordship of the Isles during the first half of the sixteenth century. Moreover, many of the vassal kindreds who gave their allegiance to Clan Donald in return for its protection, and especially the MacLeans of Duart and the MacLeods of Lewis, allied themselves with Clan Donald in its efforts to reassert its historic role as the headship of the Gael.

Even so, the death in 1545 of Donald Dubh, grandson of the fourth and last Lord of the Isles, while serving Henry VIII of England, brought not only the direct line of the Lords of the Isles to an end, but also ended any chance of Clan Donald regaining the lost glory of the Lordship. Afterwards, the Highlands and Western Isles became increasingly disturbed by the 'monstrous, deadly feuds' waged between the Highland clans as they struggled amongst themselves for power and influence, and especially territory. Only the septs of Clan Donald preserved a united front, rarely if ever feuding with one another.

Even so, Highland society was starting to fragment. The vassal kindreds who had flourished under the Lordship of the Isles, such as the MacLeans and the MacLeods, along with many others, came to regard themselves as distinct clans with their own distinct interests, quite independent of the various septs of Clan Donald. The feuds that broke out among these various clans in the latter part of the sixteenth century mostly concerned the possession of land, or its inheritance. Indeed, a clan without land became known as a 'broken clan', while a man without a clan was a 'broken man', often reduced to able-bodied vagrancy or even brigandage.

Lack of Central Authority

Such disorder ultimately reflected the continued weakness of the Scottish crown, as it struggled during the sixteenth century to exert its authority over the Highlands and Western Isles. Indeed, the country suffered from long periods of minority rule, since the Stuart monarchs often succeeded one another long before they came of age. As they were unable to rule in their own right, the country was then governed in their place by 'Guardians'. They almost inevitably neglected the wider interests of the country in their internecine struggles at the Scottish court, granting out power and patronage to their friends and allies to win their support and favour. Even when the Stuart kings came of age, they had first to impose their own authority on an oligarchy of powerful nobles, before they could address the problems faced by the country as a whole. All too often, their early deaths plunged the country into more factional infighting among the nobility, so undoing whatever they had achieved in all too short a personal reign.

Legacy of the Reformation

Such difficulties were compounded by the religious conflicts generated by the Scottish Reformation of 1560, when Parliament rejected Papal authority over the established Church in favour of the Calvinist doctrines of John Knox. But episcopacy was never abolished, even though the Apostolic Succession of the Bishops was explicitly denied. Subsequently, Andrew Melville attempted in 1581 to introduce a strict form of Presbyterian government to the Church, while asserting that its power and authority derived directly from God according to the Scriptures. He regarded James VI merely as 'God's sillie [weak] vassal', asserting that his worldly kingdom belonged instead to Jesus Christ and His Church, as represented no doubt by such true believers as himself.

Moreover, when James VI came to rule in his own right in 1587, he faced the overweening power of an unruly aristocracy, exacerbated by the years of political turmoil since the abdication in 1567 of his mother Mary Stuart, Queen of Scots. Confronted with the task – even harder than that which faced his predecessors – of exerting his authority over the country, James VI turned to the landed gentry and the burgesses for their support against the aristocracy. Meanwhile, he reinforced his own authority over the Reformed Church by restoring its episcopalian structure, appointing bishops to act in the interests of the Crown, and allowing them to exercise political power in Parliament.

James VI and the Highlands

Even while he struggled to exert his authority over Church and State, James VI of Scotland had enacted legislation in 1597, intended to bring law and order to the more disturbed parts of his kingdom, and especially the Highlands and Western Isles. All the clan chiefs and landowners were required to exhibit their title-deeds in 1598 before the Privy Council in Edinburgh. Several chiefs had no charters to exhibit, holding their lands by the edge of a sword, while others dared not appear in Edinburgh for fear of arrest. Their lands and title were promptly forfeited to the Crown.

However, it was only after 1603 and the Union of the Crowns that James VI of Scotland was strong enough to put these measures into effect. By then, the balance of power had shifted significantly between Gaeldom and what was now his kingdom of Great Britain. James VI now had the military and financial resources he needed to force the Highland clans to accept the authority of the Crown. In particular, the warships of the English navy gave him command of the sea-lanes around the Western Isles, finally eclipsing the power of the Hebridean galley. Moreover, events in Ulster had left the Highland clans without any Gaelic-speaking allies in Ireland after 1607, once Hugh O'Neill, Earl of Tyrone, and Hugh O'Donnell, Earl of Tyrconnel, had fled the country in the 'Flight of the Earls'. No longer would the Highland clans be able to present a united front with their Irish counterparts to resist the authority of what what now the British Crown.

By 1609, James VI had brought the principal chieftains of the Western Isles under the authority of the Privy Council in Edinburgh by forcing them to sign the Statutes of Iona. This agreement marked the culmination of the Crown's repeated attempts to impose its control over the Western Isles and the adjacent seaboard of the Scottish Highlands. It required the chiefs to recognise the supreme authority of the King in all matters of Church and State, to obey the laws of the realm, and to maintain ministers of the Reformed Church, which was now an Episcopalian Church ruled by bishops appointed by the King.

After 1609, James VI of Scotland was powerful enough to force the Highland clans to settle nearly all the major feuds that had existed between them, often to the advantage of the Campbells, Earls of Argyll, or the cadet branches of the family. When his reign ended in 1625, only the MacIntoshes of Clan Chattan still laid claim to the lands of Cameron of Lochiel and MacDonald of Keppoch. Thus, when Charles I came to the throne, the Gaelic-speaking society of the Scottish Highlands and Western Isles looked set to enjoy a welcome era of peace and tranquillity, imposed upon it by the Crown.

Septs of Clan Donald

By bringing the various feuds among the Highland clans to an end, James VI radically altered the balance of political power and territorial influence in the Highlands. Clan Donald at the end of the sixteenth century still consisted of the various septs that had survived the death of Donald Dubh in 1545. Since then, however, they had come into conflict with the erstwhile vassals of Clan Donald, and particularly with the MacLeods of Dunvegan and the MacLeans of Duart. A bitter feud over the lands of Trotternish in the north of Skye, claimed by the MacLeods of Dunvegan, was finally settled in 1617, when the MacDonalds of Sleat received a charter confirming their possession of Trotternish, as well as of the lands of Sleat and North Uist. The MacLeods of Dunvegan had already received a charter in 1611, confirming their possession of Dunvegan and Harris, as well as Glenelg, while the MacDonalds of Clan Ranald had gained a charter in 1610 to their lands of Moidart, Arisaig, Morar, Eigg, South Uist and Benbecula.

Farther south, the Rhinns of Islay were the subject of a deadly feud between the MacDonalds of Dunyvaig and the Glens, and the MacLeans of Duart, which drew in a number of other clans in support. It ended with the defeat of the MacLeans at the bloody battle of Gruinart in 1598. Afterwards, however, the MacDonalds of Dunyvaig and the Glens brought about their own destruction by quarrelling amongst themselves. This internecine feud allowed the Campbells, Earls of Argyll, to gain possession of their lands of Kintyre and Jura, which they later planted with devout Presbyterians from the Lowlands of Scotland. Meanwhile, the Campbells of Cawdor had succeeded in supplanting the MacDonalds in Islay, once the heartland of Clan Donald.

The MacDonalds of Dunyvaig and the Glens became extinct in 1626, leaving the MacDonalds, Earls of Antrim, to represent their branch of Clan Donald in Ulster. Despite their Catholic faith, they benefited greatly by supporting the efforts of the Crown to bring 'civility' to Ulster after the Flight of the Earls in 1607. Several other branches of Clan Donald had also died out by this time, including the MacIains of Ardnamurchan, whose lands passed to the Campbells. By then, a triumvirate of powerful clans was established among the surviving septs of Clan Donald, consisting of the MacDonalds of Clan Ranald, the MacDonalds of Sleat and the MacDonalds of Glengarry.

The latter was once a sept of Clan Ranald, but had now become an independent clan in its own right, holding land under charter from the Great Glen as far west as Knoydart. Elsewhere, the other remnants of Clan Donald were represented in Lochaber by the MacDonalds of Keppoch, and farther south by the MacDonalds (or MacIains) of Glencoe, who had both entered into the spirit of the times by abandoning their lawless ways, at least for the time being.

Vassals of Clan Donald

Several vassals of Clan Donald, powerful at the time of the Lordship, were eventually forced to accept the superiority of the Campbells, Earls of Argyll, during the course of the seventeenth century. The MacLeans with their territories in Mull and the nearby islands already consisted of several distinct septs when the Lordship was forfeited in 1493. Afterwards, the MacLeans of Duart struggled to exert their authority against the aspirations of the MacLeans of Lochbuie and Coll. Defeated at the battle of Gruinart in 1598, the MacLeans were eventually forced to accept Argyll as their feudal superior. However, they kept hold of their lands in Mull, Morvern, Ardgour, Coll, and Tiree until the 1670s, when they were dispossessed by the Campbells, Earls of Argyll.

Another powerful clan that came under the feudal superiority of the Campbells, Earls of Argyll, were the Camerons of Lochiel. Once loosely allied to Clan Donald as the vassals of the Lordship, they had broken away in 1429 when the third Lord of the Isles had risen in arms against James I. However, they later lent their support to the MacDonalds of Clan Ranald in their disputes with the Crown. Even though they had once held a charter to their lands in Lochaber as the barony of Lochiel, their chief in 1598 was a rebel beyond the law, who dared not appear before the Privy Council in Edinburgh. The Camerons of Lochiel were therefore forced to seek the protection of the Campbells, Earls of Argyll, while surrendering the superiority of their other lands in Lochaber to the Gordons, Earls of Huntly.

However, the Camerons of Lochiel were still vulnerable, since the MacIntoshes of Clan Chattan had laid claim to their lands of Glen Loy and Locharkaig, dating back to a charter of 1433. Indeed, tradition had it that these lands had once belonged to the distant ancestors of Clan Chattan. However, they had established themselves in Badenoch by the fourteenth century, while even later they came to occupy the valleys of Strathnairn and Strathdearn, forming the hinterland to the lowlands of Moray. By then, their chiefs had placed themselves at the head of the confederacy of Highland clans known as Clan Chattan, among which the MacPhersons of Cluny, and the Farquharsons of Invercauld, were the most powerful.

Challenging the MacLeans and the Camerons as equally powerful vassals of Clan Donald at the time of the Lordship were the MacLeods. As already recounted, the MacLeods of Dunvegan received a charter in 1611 from James VI of Scotland to their lands in Skye and the Outer Hebrides. The other MacLeod septs of Raasay, Assynt and Gairloch also managed to survive. However, a long-lasting and very bitter quarrel among the MacLeods of Lewis brought about their forfeiture by James VI of Scotland in 1598. Their lands were leased to the 'Fife Adventurers', but this company failed to colonise Lewis with Lowland settlers as the King had intended. By 1611, the island had passed to the MacKenzies of Kintail.

Aggrandisement of the MacKenzies

In fact, the island of Lewis was the last prize acquired by the MacKenzies during what was a long campaign of territorial aggrandisement, which started after the forfeiture of the earldom of Ross in 1475. Although they originally held the lands of Kintail, which was made into the barony of Eilean Donnan in 1509, they gained many of the lands once held in Easter Ross by Clan Donald during the late fifteenth and early sixteenth centuries. Then they claimed the lands of Lochalsh, Lochcarron and Lochbroom in Wester Ross, once held under the Lordship of the Isles, which had passed by the mid-sixteenth century to the MacDonalds of Glengarry. A bitter feud between the two clans saw the MacDonalds ousted, and afterwards the MacKenzies seized the lands of the MacLeods of Gairloch. The final accolade came in 1623 when the chief of the MacKenzies was made the first Earl of Seaforth.

Conflicts among the Northern Clans

Farther north, power lay in the hands of the Gordons, Earls of Sutherland, who had ousted its ancient line in the early sixteenth century. However, their position was challenged by the MacKays of Strathnaver, and the Sinclairs, Earls of Caithness. The Earls of Sutherland had long claimed to be the feudal superiors of the MacKays, but it was not until 1589 that the MacKays finally accepted the inevitable, allying themselves with the Earls of Sutherland against the Sinclairs, Earls of Caithness. By then, the Sutherlands of Duffus, the Rosses of Balnagown, the Munros of Fowlis, and the Gunns of Kildonan had all come under the feudal superiority of the Earls of Sutherland. However, it was another twenty-four years before the power of the Sinclairs, Earls of Caithness, was finally broken, leaving the Earls of Sutherland to rule supreme as 'the Cocks o' the Far North'.

Gordons, Earls of Huntly

Farther south, the Gordons, Earls of Huntly, and Lords of Badenoch, repre-sented the senior branch of the Gordon family. They had dominated the north-east of Scotland ever since their elevation to the peerage in 1445. They were among the more recent of the Anglo-Norman or Flemish fami-lies, whom David I (1124–53) and his successors had planted around the fringes of the Highlands. The Frasers, the Chisholms and the Grants (later of Strathspey), who all held their lands around Loch Ness at the north-eastern end of the Great Glen, had such an ancestry, as did the Sinclairs, the Menzies and the Murrays. Indeed, even the Stuart dynasty had such an ancestry. Where they settled around the fringes of the Highlands, these families often adopted the customs and traditions of their Gaelic-speaking neighbours, eventually coming to regard themselves as Highland clans in their own right. Such a process of cultural assimilation quite possibly reflected the unsettled state of the country during and after the Wars of Scottish Independence, accentuated by the resurgence of Gaelic culture and society that occurred at the same time under the Lordship of the Isles.

The Gordons, Earls of Huntly, reached the pinnacle of their power and influence in the mid-sixteenth century as King's Lieutenants north of the Forth, acting as the agents of royal authority in the Highlands. However, after the Scottish Reformation, they did not convert to Protestantism, unlike the Gordons, Earls of Sutherland. Their adherence to Roman Catholicism made them suspect in the eyes of the Reformed Church, while attracting the enmity of the extreme Presbyterian party. Even though the sixth Earl of Huntly was made Marquis of Huntly by James VI of Scotland in 1599, power in the north of Scotland had by then passed to the Gordons, Earls of Sutherland.

Campbells, Earls of Argyll

The Campbells, Earls of Argyll, were even more powerful agents of royal authority than the Gordons, Earls of Huntly, exercising vice-regal powers on behalf of the Crown in the south-western Highlands and the Western Isles. While their roots probably lay in the ancient British kingdom of Strathclyde, their ancestors had settled around Loch Awe by the mid-thirteenth century. The next two centuries saw their descendants growing slowly but steadily in power and influence, especially after they had supported King Robert the Bruce in the struggles for Scottish independence against the MacDougalls of Lorne. By the time the first Earl of Argyll was elevated to the peerage in 1457, the Campbells held all of Argyll to the north of Knapdale, including the Lordship of Lorne, as well as lands in Cowal, where such ancient clans as the Lamonts and the MacLachlans came under their domination.

Another branch of the Campbell family obtained the lands of Glenorchy, once held by the MacGregors. By the end of the sixteenth century, their descendants held lands lying in the wide swathe of the Perthshire glens around the upper reaches of the River Tay, making up the Highland district of Breadalbane. After founding such cadet families as the Campbells of Lawers and Glenlyon, the main branch of the Campbells of Glenorchy were eventually created Earls of Breadalbane in 1677. Yet another branch of the Campbells had obtained the lands of Cawdor near Inverness by abducting the infant heiress of the last thane of Cawdor in 1499, and then marrying her when she came of age in 1510. The Campbells of Cawdor later gained Islay from the remnants of Clan Donald.

The Campbells derived their strength from the close identity and unity of purpose displayed by their many branches, all owing allegiance to the Earls of Argyll at their head. Moreover, the territorial power of the Campbells, Earls of Argyll, was greatly enhanced by the powerful position they had established for themselves at the heart of central government. Indeed, their hereditary position as Masters of the Royal Household, first granted in 1464, mirrored that previously enjoyed by the Stewarts before they gained the throne of Scotland in 1371. Then in 1514, the third Earl of Argyll was made Justice-General of Scotland, and his descendants held this hereditary office until 1628, when it was finally surrendered to the Crown.

Agents of Royal Authority

Even before they were created Earls of Argyll in 1457, the Campbells of Lochawe had acted as King's Lieutenants for Argyll. They continued to act as agents of royal authority, attempting to tackle with varying degrees of success the rampant disorder that had spread throughout the Western Isles during the Age of Feuds and Forays. Nearly every insurrection to restore the Lordship of the Isles after its forfeiture in 1493 took advantage of the unsettled state of Scotland during periods of minority rule. Almost inevitably, the 'Governors' of Scotland sought the help of the Campbells, Earls of Argyll, to bring the rebellious septs of Clan Donald into submission. After the death of Donald Dubh in 1545, leaving the Lordship with no obvious heir, the Campbells, Earls of Argyll, laid claim to the headship of the Gael, once held by Clan Donald. Indeed, they arranged a series of judicious marriages to bind together the MacDonalds of Dunyvaig and the Glens, and the MacLeans of Duart, in a close alliance with the family of the fourth Earl of Argyll at the heart of Gaeldom.

Backed by this alliance, and under the leadership of the fifth Earl of Argyll, the MacDonalds and the MacLeans provided a ready source of mercenary soldiers to fight the wars waged in Ulster between its Gaelic-speaking Earls and the English crown during the latter half of the sixteenth century. This involvement of the Highland clans in the affairs of Ulster lasted until 1595, when the last great expeditionary force of 'redshanks', numbering around four thousand men, was scattered by the ships of the English navy. By then, however, the MacDonalds and the MacLeans had once again resorted to violence in their long-lasting feud over the Rhinns of Islay, drawing on several other clans for support.

As disorder spread in the Western Isles, the Campbells became 'the masters of aggressive feudalism', especially under the eighth Earl of Argyll. Suspected of fomenting disorder and unrest among the western clans to justify his intervention on behalf of the Crown, his actions were largely responsible for the bitter enmity that subsequently divided the Campbells from the other clans in Argyll and the Western Isles, and especially the septs of Clan Donald. As we have seen, the territorial aggrandisement of the Campbells was directed in particular against the MacDonalds of Antrim and their allies in the Western Isles. However, the eighth Earl also profited greatly from the commission of fire and sword granted to him by the Crown against the MacGregors, following the battle of Glen Fruin in 1603. The MacGregors were driven from their ancestral lands of Glen Orchy, Glen Lochy and Glen Strae as the climax of their long-continued persecution by the Campbells over the previous century. They were outlawed and forbidden to take the name of MacGregor, and the penal laws against the clan were only repealed in 1774.

Strength of the Clans

The contempt shown by the chiefs of the Highland clans for central authority throughout the Age of Feuds and Forays, and the difficulty in bringing them under the King's peace, testify to their fighting strength. Even at the time of the Lordship of the Isles, Clan Donald could challenge the power of the Crown, bringing armies of several thousand men into the field. Moreover, the forfeiture of the Lordship apparently had no effect in reducing the military power of the clans. In 1545 Donald Dubh sailed to Knockfergus in Ulster in a fleet of 180 galleys, accompanied by an army of 4,000 men. Among them were a thousand 'tall mariners, that rowed in the galleys', and three thousand footmen, described as 'very tall men, clothed in habergeons of mail, armed with long swords and long bows, but with few guns'. He left behind an equal number of men to guard the Highlands.

The mercenary forces of 'redshanks' that fought in the Ulster wars during the late sixteenth century were often just as strong. Indeed, the last great expeditionary force that sailed to Ulster in 1595 in a fleet of fifty galleys was 4,000 strong. As it was raised by MacDonald of Sleat, it perhaps only consisted of the clansmen of Clan Donald, suggesting that the fighting strength of the Highland clans as a whole was very much greater. In fact, when General Wade reported on the state of the Highlands in 1724, he estimated that the Highland clans as a whole could raise 22,000 men in arms, mostly in support of the Jacobite cause.

Given the clans' need to defend their own territories against their neighbours, it is hardly surprising that Highland society had its own peculiar features. Quite possibly, these features may represent the archaic relics of Celtic society, brought across the North Channel from Ireland by the Gaelic-speaking

Scots of Dalriada when they settled in Argyll around AD 500. But just as likely, they may have evolved in response to the political power vacuum that developed in the Highlands during and after the fourteenth century. Indeed, contemporary observers made little or no distinction between the Highlands and the Lowlands before the start of the fourteenth century, as Professor Barrow has asserted, so it seems the two societies must have shared much in common.

Nature of the Feudal System

As far as the Lowlands were concerned, society throughout these centuries was based on the feudal system, first introduced into the ancient Celtic kingdom of Scotland by David I (1124–53) and his immediate successors. Land was held by feudal charter, granted by the King to his most powerful subjects in return for their military service and other payments in kind, mostly food rents. Such a fiefdom could then be granted out in its turn to their vassals, who then held the land from a feudal superior. However, feudal tenants only held a life interest in the land, which reverted on their death to the Crown or to their feudal superior, at least in theory. However, it soon became common practice for such feudal grants to pass from father to eldest son according to the law of primogeniture, while younger sons were often granted out land from their father's estate, so becoming the vassals of their elder brothers. Feudal society thus evolved so that kinship became its essential feature.

The feudal system had encroached upon the Scottish Highlands during the course of the late twelfth and early thirteenth centuries, since feudal charters were granted to the Anglo-Norman and Flemish families planted around its fringes by the Canmore kings. The practice spread during the fourteenth century, as it became increasingly common for Highland magnates to hold their lands as feudal vassals of the Crown. Among the recipients of these early charters were the Campbells of Lochawe, the MacDonalds of Islay, the MacDougalls of Lorne, and the MacLeods of Lewis. Afterwards, all the MacDonald Lords of the Isles held their lands by feudal charter. Even their claim to the earldom of Ross in the early fifteenth century, which culminated in the battle of Harlaw in 1411, was founded on feudal principles of inheritance.

Divisions within the Country

Significantly, only as the monarchy declined in power and authority, from the fourteenth century onwards, did the divisions within the country become apparent. At first, they were based essentially upon language and culture.

However, they then took on a political dimension, as the very existence of the powerful Lordship of the Isles at the heart of Gaelic-speaking Scotland sowed distrust and suspicion in the minds of Lowland Scots. Even so, it was a time of 'great peace and wealth in the Isles through the ministration of justice', to quote the words of Dean Munro, writing in 1549. Only after the forfeiture of the Lordship in 1493 does the word 'clan' even enter the historical record, apart from Wyntoun's early reference, dating from around 1420, to the two clans that fought one another to the death in judicial combat upon the North Inch at Perth in 1396. Moreover, the chroniclers, apart from John Fordoun in the 1380s, only began to emphasise the striking differences between the lawless behaviour of the 'wild Scots' and their Lowland counterparts during the sixteenth century.

Feudalism and the Clan System

Arguably, it was the forfeiture of the Lordship itself that forced the kin-based society of the Highlands and Western Isles to fragment into what became known as the Highland clans. Denied its protection, and forced to fend for themselves, they could only survive and prosper if they were strong enough to counter the territorial ambitions of their neighbours. The fighting strength of a Highland clan was thus crucial to its survival. Yet holding their own lands by feudal charter from the Crown gave them a natural advantage over their rivals, so that feudalism was also an essential component of the clan system.

Moreover, the Highland clans could exploit the feudal system by gaining charters to lands forfeited by their rivals, as long as they were favoured by the Crown. Indeed, they could force their weaker neighbours to accept their feudal superiority, and they were often rewarded in this way for services rendered to the Crown. Marriage could also be employed to widen territorial influence, while other alliances were cemented by bonds of friendship between equals, binding them to act together in support of one another, or by bonds of manrent, whereby a lesser man gave his support to a greater man in return for his protection.

Emergence of the Clan System

Yet these aspects of Highland society did not make it fundamentally different from Lowland society. Instead, what distinguished the Highland clans from the equally powerful kindreds in the Lowlands was the increasing emphasis they placed upon kinship, even while such bonds were weakening in the Lowlands under the impact of social and economic change. Accordingly,

Highland clans came to differ from their Lowland counterparts in their hier-archical structure. The chief of a Highland clan occupied the very apex of this hierarchy by virtue of his illustrious descent from the clan's distant progenitor. He typically succeeded as the eldest son of the previous chief, according to the feudal principle of primogeniture. However, should a chief prove unequal to the task, it was not unknown, even in the sixteenth century, for a clan to revert to the ancient Celtic tradition of inheritance, whereby all the descendants of an earlier chief had the right to succeed, down to the fourth generation.

The chief's kinsmen formed the clan gentry, who constituted the nucleus of its fighting strength. Typically, the leading figures among the clan gentry had Crown charters to their estates, while the lesser gentry held their lands by lease as the tacksmen in charge of the townships, looking after the work-ing of the land by the ordinary clansmen. Belonging as well to this class of lesser gentry were the household men, or *buannachan*, who were especially numerous among the clans of the Western Isles and the adjacent seaboard of the Scottish Highlands. They were charged as a military elite with defending the clan territories from the depredations of their neighbours.

However, members of this elite of fighting men were also employed as the mercenary soldiers known as 'redshanks'. They lent their services in particular to the Irish earls of Tyrone and Tyrconnel, who were engaged during the late sixteenth century in a bitter struggle against the English colonisation of Ulster. Since the clans involved in such mercenary activity received in return a useful supply of food and money, they had every incen-tive to increase their fighting strength. According to an English estimate, well over 6,000 men belonged to this military caste by the 1590s. They were typically billeted at free quarter upon the lands of the ordinary clansmen. Indeed, as was recorded at Islay around this time, 'Each merkland man sustain daily and yearly one gentleman in meat and cloth, who does no labour . . . as one of their master's household men, and [who] must be sus-tained and furnished in all necessities by the tenant, and he must be ready to his master's service and advice.' Even later, it was said that there were 100 gentlemen quartered for the winter months on the MacLean lands of Tiree.

The lowest levels of clan society consisted of the ordinary clansmen who owed allegiance to their clan chief, and supported the clan gentry with food by labouring in the fields. Contrary to popular belief, they rarely had any blood ties of kinship with the clan chief, merely taking his name when surnames came into common use in the sixteenth and seventeenth centuries. But by the eighteenth century, the myth had arisen that the clan as a whole was descended from a common ancestor, given that 'clan' in Gaelic means children or offspring. However mistaken, such a belief strengthened the institution of clanship itself. By recognising his clansmen as his own kin, the chief of a clan flattered them, so making them more likely to accept his own authority as the father of their clan.

Statutes of Iona

Such was the nature of the clan system which James VI of Scotland tried to restrain by means of the Statutes of Iona, coupled with several other measures as adopted later by the Privy Council. They represented a sustained attack upon the large retinues and liberal households maintained by the chiefs, in order to impress their rivals with prodigal displays of 'feasting and feuding'. The Statutes first attempted to restrict the size of a chief's household according to his rank and status. Only the chief of Duart was allowed to maintain as many as eight gentlemen as members of his household. The other chieftains had to content themselves with even fewer retainers. Moreover, each member of the chief's household was only allowed two youths in his service, most likely recruited from the sons of other gentry. By restricting their numbers, it was evidently hoped that the military strength of the clan itself would be reduced. Even so, the very size of the Highland armies subsequently raised in support of the Stuart dynasty shows these measures had little or no effect.

Several other statutes were directed against the very existence of this military elite. They were no longer allowed the use of any firearms, except for sporting purposes within the strict confines of the policies around their own residences. Clan chiefs were required to maintain their households solely from their own resources. The practice of 'sorning' was forbidden, whereby the threat of force was used to quarter their armed retinues upon their tenantry. Hostelries were to be established instead throughout the Western Isles, catering not just for travellers and other visitors, but designed to relieve the common people from providing food and lodging to 'other idle men without any calling or vocation'. Yet another statute required all clansmen dwelling in the Western Isles to have a sufficient income of their own to support themselves unless they had a lawful trade or profession, whatever their station in life. Together, these two measures attempted to reduce the numbers of idle men, whether they were mere vagrants or the members of a chief's household. James VI had already decreed that members of a chief's retinue should 'take themselves to industry', or face transportation to the colonies.

While these measures tackled the military basis of clanship, which was arguably the cause of feuding between the clans, another set of statutes was directed against the social customs that sustained clanship. One statute attempted to curb the displays of extravagant hospitality on the part of the clan chiefs by prohibiting them from patronising 'vagabonds, bards, jugglers, and such like', who entertained the clan on such occasions, and, indeed, flattered their patrons. It seems this statute made little distinction between the professional bards and seannachies, whose presence within a chief's household gave him prestige and status, and what were just vagabond bands of strolling players.

Another statute tried to stem the 'extraordinary drinking of strong wine and aquavitae [whisky]', especially among the common people. The clan chiefs and their gentry could still import wine and whisky for their own use from the Lowlands, being allowed to consume within their households what seem to be very liberal quantities, measured in barrels rather than bottles. However, their tenants were not to drink any wine at all, even though they were still allowed to distil their own whisky, or to brew their own beer. When Martin Martin wrote *A Description of the Western Isles of Scotland* in 1703, he commented that the ancient traditions of feasting and drinking on an epic scale were already a thing of the past, perhaps as a result of these measures. However, it may equally well reflect the gulf that had opened up between the clan elite and their clansmen by then.

The cultural foundations of clanship were further undermined by a statute that required anyone who possessed more than sixty cattle to send his eldest son, or eldest daughter if he had no sons, to school in the Lowlands, so that they might learn English. No son was allowed to inherit from his father, or to become a tenant of the Crown, unless he had received such an education. By this means, it was evidently hoped to absorb the clan chiefs into the landed society of lowland Scotland. Interestingly, however, there is no mention of the widespread practice of fostering a chief's children upon his clansmen as a means of strengthening the bonds of kinship within the clan itself.

The clan chiefs were later required to live in a fixed place as agreed with the Privy Council. They were to build 'civil and comely' houses as their chief residences, presumably instead of fortified tower-houses, which were still such a characteristic feature of Scottish architecture at this period. The surrounding land was to be taken into their own cultivation as a mains or home farm, while all their other land was to be leased out at a fixed rent, without imposing any other duties. They were allowed only a single galley for their own use.

Appearance before the Privy Council

Finally, the principal chieftains from the Western Isles were required to make an annual pilgrimage to Edinburgh, so that the Privy Council could enquire into their own conduct, and the good behaviour of their tenants and other dependants. This measure only became effective in 1616, when financial sureties were taken from the chiefs, amounting to £10,000 Scots at the very most, that they would appear in Edinburgh, accompanied by the leading members of their gentry. It acted to restrain the chiefs from embarking upon any lawless conduct, while giving them every incentive to reduce their tenants and other followers to 'civility'. Moreover, it provided the Crown with a useful source of income should the chiefs not meet their obligations to the Privy Council. When Charles I acceded to the throne in 1625, these sanctions were extended to make sure the chiefs and their gentry paid all the rents and other revenues they owed to the Crown. A concession was however made in 1628 by writing off all their arrears of rents and taxes prior to 1621.

The principal chieftains of the Western Isles continued to appear each year before the Privy Council in Edinbugh to give an account of themselves. The practice only lapsed when civil unrest threatened the country after the signing of the National Covenant in 1638. By then, it was the Scottish Highlands rather than the Western Isles that were racked by disorder, mostly fomented by lawless bands of outlaws and other broken men. The Privy Council reacted at first by requiring all landowners and bailies in the Highlands to give surety for the good conduct of their tenants and other dependants. Then, it resorted in 1635 to the measure which had proved so successful in the Western Isles, requiring all the landlords in the Highlands to appear each year before the Privy Council in Edinburgh. It followed the burning of Frendraught House in 1630, when George Gordon, sixth Earl and first Marquis of Huntly, became embroiled in a bitter feud with the Crichtons, following the death of his son, Lord Aboyne.

Whether such measures would have quelled the endemic lawlessness in the Highlands and Western Isles will never be known. Any likelihood that law and order could be established by such means ended with the emergence of the Covenanting movement in 1638. It ushered in decades of bitter civil and religious conflict, which pitted the Presbyterian Church against the Stuart dynasty. By providing a ready source of military manpower, drawn upon by both factions, the Highland clans finally emerged onto the national stage.

Chapter Two

PRELUDE TO CIVIL WAR

Scottish society changed profoundly in the thirty-five years between the Union of the Crowns under James VI in 1603, and the signing of the National Covenant in 1638. The union of the two countries was a political and diplomatic triumph for James VI, who now styled himself King of Great Britain, France and Ireland. But although it added greatly to his wealth and status, its beneficial effects in Scotland were much less obvious. In particular, the nobility lost much of their power and influence when the Scottish court moved south to London, where they were often greeted with ill-disguised contempt. Indeed, the once-proud kingdom of Scotland was virtually relegated to the status of a province. But this unpalatable truth was perhaps not immediately apparent to the Scots, proud that James VI now ruled over their 'auld enemy'.

James VI on arriving in London first entertained the dream of a united nation with a single Parliament. But his arguments for such a 'perfect union', made with passion against mounting hostility, were soon foiled by the English Parliament at Westminister, anxious to protect its own entrenched interests. Afterwards, James ruled Scotland in his absence through the Privy Council, packed with his own officers of state. His own nominees came to dominate the business of the Scots Parliament in Edinburgh through the committee known as the Lords of the Articles. He was equally successful in proscribing the meetings of the General Assembly until he had restored the full office of bishop to the Reformed Church of Scotland in 1610. Appointed by the King, their return was detrimental to the interests of the nobility, since they came to dominate the proceedings of Parliament. But the radical clergy were even more offended by the restoration of bishops to govern the Church, which ran counter to all their most deeply held beliefs. It would open up a deep schism within Scottish society which lasted for well over a hundred years.

Ecclesiastical Policies of James VI

Moreover, once James VI came to rule over England after the Union of the
Crowns in 1603, he benefited greatly from the fundamental differences in
ecclesiastical doctrine and discipline between the two countries. The English
Reformation had occurred long before Calvinist doctrines could be embraced
as whole-heartedly as happened in Scotland. The Tudor monarchs simply
replaced the Pope as the supreme governors of the Church of England. The
Reformed Church in England thus came under the supremacy of the Crown,
and religious dissidents were persecuted as enemies of the State. It is hardly
surprising that James VI, after the Union of the Crowns, came to embrace
whole-heartedly the doctrines and discipline of the Church of England,
and especially its High Anglican principles. They merely served to confirm
his belief in the supremacy of the King in all matters, both spiritual and
temporal, which was first expressed in the *Basilikon Doron*, written in 1599
as a manual of instruction for his eldest son, Prince Henry.

As far as Scotland was concerned, James VI brought his influence to bear
upon the General Assembly, forcing it to restore bishops to their full authority
over the Church in 1610. Nominated by the King, they had already regained
their former position in Parliament, where they came to act as the agents of
royal power. The imposition of Episcopalian government upon the Church
of Scotland was followed by liturgical and other changes which further
offended strict Presbyterians, embodied in the Five Articles of Perth (1618).
James VI managed to pursue his ecclesiastical policies so skilfully that the
underlying discontent was never really apparent. But when he died in 1625,
he left a political legacy that would destroy his son and heir, who succeeded him
as Charles I, ruling over the three kingdoms of England, Scotland and Ireland.

Accession of Charles I

Ascending the throne as a young man of twenty-five years, Charles I knew
nothing of Scotland, which he had left for England with his father in 1603.
Moreover, he lacked his father's personable qualities. He was described as
cold and withdrawn, prudish and fastidious, shifty and devious, and given
to secrecy, quite unlike James VI. Believing that deeds spoke louder than
words, Charles I felt he had no need to explain his actions. Neither were they
tempered in any way by political expediency, which James VI had pursued
with great skill throughout his life.

Above all, Charles I was stubbornly doctrinaire and autocratic. Just like
his father before him, he was convinced of the Divine Right of Kings to rule
with absolute authority as 'God's vicars on Earth'. But by means of skilful

diplomacy and political manipulation, James VI had countered the Calvinist claim to establish a theocratic state on Earth by accepting that the royal prerogative was subject to the 'laws and customs of the realm'. He thus acknowledged that it could only be exercised under the rule of law, even though his authority was ultimately derived from God.

Charles I thus lacked the consummate skills of his father, and he pursued policies in Scotland which alienated not only the Presbyterian extremists, but the aristocracy as well. Indeed, after first refusing to entertain any changes to the Episcopalian government of the Reformed Church, he then proceeded to revoke all the charters made by the Crown since Mary Stuart, Queen of Scots, ascended the throne in 1542. The lands so affected had mostly belonged to the Church before the Reformation, and they had mostly passed into the hands of the nobility. Even though Charles I intended to improve the stipends of the clergy by this measure, which was itself implemented in none too rigorous a manner, it affected nearly every member of landed society in Scotland.

Then, by elevating bishops to positions of extreme power, especially in the Privy Council, at the expense of the nobility, he lost the support that the higher aristocracy had always given to the Crown. Indeed, he rode roughshod over the Scottish Parliament in just the same way as he had reigned over England without any Parliament at all after 1629. By refusing to temper his policies with any sense of diplomacy, he forged what proved to be a temporary alliance between the aristocracy and the extreme Presbyterians, which lasted until Charles I was executed in 1649. It allowed Parliament and the General Assembly to impose what was a revolutionary settlement upon Church and State, founded on Presbyterian principles. It could only be accepted by Charles I if he renounced his own powers as an absolute monarch, founded upon his unwavering belief in the Divine Right of Kings, and this he absolutely refused to contemplate.

Religious Policies of Charles I

While Henrietta-Maria as his Queen was a practising Catholic, Charles I was much closer in his religious beliefs and liturgical practices to what would now be regarded as High Anglican, verging on Anglo-Catholicism. Indeed, when Charles I first visited Scotland in 1633 to be crowned King, eight years after his accession, he elevated Edinburgh into a bishopric, and he revived the Five Articles of Perth, first promulgated by James VI in 1618. They prescribed the rites of private baptism, private communion, confirmation by bishops and observance of holy days, along with other Anglican practices, like the wearing of surplices and the custom of kneeling at communion.

Worse followed when the Book of Common Prayer was introduced in 1637, designed as a compromise by the Scottish bishops to bring the liturgical practices of the two kingdoms into line with one another. Its introduction alienated the Scots people, who mostly held fast to their Presbyterian beliefs, especially in the Lowlands. Not only did it contain the detested Five Articles of Perth, along with various other articles of faith suspiciously reminiscent of Roman belief, but its use was imposed under the royal prerogative without approval by the General Assembly or even the Scots Parliament.

When it was first used in a service on 23 July 1637 at St Giles Cathedral in Edinburgh, many townsfolk in the congregation walked out in protest. A riot followed in which stools were hurled. One, thrown by Jenny Geddes, an Edinburgh housewife and greengrocer, supposedly struck the clergyman conducting the service. Other disturbances against the book's use occurred at the same time in other Edinburgh churches, orchestrated no doubt by the radical ministers bitterly opposed to its introduction.

As agitation against the Book of Common Prayer spread throughout the Lowlands, Charles I in London reacted with cold anger, ordering the Privy Council to insist on its use. Almost immediately, the clergy were joined in their opposition by members of the nobility, who had their own quarrels with the King over his 1625 Act of Revocation. They were supported by the gentry and the burgesses of the towns, and petitions and supplications flooded into Edinburgh. Feelings ran so high that the Privy Council took to meeting away from the Scottish capital, so that it could avoid the fury of the mob. But, isolated in this way, it could no longer exert any influence on the course of events. The King's religious opponents started to organise themselves into the committees of delegates that later became known as the 'Tables', petitioning the King not just against the Book of Common Prayer, but now attacking the very existence of bishops as well.

Signing of the National Covenant

Prompt and decisive action was now required if the situation was not to get out of hand. However, several months passed before Charles I finally issued a proclamation in February 1638, which made absolutely no concession to the protests of the Scottish people. Just a week later, it was proposed that the Confession of Faith first signed by James VI in 1581 be renewed. Known as the National Covenant, and welcomed as 'that glorious marriage of the Kingdom [of Scotland] with God', it asserted the people's support for the Protestant religion, and their abhorrence of the Catholic faith. Signatories to the document pledged themselves to defend their true religion against all changes not sanctioned by Parliament and the General Assembly of the

Reformed Church of Scotland, entering into a covenant with God just like the people of Israel in the Old Testament.

Once the document was approved, it was first signed by nearly all the Scottish nobility and then by representatives of the landed gentry on 28 February 1638 in the churchyard of Greyfriars in Edinburgh. James Graham, fifth Earl and later first Marquis of Montrose, was among the first to sign the 'Noblemen's Covenant', as it became known, after John Gordon, thirteenth Earl of Sutherland, had exercised his own right to precedence. Next day, nearly three hundred ministers and burgesses added their names to the document, followed on the next two days by many of the common people of Edinburgh. After copies of the document were circulated throughout the country, it was eventually signed by some 300,000 people, even if not all did so of their own free will.

Revolution in Scotland

Faced with such a challenge to his authority, Charles I evidently decided that conflict was inevitable. Even so, playing for time, and still full of bluster, he made half-hearted concessions, attempting to appease his opponents in Scotland, who merely escalated their own demands. The train of events now took on a momentum of its own, ending in November 1638 with a month-long meeting of the General Assembly in Glasgow. None of the bishops attended the meeting, and only 140 ministers, out of nearly a thousand, mostly from the Lowlands. It condemned the Five Articles of Perth and the Book of Common Prayer, and then deposed all the bishops and archbishops of Scotland, excommunicating eight of their number. Ministers of religion were banned from all civil office, while kirk sessions, presbyteries, synods and general assemblies were established to form the basis for the future government of the Reformed Church of Scotland. Even so, it was not until the 1707 Act of Union with England that Presbyterianism was finally established in Scotland.

Support for the National Covenant

But while the National Covenant had the character of a national movement, the Covenanters, as its supporters became known, did not have the support of the whole country. The Covenant was formally condemned by the Universities of Aberdeen and St Andrews. Many of the leading men in the far north of Scotland were only persuaded to put their names to the document by a meeting at Inverness on 25 April 1638, attended by John Gordon, thirteenth Earl of Sutherland. They included John Sinclair, Master of

Berriedale, grandson and then heir of the exiled Earl of Caithness, and Donald MacKay of Strathnaver, first Lord Reay, along with many other gentry by the names of Sutherland, Ross, Munro, Fraser and MacKenzie. Even so, George MacKenzie, second Earl of Seaforth, would not sign the Covenant himself as he remained loyal to Charles I as a member of the Privy Council.

Elsewhere, the north-east of Scotland stood out in its resistance to the Covenanting movement, influenced no doubt by the Royalist sympathies and Catholic faith of George Gordon, seventh Earl and second Marquis of Huntly, who had succeeded to his father's titles in 1636. The opposition was led by a group of ministers known as the 'Aberdeen Doctors', who supported the religious policies of Charles I. They regarded the National Covenant as marking a breach from the rest of Protestantism and the ancient Church, describing it as illegal and disloyal. Although James Graham, fifth Earl of Montrose, visited Aberdeen in July 1638, he had little success in getting even the clergy to sign the National Covenant without reservation. It was the rival document, known as the King's Covenant, that subsequently attracted many thousands of signatures in the north-east, largely through Huntly's efforts.

Outbreak of the Bishops' Wars

When the General Assembly ended its meeting in Glasgow on 20 December 1638, the Covenanters had already disowned their allegiance to Charles I. It was only a matter of time before hostilities broke out in what later became known as the 'Bishops' Wars'. Predictably, the first skirmishes occurred in the north-east, where Charles I had appointed George Gordon, second Marquis of Huntly, to defend his interests as the King's Lieutenant in the north. Moreover, Aberdeen was still loyal to the Crown, and the burgh council decided to arm and train men in the King's service.

However, the very presence of Huntly at the head of the Royalist forces encouraged others to support the National Covenant, whatever their religious and political inclinations. Chief among them were the Master of Forbes, James Crichton of Frendraught, and Lord Fraser, who all had their quarrels with the Marquis of Huntly and his family, following the burning of Frendraught Castle in 1630. Joining them in support of the National Covenant were the Keiths, the MacKenzies and the Grants, among several other clans, giving them the command of several hundred men.

Almost the first act of the Covenanters was to seize arms and ammunition from the royal castle of Inverness. This was followed a week later by a confrontation between the two sides at Turriff. It came to nothing as Huntly, perhaps restrained by the King's orders, would not attack the Covenanters, who were evidently prepared to fight. Indeed, he eventually disbanded his own forces at Inverurie after six weeks of stalemate.

Meanwhile, the 'Tables', which had now replaced the Privy Council as the only effective instrument of government in Scotland, had already despatched a small force of 200 men north under James Graham, fifth Earl of Montrose. He was accompanied by Field Marshal Alexander Leslie, even though Leslie had earlier offered his services to Charles I as a mercenary soldier and veteran of the Swedish Wars. Together, they recruited even more men, so that a Covenanting army nearly 11,000 strong was able to occupy the city of Aberdeen without any opposition on 30 March 1639. It was the last stronghold of the Royalist forces to fall in Scotland, since during the previous three weeks the royal castles at Edinburgh and Dumbarton had been seized, and all the other Lowland castles that might be held for Charles I captured, apart from Caerlaverock and Threave.

Arrest of Huntly

Montrose then left Aberdeen under a garrison, and marched north-west with his army towards Strathbogie, while Huntly sought refuge at Balvenie Castle. Realising the Gordon territories could well be plundered and laid waste, Huntly was now prepared to come to an accommodation with the Covenanters, but only if his honour was satisfied. After meeting Montrose at Inverurie, Huntly most likely agreed to adhere to the 1581 Confession of Faith, while allowing his followers to sign the National Covenant. However, this undertaking did not satisfy the more extreme Covenanters, who demanded that Huntly should come to Aberdeen under a safe-conduct.

There, Huntly was placed under virtual house-arrest, despite an assurance previously given him by Montrose that he was free to return to Strathbogie whenever he wished. This betrayal of confidence would sour the relations between the two men, after Montrose had changed sides and declared his allegiance to Charles I, greatly damaging the Royalist cause. Then, after the Covenanters made quite impossible demands of him, Huntly was 'invited' to visit Edinburgh. Since he would otherwise be taken there as a prisoner if he did not go voluntarily, he accepted the inevitable, agreeing to travel south with Montrose. On arriving in Edinburgh, he was warded in the castle with his eldest son George, Lord Gordon, who had accompanied him south.

Repercussions in the North-East

Such dishonourable treatment of George Gordon, second Marquis of Huntly, had repercussions in the north-east, where James Gordon, Viscount Aboyne

and the Marquis's second son, was still at liberty. He joined Sir George
Ogilvie of Banff in resisting the Covenanters at the head of 2,000 men.
However, after learning that a royal fleet had reached the Forth, he went
south disguised as a fiddler to consult with Charles I at Newcastle.
Meanwhile, the first blood of the Civil War was shed on 10 May 1639. Sir
George Ogilvie of Banff and several other Royalist lairds, including Sir
Thomas Urquhart of Cromarty, Sir John Gordon of Haddo, and Sir John
Gordon of Gight, attempted to recover some arms from the castle of Tollie
Barclay, which was defended by Lord Fraser and the Master of Forbes.
One of Gight's servants, known as David Prat, was shot dead in the fracas.
Three days later, the Royalists were successful in preventing a meeting of
Covenanters at Turriff, driving them out of the burgh after a short fight. It
later became known as the 'Trot of Turriff'.

Encouraged by this success, the Royalist forces then marched on
Aberdeen, which they occupied on 15 May 1639. However, they had no
coherent plan of campaign as they had only risen in arms to avoid being
disarmed by the Covenanters and forced to sign the National Covenant.
Although they were joined by other lairds and their followers, they abandoned Aberdeen after five days to return to their own homes, disbanding
their forces. Within a few days, Aberdeen itself was reoccupied by an army
of 2,000 Covenanters under the Earl Marischal, reinforced by another 4,000
men sent north under Montrose.

Montrose now marched north once again to deal with the Royalist lairds,
but hardly had he left Aberdeen than several of the King's ships appeared off
the coast. Among those on board were James Gordon, Viscount Aboyne, as
well as the Earls of Tullibardine and Glencairn, and several of the Royalist
lairds, who had fled south by ship. Montrose and the Earl Marischal suspected that the naval expedition was intended as a decoy to draw attention
away from a Royalist landing farther south, since James Stewart, Marquis of
Hamilton, was lying with another fleet off the Firth of Forth.

They therefore marched south with all their forces, leaving Aberdeen to
be occupied on 6 June 1639 once again by Royalist forces under the command of James Gordon, Viscount Aboyne. He was now acting as King's
Lieutenant in the North in place of his father. The Gordons of Strathbogie
now rallied to the Royalist cause, as did the Farquharsons of Invercauld, so
that a force of more than 2,000 men was soon in possession of Aberdeen.
Montrose was now ordered back north by the 'Tables'. He arrived on 18
June 1639 to find the Royalist forces defending the Brig O'Dee over the
swollen waters of the River Dee, which guarded the southern approaches to
Aberdeen itself.

Battle of Brig O'Dee

Montrose now fought the first battle of his military career, although it was only a minor engagement. A heavy but ineffectual barrage of cannon was first mounted against the Royalist forces, followed by an assault on the bridge itself, which was easily repulsed. After night fell, Montrose moved his cannon closer to the enemy under the cover of darkness, so that he could direct their fire all the more accurately the next day. Even so, the Royalist forces withstood the pounding, still in command of the north bank of the Dee.

Montrose now adopted a tactic that served him well in later years by setting a trap with himself as bait. By leading his horsemen upstream, apparently intending to cross the river higher up, he drew away the forces of Viscount Aboyne from the Brig O'Dee itself along the opposite bank. Meanwhile, the barrage continued to devastating effect, and eventually a party of Covenanters under John Middleton stormed the bridge, putting its defenders to flight. The victory allowed Aberdeen to be occupied once again by the Covenanters, and while much damage was done, the city was not put to the flames.

Actions of Charles I

While these events were unfolding in the north-east, Charles I had embarked on a grandiose plan to put down the rebellion in Scotland. Involving a three-pronged attack on Scotland, it never looked likely to succeed. 5,000 men were first to land at Aberdeen to join the Marquis of Huntly, who would then march south after securing the north-east. However, the royal fleet of nineteen ships under the command of the third Marquis of Hamilton never sailed farther north than the Firth of Forth, and his ill-trained forces never attempted to land upon its shores. Indeed, any such landing would have been opposed in strength by an army of 20,000 Covenanters, and not least by Hamilton's own mother, herself a staunch Covenanter, who vowed to shoot her wayward son should he land.

The other two elements in Charles I's plan for an invasion of Scotland also failed to materialise. Ten or twelve thousand men from Ulster were to land in Argyll under the command of Randal MacDonald, second Earl of Antrim. However, it would be several more years before he finally made good his promise of support for Charles I. Even so, the threat from Ulster was serious enough to pin down Archibald Campbell, eighth Earl of Argyll. He raised a force of 900 men to oppose any such landing in Argyll, which would obviously threaten his own territories. Finally, Sir Thomas Wentworth, Lord Deputy of Ireland, would land at Dumbarton with a third force from Ireland after establishing a base on the island of Arran, which belonged to the Marquis of Hamilton. However, Wentworth was not ready until the end of June, long after the royal castle of Dumbarton was captured, and Arran occupied by the Covenanters under Argyll, so this plan came to nothing as well.

Charles I therefore resorted to raising an army in England, but lack of money reduced its strength to only 21,000 men, while its ranks were poorly trained and far from enthusiastic. After mustering his army at York, Charles I advanced to the Scottish border just west of Berwick. There, he found the Scots army of the Covenant encamped near Duns, several miles to the north. It had marched out of Edinburgh on 21 May under the command of Alexander Leslie. Although strengthened by a core of professional soldiers who had seen military service on the Continent, its ranks were just as badly fed, poorly equipped and ill-trained as the English army. But its morale was far higher, fired by the prospect of fighting a holy war for what was seen as a just and righteous cause in support of the National Covenant.

Charles I now found to his dismay that he lacked the support of the English nobility or even his military commanders to launch a full-scale attack upon Scotland. Forced to negotiate with the Covenanters, the Treaty of Berwick ended the First Bishops' War on 18 June 1639, only a day before Aberdeen had fallen to Montrose after his victory at the Brig O'Dee. It marked an uneasy truce between the two sides, which soon broke down in mutual recrimination. Both armies were to be disbanded, and the royal castles in Scotland surrendered to the King, leaving only two English garrisons on the border, and a Covenanting regiment in arms under Colonel Robert Munro around Edinburgh. Charles I agreed to call a meeting of the General Assembly, which opened on 12 August 1639 in his absence.

Meeting of the General Assembly

The General Assembly now proceeded to make even more insistent demands upon the King. It first ratified all the acts passed at the General Assembly of the previous year, declaring Episcopacy to be against God's will, and asking the Privy Council to make the signing of the National Covenant mandatory on all his Majesty's subjects in Scotland. After approving the acts of the General Assembly, over which it had authority, Parliament then laid the foundations for a constitutional revolution that reached its climax in 1641. Its proceedings so alarmed Charles I that he ordered that Parliament be prorogued until 2 June 1640, evidently hoping by then to have subdued the Covenanters by force.

Charles I now ordered Edinburgh Castle to be repaired. However, when a salute was fired from its batteries to celebrate the King's birthday in

November, pomp and royal dignity crumbled as a section of the walls collapsed. Repairs continued until February 1640, when the castle itself was fortified with supplies of ammunition and provisions, and its garrison reinforced with a hundred English soldiers. However, the need for even more repairs was emphasised later that month when long stretches of the outer walls fell down again. It was hardly a good augury for the Royalist cause.

Charles I now prepared for a renewed offensive against the Covenanters. However, the lack of money to pay his army now forced him to recall what became known as the 'Short Parliament' at Westminster, which only lasted from 13 April to 5 May 1640. It refused to vote to allow the King to raise any taxes for waging war against Scotland unless its own grievances were first settled in England. It thus fatally undermined the plans of Charles I to invade Scotland. Nearly a month later, the Scots Parliament was recalled on 2 June 1640 without the King's authority. It proceeded to make a constitutional revolution in a sitting that lasted for only nine days, effectively destroying the power of Charles I to rule as an absolute monarch in Scotland, while preparing for an invasion of England.

Suppression of Royalist Resistance

But before the Scots army of the Covenant finally invaded England to force Charles I into accepting their demands, the Covenanters had first to deal with the remaining pockets of Royalist resistance within the country. Already, the Covenanters had strengthened their hold on the north-east, where General Robert Munro had occupied Aberdeen and the surrounding districts with a thousand men, seizing many Royalist lairds with the help of the Earl Marischal, and breaking down castles and fortified houses to render them indefensible. In August his forces moved north to Banff, where they plundered the lands of Sir George Ogilvie. They met no resistance from the Gordons, since Huntly was now living in London, where he had gone after being released from Edinburgh Castle in June 1639.

Elsewhere, Archibald Campbell, eighth Earl of Argyll, received a commission of fire and sword, giving him authority from the Covenanting regime to subdue the Earl of Atholl, Lord Ogilvie, and the Farquharsons of Braemar, as well as the inhabitants of Badenoch, Lochaber, Rannoch, and the Braes of Angus. Unlike his father, who had died a Catholic, the eighth Earl of Argyll was a staunch Presbyterian. Indeed, by now, he was amongst the foremost leaders of the Covenanters. However, he did not sign the National Covenant until April 1639, worried that he might be disinherited before he had succeeded his father in all his estates.

Argyll had evidently anticipated his commission, since he was able to muster 4,000 men just a week after it was issued. Indeed, he was already planning an expedition to Lochaber and Badenoch, which he had received by the form of mortgage known as wadset from the debt-ridden Marquis of Huntly, intending to collect his rents there by force. After raising his forces, Argyll marched through Atholl and the Braes of Mar to the Glens of Angus, and then through Badenoch, Lochaber and Rannoch. He enforced the signing of the National Covenant, arresting anyone who refused to do so, while plundering their lands.

However, Argyll's commission to subdue Atholl and the Ogilvies of Airlie had greatly offended Montrose, who then had command of the Covenanting forces throughout the shires of Perth and Forfar. Acting on his own initiative, he decided to forestall Argyll by taking possession of Airlie Castle himself, allowing Lord Ogilvie, eldest son of the Earl of Airlie, to escape. Montrose then garrisoned Airlie Castle with his own men, but they were expelled when Argyll appeared on the scene. Airlie Castle was put to the flames, as commemorated in the ballad 'The Bonnie House of Airlie'.

Invasion of England

The Covenanters were now strong enough to invade England, and indeed they had to act quickly if their forces were not to disintegrate. The army entered England on 20 August 1640 in what became known as the Second Bishops' War, crossing the River Tweed at several places, and then marched steadily south, reaching Newcastle Moor on 26th August. As the city of Newcastle was found to be fortified and well-defended, the Scottish army under the command of Alexander Leslie now decided to turn the enemy's flank, intending to cross the River Tyne at Newburn, five miles upstream from Newcastle.

The southern banks of the Tyne were defended by the King's forces of five or six thousand men, but they were no match for the Scottish army, consisting as it did of some 22,000 foot-soldiers and 500 cavalry. They fled with only slight losses after a brief engagement, which marked the first battle of the Civil War in England. After the Scots had crossed the river, the Royalist garrison abandoned Newcastle in panic and fled south, first to Durham and then into Yorkshire. The Scots army entered Newcastle after it had surrendered on 30 August 1640.

The Long Parliament

After occupying Durham, the Scots resisted the temptation to advance any farther south. They demanded instead that they should be paid £850 a day while their army remained in England. Charles I was now powerless to resist the demands of the Covenanters, since he had no effective army. He was thus coerced into summoning what later became known as the 'Long Parliament' at Westminster, which first met on 3 November 1640. It attempted to sweep away the institutions and prerogatives sustaining the King's power outside Parliament, while its distrust and suspicion of Charles I deepened into outright hostility. The Commons came to demand the same concessions as the Scots Parliament had already passed in 1640. Then, after protracted negotiations, the Second Bishops' War came to an end when Charles I was forced to ratify the Treaty of London on 10 August 1641. By this treaty, he finally agreed to all the Acts passed by the Scots Parliament in 1640. Not long afterwards, the Scots army of the Covenant marched home with £300,000 to its credit.

The King now decided to visit Scotland in person, hoping to exploit the open divisions that had now appeared among the ranks of the Covenanters. But his visit was overshadowed by the 'Incident', apparently a Royalist plot to kidnap several of the Covenanters' leaders, which came to nothing, and then by the outbreak of a serious rebellion in Ireland in October 1641. Whether or not Charles I was implicated in the 'Incident', he was certainly suspected of encouraging the Irish to rise up against the Protestant colonists of Ulster in defence of their Catholic religion. Charles I returned to London to deal with this new crisis, but before he did so, he attempted to buy off his opponents in Scotland with honours. He created Archibald Campbell, eighth Earl of Argyll, the first and only Marquis of Argyll, while Field-Marshal Alexander Leslie became the first Earl of Leven.

Outbreak of the English Civil War

The need to put down the rebellion in Ulster now placed Charles I in an impossible situation. The English Parliament was not prepared to provide the King with an army, which might be used against Parliament itself. In despair, the King turned to Scotland, where an army of 10,000 men was raised under the command of Major-General Robert Munro for service in Ulster. It had secured Antrim and County Down by the summer of 1642, but only after atrocities were committed by both sides. By then, however, the political and religious divisions within the country had brought England to the verge of civil war.

Charles I abandoned London in January 1642, after a rash and ill-fated attempt to arrest his leading critics in the House of Commons. Even so, it was not until 22 August 1642 that he eventually raised the royal standard at Nottingham. Apart from the earlier engagement at Newburn, the first battle

of the English Civil War was fought at Edgehill in October, but it was inde-
cisive, revealing weakness and incompetence on both sides. Thus, after a
winter of stalemate, it was not until 1643 that full-scale hostilities broke out,
and Royalist forces won a string of victories. By then, however, the Scots had
entered into the Solemn League and Covenant with the English Parliament,
which agreed to reform the Church of England along Presbyterian lines,
and to abolish the Catholic Church in Ireland. It convened an assembly of
laymen and clergy, together with representatives from Scotland, which three
years later in 1646 produced the Westminister Confession of Faith, on which
Presbyterian churches still base their doctrines.

A Scots army under the command of Alexander Leslie, first Earl of Leven,
now entered England, where it helped to defeat the Royalist army at the critical battle of Marston Moor in June 1644, after which the military struggle
increasingly favoured the Parliamentary forces, especially after their victory
at Naseby in July 1645. It was only now that the Highland clans were finally
drawn into the conflict in support of Charles I under the leadership of James
Graham, fifth Earl of Montrose, who by then had abandoned his erstwhile
support of the Covenanting regime.

Chapter Three

CLAN DONALD AND
THE EARL OF ARGYLL

The Statutes of Iona of 1609 are cited by some historians as marking a watershed in Highland history, after which the Highland clans abandoned their troublesome ways and gave their wholehearted allegiance to the Stuart dynasty. Admittedly, after the final collapse of the revolt of Sir James MacDonald in 1615, the Highlands and the Western Isles remained at peace for almost the next thirty years, apart from the abortive rebellion of the MacIains of Ardnamurchan against the aggrandisement of the Campbell family in 1625. Indeed, the heavy cautions demanded of them as financial sureties virtually guaranteed their own good behaviour, while ensuring that they had every incentive to keep control of their tenants and other dependants.

Even so, the Statutes of Iona seemingly did little more than bring the Highland chieftains into closer contact with Edinburgh society through their visits each year to the Scottish capital. There, they were often tempted into extravagant spending, vying with one another to live in a manner appropriate to their status, as they saw it. Although their elder sons (or their elder daughters if they had no sons) were now to be educated in English away from the Gaelic-speaking Highlands, it is difficult to believe that this policy in itself would have transformed the once-lawless chiefs of the Highland clans into loyal supporters of the Stuart dynasty within a single generation. After all, it was the Stuarts themselves under James VI who introduced this punitive policy in an attempt to destroy their ancient Gaelic traditions and culture.

Indeed, the measures taken by James VI did not prevent Gaelic poetry and other arts from flourishing throughout the seventeenth century, while the munificence of the chiefly households seemed little diminished. Bards still flourished with enough heroic deeds for them to praise, and even the Campbell Earls of Argyll maintained the MacEwans as their hereditary family of bards and seannachies at Inveraray. Even attempts to disarm the Highlanders evidently had little effect, to judge by subsequent events, since arms could easily enough be hidden, or smuggled into the country if they were needed. No doubt, the great chiefs played down their own conduct when they appeared each year before the Privy Council in Edinburgh, giving accounts of their own households which could not easily be checked.

Divisions within Gaeldom

It was hardly the civilising effects of the Statutes of Iona that prompted many Highland clans to support the Stuart dynasty when it was first threatened with destruction in the years after 1638, and then overthrown in 1688, never to be revived. Instead, the Highland chiefs had their own motives for supporting what was essentially an alliance of mutual self-interest with the Stuarts. Significantly, the Jacobite clans still found themselves opposed to the overweening power and influence of the Campbell Earls of Argyll. No doubt, it was the central role played in the Covenanting movement by Archibald Campbell, Lord Lorne and afterwards the eighth Earl and first Marquis of Argyll, which determined their own reactions to the momentous events that followed the signing of the National Covenant in 1638.

Ever since Archibald Campbell, Lord Lorne, had come of age in 1628, he had acted as guardian of the Campbell interest in the absence of his father, the seventh Earl, who had fled the country in 1617 after becoming a Catholic. Although Lord Lorne had then surrendered his hereditary office as Justice-General of Scotland to the Crown, he still remained Justiciar of Argyll and the Western Isles. By then, Campbell hegemony stretched over much of present-day Argyll and beyond from Kintyre in the south to Ardnamurchan in the north, while the influence of the Campbells of Glenorchy had spread eastwards into Breadalbane. By supporting Charles I against the Covenanters, many Highland chieftains evidently hoped to shake off the feudal superiority of the Campbells, Earls of Argyll, under whom they held their lands, while others may even have hoped to recover lands lost by their forebears. Chief among the latter was Randal MacDonald, second Earl of Antrim, who stood at the head of a powerful family that had replaced the MacDonalds of Dunyvaig and the Glens as the southern branch of Clan Donald.

Revival of Catholicism

Equally important were the religious differences which separated the two factions. Since the Campbells were staunch Presbyterians, it is perhaps not surprising that the remnants of Clan Donald in the Western Isles were a fertile ground for the proselytising work of the Catholic Church. Gaelic-speaking missionaries of the Franciscan order first appeared in the years after 1619, when their mission to the Western Isles was most likely encouraged by Randal MacDonald, first Earl of Antrim. Not only was he a Catholic, but he also sought to revive the ancient unity of Clan Donald under his leadership. In any event, the Franciscan priests established their mission at the old friary of Bonamargy near Ballycastle in the north of Antrim, where the Earls of Antrim were buried.

The Franciscans travelled widely throughout the western Highlands and Islands, often in danger of their lives, visiting the Uists and Barra in the Outer Hebrides; Canna, Eigg, Rhum and Muck as well as the Ross of Mull, Oronsay, Colonsay and Jura in the Inner Hebrides; and Kintyre, Moidart and Glengarry on the mainland. Oddly enough, Sir John Campbell of Cawdor was an early convert on Islay, perhaps emulating the example of the seventh Earl of Argyll, who had married a Catholic as his second wife.

But it was the revival of Catholicism among the MacDonalds which was politically more significant. It marked a return of the close links which had existed between Ulster and the Western Isles during the sixteenth century. Indeed, after 1631, when travelling to the Western Isles became too hazardous for the Franciscan missionaries, many hundreds if not thousands of MacDonald clansmen visited Bonamargy each year at Easter to receive the sacraments of the Catholic Church. Prominent among these converts was John MacDonald, Captain of Clan Ranald, who wrote from Uist to the Pope in 1626 offering to drive 'the turbulent, detested followers of Calvin' from his territories if he was given military help.

More significantly, John MacDonald, Captain of Clan Ranald, promised the Pope that 'all the Gaelic-speaking Scots and the greater part of the Irish chieftains joined to us by ties of friendship will begin war in each his own district to the glory of God'. Nothing came of his grand promise for the time being, but it was honoured in the years after 1638, when the Covenanting movement made ever more strident demands in response to the intransigence of Charles I. By then, Gaelic-speaking Highlanders, and especially the Catholic chieftains of the western Hebrides, had come to reject the extreme Presbyterianism imposed upon them by the Covenanters. They viewed it as yet another attempt by a Lowland government to destroy their ancient traditions and culture.

Machinations of the Earl of Antrim

The Gaelic chieftains of the western Highlands mostly held aloof from national affairs in the years that followed the signing of the National Covenant in February 1638. However, Randal MacDonald, second Earl of

Antrim after 1636, realised that he might regain the ancestral lands of Clan Donald if he were to offer his services to Charles I as the heir to James MacDonald of Dunyvaig and the Glens.

The first Earl of Antrim already held vast estates in Antrim, inherited from his father, Sir Randal MacDonald of Dunluce, who had himself received them from James VI, just after the Union of the Crowns in 1603. Even before the ancestral lands of Clan Donald in Islay finally passed from their hands, Sir Randal MacDonald had managed to obtain a seven-year lease of the island in 1612, only to provoke the rebellion that finally lost Islay to Sir John Campbell of Cawdor in 1614. Then, after being created Earl of Antrim in 1620, he attempted without success to buy back the island in 1627. Three years later, the barony of Kintyre with its lands on Jura was offered for sale. Eventually, it was agreed that Sir Randal MacDonald should purchase it on behalf of his eldest son, but again the bargain was annulled in 1635 after Archibald Campbell, Lord Lorne, had intervened to prevent its sale.

Given this background, it is hardly surprising that Randal MacDonald, second Earl of Antrim, approached Charles I in June 1638 to propose that he should seize the Campbell territories in the western Highlands and Islands in return for their restoration to Clan Donald. Archibald Campbell, Lord Lorne, had already greatly offended Charles I with his outspoken remarks when summoned to London to explain Scotland's grievances, soon after the signing of the National Covenant. Indeed, Charles I was so hostile that Lord Lorne had already started to muster men and arms for the defence of his own territories in Argyll, long before he finally declared his support for the National Covenant in December 1638. By then, his father had died in London, so removing any danger that he might be disinherited if he did so.

Rallying the Clans

Meanwhile, James Hamilton, third Marquis of Hamilton, acting as the King's Commissioner in Scotland, had realised that the widespread hostility to the Campbells among the Highland clans, and especially among the remnants of Clan Donald, might well be harnessed in the Royalist cause. He therefore encouraged Sir Donald Gorm MacDonald of Sleat to take soundings in the western Highlands and Islands. He wrote back in August 1638 with the gratifying news that John MacDonald, Captain of Clan Ranald, and Donald MacDonald of Strome, Chief of Glengarry, along with the 'whole name of Clan Donald', had sworn to live and die with him in the King's service. Meanwhile, the King's Commissioner had already dispatched George MacKenzie, second Earl of Seaforth, to garner Royalist support among his own clansmen in the north-west Highlands. Seaforth was later promised the office of Justice-General of the Western Isles in place of Argyll. It was even thought that Lord Reay, Chief of MacKay, might be equally sympathetic to the Royalist cause, despite his support for the National Covenant.

So the makings of a King's party evidently existed among the Gaelic clans opposed to Campbell dominance over the western Highlands and Islands. If Randal MacDonald, second Earl of Antrim, had made good his offer to invade Argyll in 1638, the Covenanters might well have been faced by a major revolt in the Highlands, as other disaffected clans were likely to join Clan Donald in fighting their traditional enemies. However, it was soon clear that the Earl of Antrim lacked the resources to mount such an invasion without the government in Ireland providing him with men and arms. Such help was never likely to be forthcoming, given the implacable opposition of Sir Thomas Wentworth, Lord Deputy of Ireland. Indeed, the plan itself was inimical to the King's own interests, since the employment of Catholics like Randal MacDonald to further the Royalist cause could only deepen the religious divisions that already existed between Charles I and the Covenanting movement.

Meanwhile, Archibald Campbell, now the eighth Earl of Argyll, evidently felt threatened by such an alliance between Charles I and the Earl of Antrim. He strengthened his own hold on Islay and Kintyre, expelling any remaining MacDonald clansmen from his territories. Indeed, after Argyll had purchased a frigate from Holland, Sir Thomas Wentworth remarked drily that it now looked more likely that the Earl of Argyll would invade Antrim, rather than the other way round.

Royal Promises to the Clan Chiefs

One consequence of Argyll's actions was that Sir Donald Gorm MacDonald of Sleat accompanied the second Earl of Antrim to visit Charles I at Berwick, after he had landed in Ulster with 300 MacDonalds expelled from Kintyre and Islay by the Campbells. After their arrival at Court, and even while he was negotiating terms of peace with the Covenanters to end the First Bishops' War, Charles I issued commissions to Antrim and MacDonald of Sleat appointing them jointly to act as King's Lieutenants and Commissioners in the Highlands and Isles against his enemies. In return for their support, Antrim was promised possession of Kintyre and Jura, while MacDonald of Sleat was to receive the islands of Rhum, Eigg, Muck and Canna, the lands of Sunart and Ardnamurchan, and the lands of Strathordle on Skye. The King had already written to William MacIntosh, Captain of Clan Chattan, promising to remove him from the feudal superiority of Argyll if he would obey George Gordon, second Marquis of Huntly.

Armed with his commission, Sir Donald Gorm MacDonald of Sleat then persuaded a number of chiefs to sign a bond of loyalty to the King. They included, among several others: Sir James Lamont of Lamont; Sir James Stewart, Sheriff of Bute; John MacDonald, Captain of Clan Ranald; George MacKenzie, second Earl of Seaforth; John MacLeod of Dunvegan; and Sir Lachlan MacLean of Duart. Together, they agreed to resurrect the earlier plan for an invasion of Islay and Kintyre by the Earl of Antrim, coupled with an attack on Lorne by forces loyal to Sir Donald Gorm MacDonald of Sleat. However, their plans came to nothing after they were betrayed to the Covenanters by Sir James Lamont, fearful of his dependence on the Campbells.

Raid upon Colonsay

Indeed, Argyll now apparently seized the initiative. Not content with forcing the remaining MacDonalds out of Islay and Kintyre, it seems the Campbells also raided the island of Colonsay in June 1639, which had been held for many years for the MacDonalds by Colla Ciotach, father of Alasdair macColla Ciotach MacDonald. A kinsman of the MacDonalds, Earls of Antrim, Colla Ciotach had taken a leading role in the rebellion of Sir James MacDonald in 1615, but afterwards escaped the consequences of its failure by turning King's evidence to save his own life. Tradition has it that he then engaged in a lengthy feud with the MacPhees of Colonsay, capturing their chief by an act of treachery. The feud itself ended with the chief's death in 1623 at the hands of Colla Ciotach, who then took possession of Colonsay after he had been pardoned for his crime.

Colla Ciotach thus came under the feudal superiority of Archibald Campbell, then Lord Lorne, who eventually accepted him as his tenant in return for the payment of 10,000 merks for the lease of Colonsay during his lifetime. An ardent Catholic, and a distant kinsman of the Earl of Antrim, Colla Ciotach soon became involved in planning an abortive invasion of the south-west Highlands in 1638, which however came to nothing. But the following year, after Royalist ships had been active in the Hebrides, Argyll ordered a raid in June 1639 against Colonsay by 100 Campbells from Islay under the command of Sir Donald Campbell of Ardnamurchan. They plundered the island and perhaps even captured Colla Ciotach and two of his sons. However, mystery surrounds their capture, and it may be they were lured under trust to visit Inveraray or Dunstaffnage, and then arrested. Even so, the raid was not entirely successful. Two other sons of Colla Ciotach escaped to Ireland, where Alasdair macColla Ciotach MacDonald and his brother Ranald found refuge with their kinsmen in Antrim.

Gathering Storm

Only minor disorders occurred in the western Highlands over the next two years, when the feudal superiority of Archibald Campbell, eighth Earl of Argyll, was briefly challenged by the MacDonalds of Keppoch and Glengarry. Then yet another threat to Campbell interests emerged in November 1640 when Alasdair MacDonald and his brother Ranald mounted an attack against Islay with eighty men from Antrim. However, they failed to capture George Campbell of Kilchoman, tutor to the brother of Sir John Campbell of Cawdor, whom they presumably hoped to exchange for Alasdair's father. A year later in October 1641, however, the rebellion broke out in Ulster, and Alasdair MacDonald was drawn into a military career that came to rival the exploits of James Graham, fifth Earl and first Marquis of Montrose.

Rebellion in Ulster

The insurrection in Ulster began as a reaction against the Elizabethan conquest of Ireland, and the subsequent plantation by James VI of Protestant colonists in Ulster after the 'Flight of the Earls' in 1607. As a result, many of the native Irish gentry who had once held the lands of the Catholic Earls of Tyrone and Tyrconnel now became the tenants of English settlers or Lowland Scots, especially in the six counties of Armagh, Cavan, Derry (or Coleraine), Donegal, Fermanagh, and Tyrone. They were also dispossessed in parts of County Antrim and County Down, where Lowland Scots with their Presbyterian sympathies had started to settle in strength. Only in northeast Ulster did the MacDonalds, Earls of Antrim, keep hold of their lands.

Then the Long Parliament at Westminister threatened to introduce repressive legislation against the Catholic religion in Ireland after the overthrow of Sir Thomas Wentworth, formerly Lord Deputy of Ireland, soon after Charles I made him the first Earl of Stafford in 1640. The native Irish now began to fear that the Protestant settlers in Ulster would be used to enforce these laws. Equally, the successful challenge made in Scotland by the Covenanters against the authority of Charles I encouraged them into rebellion, even if their aims were very different. The insurrection afterwards spread to other parts of Ireland, where many Anglo-Irish families shared much the same grievances as the native Irish, and it was only finally put down, with great brutality, when Oliver Cromwell invaded the country in 1649.

Randal MacDonald, second Earl of Antrim, was staying in Dublin when the Ulster rebellion first broke out in October 1641. Despite his Catholic religion, and his Gaelic origins, his father had been granted the ancient lands

of the MacDonalds in the Glens of Antrim, and farther west in the district
known as the Route. Thus, Randal MacDonald as the second Earl of Antrim
had every reason to remain loyal to Charles I, who had already shown him
favour, and very little to gain if he joined the Irish confederates in their
rebellion.

However, his followers at Dunluce Castle on the north coast of Antrim
could not so easily remain aloof from the conflict. They immediately raised a
regiment in support of the Crown under the command of Archibald Stewart
of Ballintoy, who was the Earl's agent but a Protestant. Two of the companies
in Stewart's regiment were composed of Catholics, consisting of MacDonalds
and their refugee MacDonald kinsmen from Scotland under the captaincy of
Tirlough Og O'Cahan and Alasdair macColla Ciotach MacDonald. The
other five or six companies were almost exclusively Protestant. This uneasy
alliance of Catholic and Protestant forces kept the peace for the next two
months, defending the western marches of County Antrim against the threat
of any infiltration by the Irish rebels from County Derry across the River
Bann.

Elsewhere, however, the rebel forces under Sir Phelim O'Neill soon came
to dominate much of Ulster, apart from County Antrim and the north of
County Down. Forces loyal to the government in Dublin only held isolated
strongholds like Londonderry, Enniskillen and Carrickfergus. The rebels'
success brought with it stories of Catholic atrocities, however exaggerated,
and Alasdair MacDonald evidently decided to change sides, given the distrust he now attracted within Stewart's regiment. He acted quickly, decisively
and quite ruthlessly when he did so.

Duplicity of Alasdair MacDonald

After Archibald Stewart of Ballintoy had learnt that Agivey Castle, lying just
across the River Bann in County Derry, was besieged by rebel Catholic
forces, he ordered each company in his regiment to send fourteen or fifteen
men to help relieve the castle. However, the order was refused by Tirlough
Og O'Cahan and Alasdair MacDonald, unwilling to act against the rebels
since they were led by Tirlough's brother Manus. This conflict of loyalty,
and fears for their own safety, most likely precipitated their decision to
change sides and join the Catholic rebels, since they must have known that
action would be taken against them for refusing orders.

What happened next is not entirely clear. It seems that nearly all the
Protestant companies were guarding a crossing of the River Bann at Portnaw
against a rebel incursion, when the two Catholic companies of Tirlough Og
O'Cahan and Alasdair MacDonald suddenly appeared just before dawn on

the morning of 2 January 1642, fully armed and marching towards their quarters with banners flying. Once they realised the danger, the officers commanding the Protestant companies made a desperate attempt to rally their own men, who were still asleep. By then, the Catholic companies had fanned out, firing a volley of musket shot before they charged the Protestant lines. The surprise attack routed the Protestant forces, who mostly fled in panic to safety, leaving some sixty men dead upon the field.

Origins of the 'Highland Charge'

Alasdair MacDonald and Tirlough Og O'Cahan now joined up with the Irish rebels from County Derry, and proceeded to subdue Antrim, burning the towns of Ballymena, Ballymoney and Cross. Then, an engagement on 11 February 1642 entered the annals of military history as the first recorded instance of the 'Highland Charge'. By then, Archibald Stewart of Ballintoy had retreated to the town of Coleraine with the remnants of his Royalist regiment. Desperately short of food since the town was also packed with thousands of refugees, he broke out of the loose siege around the town on 'Black Friday', as the date later became known to Protestants, with a force variously put at 600 or 1,100 men, intending to scour the surrounding countryside for supplies.

The rebels had only 600 or 700 men at their command. However, Alasdair MacDonald was able to draw off all of Stewart's forces into an ambush at Laney near Ballymoney, luring them into pursuing a rebel detachment across boggy ground. After firing just a single volley, Alasdair's men threw down their muskets, and immediately charged the enemy with bloodthirsty cries. Engaging in hand-to-hand fighting, they then used their single-handed swords or dirks as weapons, whilst defending themselves with the small rounded shield of wood and leather with a central spike, known as a targe. It was a devastating tactic that would bring Highland armies success after success against Lowland or English forces in the century ahead until it failed to break the Hanoverian lines at Culloden. The battle of the Laney itself, or the battle of Bendooragh as it is sometimes known, ended with the slaughter of nearly of all Stewart's forces, and only a pathetic remnant finally struggled back to Coleraine with their commander.

The tactic itself evolved over time since later accounts suggest that the enemy lines were often pierced by thick wedges of charging swordsmen, twelve or fourteen men deep. By first discharging a single volley of musket fire at a distance, the Highland clansmen would often provoke the enemy into firing back too soon. They then had no time to reload their muskets before they were attacked at close quarters in hand-to-hand fighting or, later in the century, to fix their plug bayonets into the barrels of their muskets to defend themselves. Such a charge could often only be defeated if fire was withheld until the Highlanders were within point-blank range, but this required great discipline to be exercised by the enemy ranks if it were to succeed. Such a method of attack might appear highly risky, but surprisingly the casualties among the Highlanders were often remarkably light, compared with the devastating effect upon the enemy ranks.

Intervention of Argyll

Meanwhile, Randal MacDonald, second Earl of Antrim, had left Dublin at the outbreak of the Ulster rebellion. He took shelter with various friends and kinsmen around the country, trying to avoid being drawn into the struggle. However, a Covenanting army from Scotland under the command of Major-General Robert Munro arrived at Carrickfergus late in April 1642 to lend its support to the defence of the Protestant settlers in Ulster. Its presence forced the Earl of Antrim to declare where his allegiance lay with regard to the Crown. More significantly, however, he faced the immediate danger of an invasion of his own territories by Archibald Campbell, eighth Earl and first Marquis of Argyll.

Indeed, after learning that Alasdair MacDonald and the other MacDonalds had joined the rebellion in Ulster, the Marquis of Argyll was granted permission by the Covenanters to send his own regiment to Ulster. Moreover, he was given power to appoint a governor of Rathlin Island, a MacDonald stronghold, thus suggesting that any invasion by his own forces would be directed against the lands of Randal MacDonald in the north of Antrim. Faced with the likelihood of an imminent attack upon his estates, the Earl of Antrim hurried back at last to Dunluce Castle. Desperate to prove his loyalty to the Crown, he immediately ordered his own tenants and other dependants to withdraw from the siege of Coleraine, and then sent food into the town to relieve its suffering. Soon afterwards, the siege itself was abandoned.

Covenanting Army in Ulster

After arriving in Ulster, Major-General Robert Munro first mounted an expedition south to Newry, and then turned his attention to subduing Antrim. The bulk of his forces left Carrickfergus on 25 May 1642 to march north along the River Bann towards Dunluce Castle, while trying without much success to cut off any rebels as they tried to escape west into County Derry. Randal MacDonald had already written to Munro at Carrickfergus in conciliatory terms, and now he tried to placate him further by laying on a 'mighty feast' at Dunluce Castle in his honour. Munro gracefully accepted the invitation, only to arrest his host as soon as the feast had ended.

Meanwhile, Argyll's regiment had occupied Rathlin Island, where tradition has it that many MacDonalds were massacred by the Campbell forces, before landing on the north coast of Antrim. Dunluce Castle was now garrisoned by Munro's own men, while the rest of Antrim's estates were occupied by Argyll's regiment, commanded by Sir Duncan Campbell of Auchinbreck. However, the liberties taken by the Campbell forces on their arrival, acting as if they had every right to the MacDonald lands of Antrim, eventually persuaded Munro to transfer Randal MacDonald to Carrickfergus by sea for his own safety, leaving Dunluce Castle to be garrisoned by Sir Duncan Campbell of Auchinbreck.

Battle of Glenmaquin

Munro's expedition north to Dunluce was evidently successful in subduing much of Antrim. It forced Alasdair MacDonald and his brother Ranald to take refuge in the Glens of Antrim, along with 1,000 of their men. However, they soon escaped west across the River Bann, where they joined the main body of Irish rebels under Sir Phelim O'Neill. Thus reinforced, the rebel army was able to move against the Protestant forces around Londonderry, which were commanded by Sir Robert Stewart. The inadequacies of Sir Phelim O'Neill as a military commander now became obvious. When battle was joined on 16 June 1642 at Glenmaquin, northwest of Raphoe in County Donegal, the Irish rebels were heavily defeated despite a superiority in numbers.

The two armies had made contact with one another on the previous day. Sir Robert Stewart fell back at first, but then advanced under the cover of darkness to a defensive position within half a mile of the Irish camp. Dawn revealed the Irish rebels occupying the opposite hillside across an area of low-lying ground. Trying to draw the Irish forces to attack his entrenched positions, Sir Robert Stewart first ordered forward a strong body of horse- and foot-soldiers. The stratagem tempted the Irish to mount a fierce if somewhat confused charge towards the Protestant forces advancing against them, who fired upon the enemy before falling back in quick order to their prepared positions.

Now thinking the enemy had been put to flight, Alasdair MacDonald continued to charge uphill towards the Protestant forces with his men, but the force of his attack was completely broken by Stewart's musketeers and pikemen behind their earthen ramparts. The Irish forces under Sir Phelim O'Neill were soon in full flight, with Alasdair's own men not far behind, as they were pursued with very heavy losses for several miles from the field of battle. Alasdair MacDonald was himself seriously wounded, but managed to escape to safety, carried away on a horse-litter.

Such a humiliating defeat might well have ended the Ulster rebellion, but the Scots army under Major-General Robert Munro lacked sufficient men and supplies to follow up its victory. Indeed, before the Scots army could be reinforced, the military balance changed significantly in August 1642 when Owen Roe O'Neill arrived in Ireland to take command of the Irish forces in Ulster. O'Neill was a professional soldier of great experience, who had served for over thirty years in the Spanish army. He set about converting the Irish forces in Ulster into a more disciplined and well-trained army. Even though his reforms did not yield quick results, they eventually led to stalemate between the two armies for the next six years, broken only occasionally by minor victories on either side.

Alliance with the Earl of Leven

Meanwhile, Alexander Leslie, first Earl of Leven, had arrived in Ireland to take command of the Scots army of the Covenant in Ulster. His arrival apparently prompted Alasdair MacDonald and his brother Ranald to betray their former allies among the Irish rebels by changing sides once again. In return for their submission, the Earl of Leven promised to obtain the release of their father Colla Ciotach and their two brothers from Archibald Campbell, first Marquis of Argyll, while they were to be restored to their lands in Colonsay.

As a pledge of their sincerity, Alasdair MacDonald and his brother Ranald were first to plunder goods and livestock from their O'Cahan hosts and kinsmen, who had given them shelter after their defeat at the battle of Glenmaquin only three months previously. This was apparently enough to satisfy the Earl of Leven, who issued orders in November 1642 that Alasdair MacDonald was to choose 300 men from among his followers for service against the Irish rebels, while his brother Ranald and their remaining followers were to remain behind as hostages against his return.

It is not known if Alasdair ever made this expedition against his former allies, as the agreement with Leven broke down not long afterwards when Argyll refused to release Colla Ciotach and his other prisoners. Alasdair MacDonald and his followers then escaped back across the River Bann into rebel-held territory. What sort of welcome they received is not recorded, but it can hardly have been enthusiastic, and another year passed before anything more is heard of them.

Setback to Charles I

Meanwhile, Randal MacDonald, second Earl of Antrim, was still held captive at Carrickfergus when Charles I raised his standard at Nottingham in August 1642, marking the start of the Civil War in England. However, Randal managed to escape from Lord Chichester's house, disguised as a servant, early in October 1642. But finding the boat he had hired from the Isle of Man could not sail because of contrary winds, he calmly returned to captivity to wait for the winds to change. Two days later, he again used the same disguise to fool his guards, and escaped to England, where he joined the Royalist camp at York.

Randal spent the following winter in England, plotting and negotiating with other Royalist sympathisers, and encouraged by Henrietta Maria, the King's Catholic Queen, who promoted her husband's interests with more zeal than good judgment. While Randal evidently did not disclose all his plans to Charles I, their full extent became clear when he was captured in May 1643 at Newcastle in County Down on his return to Ireland. He apparently hoped to reach an agreement with the rebel commander Owen Roe O'Neill on behalf of the King.

The disclosure of Randal's plans proved disastrous to Charles I, whether or not he knew anything of them. The King's enemies now believed that the King was even prepared to use such Catholic forces as the Irish rebels under Owen Roe O'Neill and the other confederate leaders, and the Gaelic-speaking Scots of Clan Donald, against his Parliamentary opponents in England. The revelations were especially damaging in Scotland, where Charles I was seen as plotting civil war against the Covenanters, but in fact Protestants throughout the whole country were horrified, whatever their political persuasion.

It was enough to lose Charles I the tacit support of the Covenanters in Scotland, who feared losing all the religious and political gains they had made since 1638. A few months later in August 1643, at the urging of the Earl of Argyll, who was now among the foremost leaders of the Covenanters, the Scots approved the religious, political and military alliance with the English Parliament known as the Solemn League and Covenant. This alliance effectively tipped the balance of power against Charles I in England, causing his defeat in the English Civil War, and ultimately his death on the block in 1649.

Campaign in the Western Isles

Once again a prisoner, Randal MacDonald, second Earl of Antrim, was held in close confinement for several months at Carrickfergus. He then managed to escape in October 1643. Helped by Lieutenant John Gordon, who had concealed a rope in his 'breeks', Randal MacDonald let himself down the castle walls, only to fall into the sea. He sought refuge in the Irish quarter of the town, even passing a soldier who remarked that 'if the Earl was not in the Castle, he would swear that was he who passed by him then'. Hunted by his enemies, the Earl of Antrim eventually succeeded in reaching Charles I at Oxford.

Randal's audacious escape perhaps allowed one small element of his original plan to be put into effect, since Alasdair MacDonald and his brother Ranald MacDonald embarked on a prolonged raid throughout the Western Isles in November 1643. Even before he was captured on his return to Ireland in May 1643, Randal had sent his brother Alexander to recruit Alasdair and Ranald MacDonald to the Royalist cause, and afterwards helped them raise the forces that were needed, numbering around 300 men.

Alasdair MacDonald evidently made first for his home territory of Colonsay, where he landed in mid-November 1643, seizing the island from its Campbell tenants. Several days later, a merchant vessel armed with six cannon was very nearly captured by Alasdair MacDonald, after it had taken shelter from a storm off the island. The ship managed to escape when the master gunner threatened to blow up its magazine, but it was afterwards wrecked off the coast near Dunollie Castle.

Meanwhile, news of this latest insurrection had reached Edinburgh, where Archibald Campbell, first Marquis of Argyll, was given a commission of lieutenancy over the Western Isles. He had the power to levy a force of 600 men, while he raised another 500 men from his own estates. As the matter was not considered serious enough to merit his own presence in the field, he appointed James Campbell of Ardkinglas to act as his deputy lieutenant.

All we know of the subsequent campaign comes from the brief report written by Ardkinglas after he had succeeded in bringing the incursion to an end. According to his account, Alasdair MacDonald and his forces were driven from island to island, and eventually forced to retreat to Ireland. Their losses were 119 men killed, or executed after they had been captured. Ardkinglas then proceeded to Mull, where he punished anyone who had sheltered the rebels by 'giving them law', a bland enough phrase for their summary execution.

By now, the rebellion appeared to be over, but Ardkinglas then learnt that Alasdair's men had captured Rathlin Island from the garrison already established there by Argyll's regiment in Ulster. He therefore attacked the island, forcing the rebels to flee to Islay and Jura, and executing over 150 of them. Alasdair MacDonald himself escaped by sheer good fortune, since he had by then been recalled to Ireland by the Earl of Antrim to take command of a new expedition against the King's enemies in Scotland.

Renewed Plans by the Earl of Antrim

When he escaped from captivity at Carrickfergus in October 1643, Randal MacDonald, second Earl of Antrim, had taken advantage of the truce agreed just a month earlier between the confederate forces under Owen Roe O'Neill, and the Royalist forces now in Dublin under the command of James Butler, thirteenth Earl and first Marquis of Ormond. Indeed, Randal fled to safety at Charlemont on the western shores of Lough Neagh, where Owen Roe O'Neill had his headquarters. He was there granted the role of Lieutenant-General of the confederate forces, even though he was not trusted with any military powers. Then, after passing through Dublin, he made his way to Charles I at his headquarters in Oxford.

Once there, Randal set about reviving his plans for a grand alliance of Royalist forces, Protestant and Catholic, throughout the three kingdoms of Scotland, Ireland and England. Charles I now needed all the help he could get, since it was only a matter of time before a Scots army of the Covenant under Alexander Leslie, first Earl of Leven, would invade England in support of his enemies, which it duly did on 19 January 1644. The King therefore now encouraged Randal MacDonald in what was a forlorn attempt to persuade the Irish confederates to raise an army of 10,000 men for the King's service in England. However, the Irish rebels had no real interest in sending an army to England to fight for the King. But they might be persuaded to raise a smaller force of two or three thousand men for an invasion of Argyll's territories in Scotland, since they were still fighting the Scots army of the Covenant in Ulster.

By 20 January 1644, a plan of action was agreed with Charles I, acting on the advice of James Graham, fifth Earl of Montrose, who was now appointed Lieutenant-General of the King's forces in Scotland. Randal MacDonald, second Earl of Antrim, was given a commission to negotiate with the Irish confederates, not only to raise 10,000 men to resist the Scots invasion of England, but to send another 2,000 men to invade Argyll's territories in Scotland with the help of George MacKenzie, second Earl of Seaforth. Both men were to act as joint justiciars of the Highlands and Isles, along with Sir James MacDonald of Sleat, who had succeeded his father in 1643.

Negotiations in Ireland

Randal MacDonald, second Earl of Antrim, then returned to Ireland at the end of January 1644. There the supreme council of the Irish confederates at Kilkenny agreed to supply him with arms, ammunition and food if he himself raised the 2,000 men he had promised for the invasion of Argyll's territories. However, the Irish insisted that the Marquis of Ormond, acting as the King's Lieutenant in Dublin, should hand over a port such as Carlingford in County Louth where they could assemble their expeditionary force in safety. Although willing to provide the ships for Antrim's expedition to Scotland, Ormond was not prepared to make any strategic concession to the Irish confederates. Indeed, they might use such a port against his Royalist forces in Ireland if hostilities ever broke out again between them.

No doubt, Ormond distrusted the motives of Randal MacDonald, second Earl of Antrim, thinking that he was perhaps more intent on regaining his own territories in Antrim, now occupied by Argyll's forces, than in mounting an expedition in an attempt to regain the ancient lands of Clan Donald in Islay and Kintyre. Ormond also doubted if the Earl of Antrim was the most suitable person to command the expedition, even though he probably never intended to lead it personally. Indeed, it seems the Earl of Antrim gave Alasdair MacDonald the King's commission, appointing him as Major-General in charge of the expedition against Argyll's territories in Scotland, after meeting him with 800 of his men in County Galway in mid-March 1644.

Expedition against the Western Isles

There was little difficulty in raising the men needed, but it was not until the end of June 1644 that three merchant ships finally set sail from the ports of Passage and Ballahack near Waterford, accompanied by the frigate *Harp*. The expedition sailing north through the Irish Sea consisted of 'hard on sixteen hundred' men, but they were well-armed and supplied. Later reinforcements from Ulster perhaps brought their number up to 2,500 men. They were divided into three regiments, commanded respectively by Antrim's brother Alexander MacDonald with the rank of Lieutenant-General; Colonel Manus O'Cahan, who had joined Alasdair MacDonald in his campaigns in early 1642 on behalf of the Irish rebels; and Colonel James MacDonald, who was a distant kinsman of the earls of Antrim.

The officers under them were mostly native Irishmen from County Antrim and the north of County Derry, made up especially of MacDonalds, along with MacHenrys, MacQuillans, O'Cahans, and O'Haras. But a significant number were English, Lowland Scots and other Highlanders, including many MacDonalds who had taken refuge in Ireland. Most had gained their military experience in the Ulster rebellion. Some at least were veteran soldiers who had fought for the Catholic armies in the Spanish Netherlands, to judge by the military discipline that they were later to show in battle. All were united by their Catholic religion, appearing to the strict Covenanters as the hordes of the Antichrist.

Early Setbacks and Successes

After anchoring in the Sound of Islay, Alasdair MacDonald learnt that the MacDonald stronghold of Rathlin Island had fallen to the Campbells, cutting off any line of retreat. He then sailed north towards Mull, hoping to rally Sir Lachlan MacLean of Duart to the Royalist cause. Already, the expedition had captured a boat sailing from Ulster to Scotland with two Presbyterian ministers on board, who were held captive for use in any exchange of prisoners. Then two English merchantmen were captured off Mull, laden with wheat, rye and sack, which had been blown off course en route to Londonderry.

However, after arriving off Mull, Alasdair MacDonald failed to persuade Sir Lachlan MacLean of Duart to join what must have seemed to him an enterprise doomed to failure. Doubtless, MacLean was aware of the reprisals taken by the Campbells during the course of Alasdair MacDonald's last raid against the Western Isles, only a few months previously. Moreover, he had already contributed a company to Argyll's regiment in Ulster. It followed his release from imprisonment by Archibald Campbell, eighth Earl of Argyll, who had earlier discovered that he had signed the band of 1639 with Sir Donald Gorm MacDonald of Sleat in support of the King.

Faced with this setback, Alasdair MacDonald now decided to take the offensive without waiting for any other chiefs to join him. His first objective was the capture of Kinlochaline Castle on the mainland of Morvern opposite Duart, now held by Campbell forces. Manus O'Cahan landed there with 400 men on 7 July 1644, and the castle surrendered on the same day. Meanwhile, Alasdair MacDonald with the rest of his expedition sailed north to Ardnamurchan, which was now held by Sir Donald Campbell of Ardnamurchan after the MacIains of Ardnamurchan were expelled in 1625.

When Alasdair MacDonald first set foot on the Scottish mainland on 8 July 1644, it was said that a supernatural noise was heard throughout the kingdom as a dreadful portent 'that a cruel, savage, and foreign enemy had invaded the country'. Perhaps it was only summer thunder. He began by plundering the surrounding countryside, before laying siege to Mingary Castle two days later. Its garrison surrendered on 14 July 1644, possibly through a lack of water.

Alasdair MacDonald now tried unsuccessfully to rally the other chieftains to the King's standard. Sir James MacDonald of Sleat was much less committed to the Royalist cause than his father, who had died the previous year, and he spurned the King's commission, as did George MacKenzie, second Earl of Seaforth, and John Mor MacLeod of Dunvegan. The failure to rally any Highland chieftains to the Royalist cause was followed by yet another blow to the expedition, when Alasdair ordered the frigate *Harp* to pursue a ship that appeared off Ardnamurchan on 17 July 1644. Two days later, the frigate reappeared, now hotly pursued by ships loyal to the English Parliament, which were patrolling the waters between Scotland and Ireland.

There are conflicting accounts about what then happened. It is usually thought that all of Alasdair MacDonald's ships were sunk there and then, so cutting off his retreat to Ireland in the face of almost certain defeat. However, the only account by an eyewitness suggests that only one ship was captured, while two others took refuge by anchoring under the guns of Mingary Castle, now in the hands of Alasdair MacDonald, where they remained until they too were finally captured on 10 August 1644, almost a month later.

March to Blair Atholl

Alasdair MacDonald now decided to take the initiative by advancing into the Highlands. His impetuous character made it quite unlikely that he ever contemplated withdrawing to Ireland, had he had the ships. Instead, he still evidently planned to join up with the Royalist forces of George Gordon, second Marquis of Huntly. He left on 29 July 1644, nearly a fortnight before the date when all his ships were most likely captured, but after he had started to negotiate an exchange of prisoners with the Marquis of Argyll.

His small army first marched into Lochaber, where Donald Glas MacDonald of Keppoch had already risen in arms earlier in 1644 to join the abortive rebellion of the Marquis of Huntly. But it had long since collapsed, and Alasdair MacDonald was unable to rally Keppoch and the other chiefs in Lochaber to the Royalist standard. He then turned north towards Kintail, reaching Glenelg by 13 August 1644, where he perhaps hoped to persuade Sir James MacDonald of Sleat, and George MacKenzie, second Earl of Seaforth, to declare their allegiance to Charles I. But they too refused to join a venture so unlikely to succeed.

Alasdair MacDonald marched east from Kintail a few days later, probably by way of Glen Shiel and Glen Moriston to Kilcumein, as Fort Augustus on the Great Glen was then known. A few MacDonald clansmen joined him from the lands of Keppoch and Glengarry, but it was not until he reached Badenoch that he resorted to more forceful methods of recruitment. Marching over the Corrieyairack Pass to avoid the Covenanters' forces advancing up Stratherrick from Inverness, he sent ahead a 'fiery cross'.

Then, after his arrival in Badenoch, Alasdair arrested the principal men of Clan Chattan, presumably in the King's name, and forced them to raise 500 men for his army. Ewen Og MacPherson, Master of Cluny, brought in 300 men, perhaps by choice, given the animosity between the MacPhersons and the MacIntoshes, hereditary captains of Clan Chattan, while Donald Glas MacDonald of Keppoch now contributed his own men freely to Alasdair MacDonald's growing army.

Alasdair MacDonald was now threatened in his rear by Campbell forces mobilising in the west, while he was still not strong enough to break out to the north or east. Already, the Covenanters had raised levies from such loyal clans in Ross and Moray as the Frasers, Grants, Rosses and Munros to oppose the likely advance of Alasdair MacDonald's forces down Strathspey towards Huntly's territories around Strathbogie. They were further reinforced by men sent south by George MacKenzie, second Earl of Seaforth, and John Gordon, thirteenth Earl of Sutherland.

Alasdair MacDonald therefore had little choice but to march his army over Drumochter Pass into Atholl, where the garrison of Blair Castle fled at his approach. There, the Stewarts of Atholl and the Robertsons of Struan were potential allies, given their Royalist sympathies and their resentment of the Marquis of Argyll, who had plundered their lands during his Highland expedition of 1640, when his clansmen had openly boasted of 'King Campbell'.

However, Lowland influences were equally strong in Atholl, especially as the Stewart Earls of Atholl, descendants of the Black Knight of Lorne, had died out in 1626, when the title passed to the Lowland family of John Murray, Earl of Tullibardine. Lacking any close ties with the western Highlands, let alone Ireland, the men of Atholl felt themselves so threatened by the Irish army under Alasdair MacDonald that they were preparing to resist the invasion of their lands when the situation was suddenly saved. As if by divine providence James Graham, fifth Earl and first Marquis of Montrose, suddenly appeared, accompanied by only three close friends and kinsmen. Together, Montrose and Alasdair MacDonald would embark on a stirring year of whirlwind victories against the Covenanters in Scotland, and especially against the Campbells of Argyll.

Chapter Four

MONTROSE AND
ALASDAIR MACDONALD

Montrose had evidently faced a crisis of conscience in 1640 when the Scots army of the Covenant first crossed the border into England at the start of the Second Bishops' War. Indeed, although he had been instrumental in drawing up the National Covenant in 1638, it was not long before his new-found loyalty was tested. The more extreme leaders of the Covenanters made ever more radical demands of Charles I, while the compulsion needed to enforce the signing of the National Covenant throughout the country clearly offended Montrose's innate sense of justice and tolerance. But he evidently still hoped that Charles I would accept the will of the Scottish people by signing the National Covenant. But when the King refused to do so, Montrose was placed in a dilemma of his own making. Unwilling to disown his sovereign, he was not alone in fearing that Charles I would be deposed as the 'lesser of two evils'.

Montrose first attempted to resolve his divided loyalties after learning of a conspiracy against Charles I for 'the shaking off of Authority, and establishing the whole power and rule of the kingdom of Scotland in the hands of General [Alexander Leslie] in the fields, and the power of all besouth of the water of Forth in [the hands of] the Marquis of Hamilton, within the country, and [in the hands of] the Earl of Argyll benorth of the Forth'. He reacted by trying to forge an ill-defined alliance between moderate Royalists and Covenanters in the Cumbernauld Band of August 1640.

But soon afterwards, the nature of the Cumbernauld Band was revealed, and it became known that Montrose had written in secret to Charles I, assuring him of his loyalty. By breaking the National Covenant, Montrose now faced the hostility of Argyll, who eventually succeeded in bringing charges of perjury and sedition against him. He was arrested in June 1641, and held captive for five months in Edinburgh Castle, only to be released in November 1641. When his trial finally took place early in 1642, Montrose was found guilty, but he gained his freedom after Charles I granted him a letter of exoneration for his actions.

Now more eager than ever to assist his King, Montrose's offers of help were spurned at first by Charles I. Faced with the full hostility of the English Parliament once the Civil War had finally broken out in England, it was now in his interest for the Scots to remain neutral. However, once the Scots had entered into the Solemn League and Covenant with the English Parliament in 1643, Charles I had nothing to lose. By thus siding with the King's enemies in England, the Covenanters set the stage for Royalist intervention in Scotland. However, any such campaign in support of Charles I did not come to fruition until early in 1644, soon after the Scots army under Alexander Leslie, first Earl of Leven, had entered England to confront the King's forces in support of the English Parliament.

Start of a Royalist Uprising

The Royalist plan of campaign was another three-pronged attack, such as Charles I had planned in 1639 at the start of the First Bishops' War. George Gordon, second Marquis of Huntly, was again appointed as the King's Lieutenant-General in the North to lead an uprising in north-east Scotland against the Covenanters. He raised 1,200 men at Aboyne towards the end of March 1644, who first seized weapons and ammunition from Aberdeen. However, the Royalist forces under Huntly were soon put to flight by Argyll, advancing from the south with an army of up to 6,000 men. Aberdeen was retaken, and the surrounding districts reduced to obedience. By the end of May, Huntly had disbanded his forces, fleeing north to Strathnaver, where he remained for the next eighteen months.

Meanwhile, Charles I had given a commission to Montrose, appointing him as Captain-General of all the King's forces in Scotland. Armed with his commission, he left Oxford at the beginning of March 1644. A month later, he entered Scotland in what was intended to be a second line of attack at the head of 1,200 men, accompanied by the Earls of Crawford and Nithsdale, and Lords Ogilvie and Aboyne. Among his party was the mysterious figure of Captain Frances Dalziel, illegitimate daughter of the Earl of Carnwath. She had taken to arms in support of Charles I at the head of a troop of horse. Despite a mutiny by his forces, Montrose managed to take Dumfries by mid-April, but he was then forced to fall back on Carlisle by a superior force under Lord Sinclair, advancing from the north. His efforts on behalf of Charles I were recognised when he was created the first Marquis of Montrose on 6 May 1644.

The third line of attack was intended to come from Ireland, where Charles

I had appointed Randal MacDonald, second Earl of Antrim, to the position of King's general for the Highlands and Islands. As already recounted, his claim that he could supply 10,000 men for the King's army in England turned out to be an empty boast. However, he was still able to recruit a much smaller force of some 1,600 men for an invasion directed at Argyll's territories in the western Highlands under the command of Alasdair MacDonald.

Montrose's Pilgrimage North

Meanwhile, James Graham, fifth Earl and first Marquis of Montrose, had further demonstrated his military abilities by successfully taking the castles at Morpeth and South Shields, before he was recalled south, arriving in Richmond only a day after the Royalist defeat in early July at the battle of Marston Moor. It was only then, after all of Montrose's troops had been requisitioned, and without any prospect of military advancement in England, that Montrose resolved to raise the royal standard in Scotland. He perhaps feared that his hour of glory would be seized by Huntly if he did not act promptly.

Disguised as a groom, he crossed the western marches to the north of Carlisle in mid-August with only two companions, and rode north through the very heart of Covenanting country to reach the fringes of Highland Perthshire. There, he stayed in hiding in the Methven Woods north-west of Perth while he took stock of the situation. In fact, Alasdair MacDonald and his forces had reached Atholl by then, after landing in the western Highlands, and the stage was set for the first great campaign of Gaeldom in support of the Stuart monarchy, driven by the traditional enmity between the MacDonalds and the Campbells.

Meeting at Blair Atholl

James Graham, first Marquis of Montrose, had quite probably made his lonely way north in order to prevent Alasdair macColla Ciotach MacDonald from seeking out the Marquis of Huntly, as indeed he was instructed to do after Montrose had failed in his attempt at an invasion of Scotland from the south in April 1644. No doubt, Montrose feared that the Marquis of Huntly would steal his own thunder in the Royalist cause if reinforced by Alasdair's men, or waste whatever resources were placed under his half-hearted and incompetent command. He had therefore hurried north, armed only with the King's commission as his Lieutenant-Governor of Scotland.

Now the fortuitous meeting between Montrose and Alasdair MacDonald at Blair Atholl utterly changed the immediate prospects of the Royalist forces in Scotland, since Alasdair MacDonald had the troops Montrose needed for a quick victory. For his part, Montrose as a Scottish nobleman of high birth gave respectability to Alasdair MacDonald's own expedition, which otherwise would surely have ended in disaster.

Indeed, disaster nearly struck when Montrose first made himself known to Alasdair MacDonald, since a great shout arose from the Irish camp, and Alasdair's men fired their muskets into the air. The Athollmen, not knowing what had caused the commotion, feared an imminent attack. Bloodshed was only averted when they learnt that Montrose had arrived in Alasdair's camp, and 700 Athollmen hastened to join him.

Montrose raised the King's standard in the late August of 1644 for 'the defence and maintenance of the true Protestant religion, his Majesty's just and sacred authority, the fundamental laws and privileges of Parliament, [and] the peace and freedom of the oppressed and thralled subject'. He then made a final appeal to the Marquis of Argyll to return to the grace and protection of his King, before he prepared to advance against the King's enemies in Scotland.

Reaction of the Covenanters

Archibald Campbell, first Marquis of Argyll, had already received a new commission in early July to raise his own forces as soon as the Covenanting authorities in Edinburgh had learnt that Alasdair MacDonald had landed in the western Highlands. Argyll mustered 2,600 men at Dunstaffnage Castle by 22 July under his own command, and he then campaigned throughout the Western Isles, Ardnamurchan, Morvern, Lochaber and the surrounding districts. However, he made little headway, except that he mounted a siege against Mingary Castle ten days after Alasdair MacDonald had left with the bulk of his forces, capturing the ships remaining at anchor under its walls.

Meanwhile, even before Argyll had returned south from this campaign, the news reached Edinburgh by 28 August 1644 that Montrose had placed himself at the head of Alasdair MacDonald's forces in Atholl. The Royalist forces now threatened to advance against Perth. Indeed, while the Covenanters were desperately trying to raise their own forces from Angus, Perth, Stirling and Fife, Montrose gave the order to march south by way of Aberfeldy, where he doubtless hoped Menzies would join him. He then avoided the obvious route to Perth along the Tay valley, marching instead from Aberfeldy to Amulree, and then down the Sma' Glen to the Hill of Buchanty. By approaching Perth from the west, he might well surprise the Covenanting forces holding the city.

Montrose now encountered an advance party of 500 Highlanders, mostly archers, among whose commanders were his kinsman Lord Kilpont; Sir John Drummond, son of the Earl of Perth; and the Master of Maderty, Montrose's own brother-in-law. They were far too few in number to oppose Montrose's advance, and their support for the Covenanting cause was only half-hearted, since they promptly decided to join Montrose, perhaps even by prior arrangement. Thus reinforced, Montrose continued his advance upon Perth on the morning of 1 September 1644, only to encounter the hastily raised levies of the Covenanters at Tippermuir (now known as Tibbermore), a few miles west of the city.

Battle of Tippermuir

The first battle in any campaign is crucial to its success. The Covenanters had perhaps five or six thousand men, roughly twice as many as Montrose, and they were better armed. But they were not well-trained or experienced soldiers imbued with a zeal for the Covenanting cause, since the bulk of the Scottish army was now fighting against Charles I in England. Lord Elcho as their commander also lacked experience, since he was standing in for the Earl of Lothian, who was away in Edinburgh.

Montrose's forces, and especially Alasdair MacDonald's Irishmen, were battle-hardened from their Ulster campaigns, and they were commanded by a core of professional officers, while the Highlanders were bred to regard their skill in fighting and their courage in battle as fundamental to their manhood. Above all, they were fired with a deep hatred for the Presbyterian Lowlanders who had inflicted past wrongs and present injuries upon them. In particular, the Irish under Alasdair MacDonald were fighting an enemy who had occupied their own lands in Ulster. No doubt, they hoped to force the Scots army of the Covenant under Major-General Robert Munro in Ulster to withdraw to Scotland.

The Covenanters under Lord Elcho drew up their infantry in a long line, perhaps six deep, defended at each end by 500 cavalry. Advancing upon the enemy, Montrose strung out his own forces more thinly in a line only three deep, so that his smaller army would not be outflanked by the Covenanters' cavalry. He placed his Irish infantry in the centre under Alasdair MacDonald, while he commanded the Highlanders from Badenoch and Atholl on the right wing, and Lord Kilpont had command of his own archers on the left wing.

The order of the day was to advance upon the enemy until within firing distance, discharge a single volley of musket shot, and then charge upon the enemy with sword and dirk. Thus, Montrose employed the tactic of the so-called 'Highland charge', already used by Alasdair MacDonald at the battle of the Laney. It denied the Covenanters any advantage from their superior firepower, since they were soon overwhelmed in hand-to-hand fighting, but it required iron discipline if the advance was made against cannon-fire.

The Covenanters were broken by the suddenness and unexpected ferocity of the Highland charge, which they were encountering for the first time. Their infantry collapsed in the centre, and the battle turned into an utter rout, which not even the cavalry could prevent. As the enemy ranks fled in panic towards Perth, they were pursued and slaughtered in their hundreds. Perhaps well over a thousand were killed before the remnant reached the safety of the city walls, and another 800 were captured, along with much baggage, arms and ammunition. An Irish officer boasted afterwards: 'God gave us the day, the enemy retreating with their backs towards us that men might have walked upon dead corpses to the town.' Perth surrendered within twenty-four hours, and Montrose garrisoned the city with his Highlanders.

Advance on Dundee and Aberdeen

Montrose stayed only a few days in Perth, since the Covenanters were now raising fresh levies for a new army, and recalling regiments from England. Abandoning his campaign in the western Highlands, Archibald Campbell, first Marquis of Argyll, arrived in Stirling on 4 September 1644 to take command of the preparations now being made against Montrose. As Montrose knew that he did not have the strength to face Argyll, he decided to march north to Dundee and Aberdeen, where he evidently hoped to obtain more recruits to the Royalist cause.

Soon after Montrose left Perth, Lord Kilpont was murdered at Collace by James Stewart of Ardvorlich after a quarrel between the two men. James Stewart of Ardvorlich had joined Montrose with Lord Kilpont, but he was probably an unwilling ally of the Royalist cause. He held his lands under the feudal superiority of the Marquis of Argyll, who had already ordered his cattle and other livestock to be plundered in retaliation for his joining Montrose. The quarrel quite possibly arose after Lord Kilpont had discovered that James Stewart of Ardvorlich was plotting against Montrose, or perhaps when he refused to support Stewart's claim for recompense for his losses. Already, the men of Atholl had gone home with their booty, although they would return, and now the murder of Lord Kilpont further depleted Montrose's forces, since Kilpont's own men insisted on returning home to bury the body of their chief.

After leaving Perth, Montrose reached Dundee by 6 September 1644, when he camped outside the town and summoned it to surrender. Meeting a refusal, he realised that his forces were not strong enough to storm its walls

without a long siege, which he could not afford. He therefore marched north
through his own territories towards Aberdeen by way of Crathes Castle,
crossing the hills to the east of the Cairn O'Mount. He thus approached
the city along the north bank of the River Dee, no doubt remembering his
previous struggle to capture the town from the south at the Brig O'Dee.

By now, Montrose had only 1,500 men under his command, while the
Covenanting forces holding Aberdeen had 2,500 men. They were mostly
Forbeses, Frasers and Crichtons from the surrounding districts, together
with the burghers of Aberdeen, and a remnant of Lowland levies who had
fled north to Aberdeen after the battle of Tippermuir. No doubt, the latter
group spread alarm and despondency among the Covenanters' ranks with
their accounts of the earlier battle, attempting to justify their flight by tales of
enemy ferocity. However, it was the poor tactics adopted by the Covenanters,
and the lack of leadership shown by Lord Burleigh as their military commander, which now caused their defeat.

Battle for Aberdeen

As Montrose's army approached Aberdeen on Friday, 13 September 1644,
Lord Burleigh decided to draw up his army outside the natural defences
protecting the burgh from the west, but where they still occupied a strong
position at the top of a steep slope. Evidently, he hoped to tempt Montrose
into attacking him so that the Royalists could be defeated in open battle.
Montrose first sent a summons to Lord Burleigh to surrender Aberdeen in
the King's name, which was refused, and the drummer-boy accompanying his
envoys back to the Royalist lines was shot dead by an over-zealous Covenanter.
Outraged by this action, Montrose ordered his men to show no mercy to
their enemy.

The battle itself started when a body of Covenanting cavalry rode towards
Montrose's lines in the old-fashioned manoeuvre known as a caracole,
wheeling away after they had fired in order to reload their pistols or carbines.
It had no effect on the enemy. Sir William Forbes of Craigievar then used the
manoeuvre which by then had largely replaced the caracole by mounting a
cavalry charge directly against the enemy, attempting to break through their
lines in order to attack them from the rear.

The tactic might have succeeded had he not directed his charge against
Alasdair MacDonald's Irish musketeers in the centre of the enemy lines, or if
he had made certain that other troops of cavalry would follow through his
own attack. As it was, Alasdair MacDonald trusted in the tight discipline of
his men when he coolly ordered them to open their ranks to allow the charge
to penetrate deep into his own lines, and then to close their ranks to cut off
its escape.

Meanwhile, full battle was joined between the two armies. Two charges against Montrose's right wing by the Frasers and Crichtons were repelled at first, but the Covenanters' onslaught on his left wing nearly succeeded before Montrose dispatched a hundred more musketeers to strengthen his line, forcing the enemy to retreat. The Irish in the centre then attacked in their traditional manner, abandoning their muskets to fight at close quarters with sword and dirk. The fighting raged for two hours before the Covenanters broke ranks and fled. The cavalry mostly managed to escape, but the infantry were not so lucky. Fleeing on foot towards Aberdeen, they were cut down in their hundreds. Soon only a small number of Covenanters remained on the battlefield, but they were cut off by Alasdair MacDonald and 400 of his men as they tried to escape south across the River Dee.

Sacking of Aberdeen

The Irish soldiers of Alasdair MacDonald's army now committed murder, rape and pillage throughout the city of Aberdeen for the next three days, without any let or hindrance. It was a legacy that would come to haunt Montrose, since he made little attempt to stop these excesses. He had entered Aberdeen, but he soon withdrew to establish a camp for his own men outside the city walls. However, the Irish continued with their orgy of destruction, even stripping their victims naked before killing them in order not to soil their clothes. Many women were raped and left for dead, or carried off as camp-followers for the later pleasures of the soldiery.

The day after the battle, Montrose returned to Aberdeen, where he lodged for the next two nights, after he had sent most of his army north to camp at Kintore and Inverurie. He issued orders for the carnage and plundering to cease, but they had little effect, and the suspicion remains that he deliberately allowed such excesses to occur in order to strike terror into his opponents. This suspicion is reinforced by his proclamation at the Mercat Cross, calling all men to arms in the King's name, when he declared that he intended to bring all the King's subjects to obedience 'by fair means, or by fire and sword'.

If it was deliberate, this toleration of violence was a gross error of judgment on Montrose's part, especially as Aberdeen was renowned for the strength of its Royalist feeling. When John Spalding wrote his account of the atrocities, which he had observed at first hand, he listed by name only twenty Covenanters who were killed in battle or later, but he gave the names of another ninety-eight dead, who had never supported the Covenanters' cause. It seems likely that they were among the more prominent burgesses of Aberdeen, and that unknown numbers of ordinary townsfolk were also killed, after they had been forced to fight for the Covenanters against their will.

Distrust of Montrose

Allowing such excesses to occur was a dreadful miscalculation that cost Montrose the support of nearly all the Lowland Royalists, who might otherwise have rallied to his cause. Instead, they were horrified that he was even prepared to ally himself with such savage barbarians from Ireland, with their Gaelic language and abhorrent religion, as made up Alasdair MacDonald's forces. Such an alliance must have recalled for them the battle of Harlaw, more than two centuries earlier. While Harlaw had not really been a battle of Highland Gael against Lowland Scot, divided by language and culture, it was no doubt later perceived as such by the Lowland Scots of Aberdeen and farther south.

Distrust of the Gaelic-speaking Highlanders had grown in the Lowlands once the cultural and linguistic divisions within Scotland became ever more marked after the Reformation of 1560, and it was further accentuated by the signing of the National Covenant in 1638. Although hardly important in itself, Montrose had perhaps made matters worse by parading through Aberdeen in Highland dress, clad in trews, shortcoat and bonnet, which he had first worn for his meeting with Alasdair MacDonald at Blair Atholl. No doubt such a trifling matter was flattering to the Gael, but it did little for the Royalist cause.

Indeed, Montrose never recovered from the atrocities committed in Aberdeen. When the city learnt of the approach of the Covenanting army under the Marquis of Argyll, 'many who loved the King were glad of the news, and others of the Covenant were no less sorry', in the words of John Spalding.

March and Countermarch

Montrose now wanted to stand and fight, but he was persuaded into a tactical withdrawal by his closest lieutenants, who argued that he still did not have the strength of numbers to face the Covenanting army under Argyll. Montrose therefore struck camp on Monday, 16 September 1644, marching north-west from Kintore and Inverurie towards the Gordon territories around Strathbogie, where he hoped to gather recruits. But only a handful of men joined him from this stronghold of Royalist support.

He now marched west towards Strathspey, only to find all the ferryboats were beached on the far bank of the river, which was held by forces loyal to the Covenanters in the north. He therefore retreated by way of Abernethy and Rothiemurchus towards Badenoch, where he fell sick for several days. By the first week of October, however, he had recovered sufficiently to reach

Atholl, where he parted company with Alasdair MacDonald for the next few weeks.

Meanwhile, the Covenanting forces under Archibald Campbell, first Marquis of Argyll, had reached Brechin on the same day as Montrose had abandoned Aberdeen. Campbell was joined there by the Earl Marischal, and Lords Gordon, Forbes, Fraser and Crichton, who were all reluctant recruits to his army. He then continued his march north to Aberdeen, where he stayed for several days before advancing towards Strathbogie, which he reached on 23 September 1644. His army engaged in a campaign of attrition as it advanced, plundering the countryside with fire and sword to deny men or supplies to Montrose. Much of Deeside, and Strathbogie and Strathisla to the north, were devastated before Argyll advanced to Forres.

Argyll consulted there with John Gordon, thirteenth Earl of Sutherland, Andrew Fraser, second Lord Lovat, and other northern lairds, even though George MacKenzie, second Earl of Seaforth, was absent. Argyll evidently suspected that Seaforth and some other lairds had communicated privately with Montrose, perhaps to explain their lack of support. Meanwhile, George Gordon, second Marquis of Huntly, remained in Strathnaver, refusing all help to the Royalist cause. Indeed, Montrose received an anonymous letter, explaining that the Marquis of Huntly had refused even to allow his own followers to join with Montrose. It was one more blow to the Royalist cause.

After a brief visit to Inverness, Argyll returned to pursue Montrose, marching up Strathspey into Badenoch. He reached Ruthven on 5 October 1644, before turning south into Atholl. There he found that Montrose had wheeled east through the Glens of Angus back towards Aberdeen, accompanied by a thousand foot and fifty horse. Montrose crossed the River Dee near Crathes Castle, and then retreated north towards Strathbogie, burning the lands of the Forbeses and the Crichtons on the way. He then made his headquarters at Fyvie in the splendid Renaissance castle of George Seton, second Earl of Dunfermline, which he reached by 27 October 1644, thinking that the Marquis of Argyll and his Covenanting army were far away to the south.

It was a near-fatal failure of intelligence, since the Covenanters were even then advancing on Fyvie itself from Inverurie, only a few miles away. However, when Argyll drew up his army of 2,500 footsoldiers and a thousand horse on the south bank of the River Ythan at Crichie, he found himself faced by Montrose's army, occupying a strong position on the opposite bank at the top of a steep slope. Argyll promptly launched a cavalry attack, but it was beaten off by the Irish under Manus O'Cahan. Discouraged, Argyll now abandoned any attempt to cross the river, and withdrew his own forces the next day. The skirmish itself, and the death of a captain of 'a troop of Irish dragoons', is best remembered in the ballad 'The Bonnie Lass o' Fyvie', in which the lass was left to lament the loss of her sweetheart.

Truce with Argyll

Montrose now went north to plunder Turriff and Rothiemay, before returning south to Strathbogie Castle by 6 November 1644. Argyll followed him there, and minor skirmishes broke out again between the two armies. However, the forces under Argyll were undoubtedly exhausted by their long route-marches through difficult country. Given the lateness of the campaigning season, Argyll came to a generous truce with some of Montrose's officers, who were given free passages and safe conducts to go wherever they pleased. Montrose himself would accept no truce. Instead, he set fire to his camp at Strathbogie, retreated west along the Deveron to Balvenie Castle, and then retired into Badenoch.

Argyll fell back to Aberdeen, where he disbanded a thousand of his Campbell clansmen on 14 November 1644. They went home for the winter by way of Strathspey, Badenoch and Lochaber, plundering as they went. Argyll himself returned to Edinburgh to resign his own commission. Montrose had perhaps already crossed the wintry passes into Atholl with his small army which, apart from the Highlanders and the Irish, now consisted of more officers than men. Despite his overwhelming victories at Tippermuir and Aberdeen, he had achieved very little, apart from evading defeat and capture.

Campaign in the West

However, Alasdair MacDonald had already transformed the situation over the previous month through the recruiting campaign he had waged among the western clans since leaving Montrose early in October. He had left Montrose and marched west from Atholl with upwards of 500 men, intending to relieve Kinlochaline and Mingary Castles, which were then still besieged by Campbell forces. Argyll had learnt on 8 October 1644 when he was camped at Ruthven Castle in Badenoch that Montrose and Alasdair MacDonald had divided their forces. Next day, he wrote to the captain of Dunstaffnage Castle, ordering him to send supplies of meal, bere or barley, biscuit, gunpowder and lead to reinforce Inverlochy Castle. The supplies were to be carried by sea in his own galley and other boats, and he warned their crews to be 'careful in their passage from the treachery of the people thereabouts'.

Argyll evidently intended his Campbell forces to muster at Inverlochy Castle, so that they could intercept Alasdair MacDonald as he marched west towards Morvern or Ardnamurchan. However, Argyll's orders came too late, since Sir Duncan Campbell of Ardnamurchan had already abandoned his siege of Mingary Castle on the night of 5 October 1644. Alasdair MacDonald apparently went first to relieve Kinlochaline Castle in Morvern, where the Campbell forces promptly withdrew at his approach. Only afterwards did he appear at Mingary Castle in Ardnamurchan on 16 October 1644.

Rallying the Highland Chiefs

Alasdair MacDonald now urged the chiefs of the local clans to rise in arms against the Campbells, encouraging them with news of Montrose's victories at Tippermuir and Aberdeen. John MacDonald, Captain of Clan Ranald, was the first to join the rebels. Raising all his clansmen of Uist, Eigg, Moidart and Arisaig, he descended on the lands of Sunart, which he plundered of all cattle and sheep. Alasdair MacDonald now joined Clan Ranald at his stronghold of Tioram Castle, leaving behind a garrison to hold Mingary Castle. Together, they first marched north to Arisaig and Morar, where they learnt that John Mor MacLeod of Dunvegan still refused to join the Royalist cause.

They then continued north into Knoydart, hoping to raise clansmen loyal to the MacDonalds of Glengarry, who held these lands. The old chief of Glengarry was now over a hundred years of age, and the affairs of the clan had devolved upon his grandson Angus MacDonald. He would not join them in person, but his uncle Donald Gorm MacDonald of Scotus raised the MacDonalds of Knoydart and Glengarry to march with Alasdair MacDonald. Returning back to Lochaber from Knoydart, Alasdair MacDonald was joined by clansmen under Donald Glas MacDonald, who later became the chief of Keppoch, and Angus MacAlan Dubh, cadet of the MacDonalds of Glencoe, along with the Stewarts of Appin and some Camerons of Lochiel.

All these Highland chieftains were united in their hostility to Archibald Campbell, first Marquis of Argyll, who held the feudal superiority of nearly all their lands. Elsewhere, such clans as the MacLeans of Duart, the MacDonalds of Sleat, the MacLeods of Dunvegan, and the MacKenzies, kept a wary neutrality, waiting to see how their interests would best be served. After Alasdair MacDonald had returned to Atholl with his well-armed reinforcements by way of Drumochter, his efforts had doubled the size of Montrose's army and he had possibly 3,000 men under his command.

Winter Campaign against Argyll

It was now mid-November, and Montrose, faced with the onset of winter, proposed to seek food and shelter in the Lowlands. However, Alasdair

MacDonald and John MacDonald of Clan Ranald now presented him with a dramatic ultimatum: he must march against the Campbell territories in Argyllshire, attacking them in a winter campaign, or they would return home with all their men. After a long debate, Montrose was quite possibly persuaded by the force of their arguments. He later wrote to Charles I after the great victory at Inverlochy, marking the culmination of this campaign: 'I was willing to let the world see that Argyll was not the man his Highlandmen believed him to be, and that it was possible to beat him in his own Highlands.' But perhaps he only took the credit when victory was achieved.

Even so, invading Argyll's territories, and especially in the depths of winter, must have looked an extremely risky venture to Montrose. Argyllshire appeared impregnable, separated from the rest of the country by 'a continuous ridge of high crags and inaccessible mountains, the straight [narrow] passes whereof might easily be kept by five hundred against twenty thousand'. Once beyond these passes, Montrose's army could be trapped by the Campbell forces until starvation forced its surrender, or until his men were left to die. But Alasdair MacDonald argued that many of the Highlanders present had an intimate knowledge of the country, and indeed Angus MacAlan Dubh MacDonald, kinsman of MacIain of Glencoe, assured Montrose that there were enough 'tight houses and fat cows as victuals to feed upon . . . [which] would answer their purpose'.

If Montrose willingly agreed to the plan of campaign now proposed by Alasdair MacDonald, he was most likely swayed by its very boldness and daring, which must have appealed to his own flamboyant nature. By striking at the very heart of his territories, Montrose would discredit the Marquis of Argyll as foremost amongst the leaders of the Covenanters in Scotland. Already Montrose had demonstrated by his victories at Tippermuir and Aberdeen that the Covenanting armies were not invincible. Now Alasdair MacDonald wanted to prove that the Campbell lands in Argyllshire were equally vulnerable to invasion. If the attack succeeded, the power of the Campbells would be greatly weakened, and 'the whole Highlanders with one consent would take arms for the King'. The proud taunt of the Campbells, 'It's a far cry to Loch Awe', would then sound very hollow.

Even so, Alasdair MacDonald had his own reasons for attacking the Campbells who

> had long been the fiercest persecutors and, whenever they could, the murderers and assassins of the Catholics in the north of Ireland and the whole of Scotland . . . The whole conduct of the war and the whole hazard of their cause turned upon this single point, and they considered they would effect nothing worthy of their efforts unless they crushed

the Campbells, devastated Argyll with fire and sword, and administered a terrible and telling chastisement to this hideous receptacle of bandits, plunderers, incendiaries and cut throats.

Clan Donald, then, embarked not just on a religious crusade to seek vengeance for the souls of their dead, but on a brutal campaign of what would now be called 'ethnic cleansing', designed to exterminate the Campbells of Argyll. Only then would Clan Donald be restored to its rightful place as the 'Head of the Gael'.

March into Argyll

Montrose's subsequent campaign against Argyllshire cannot now be followed in any detail. He left Atholl in the first week of December 1644 and marched west with no more than 3,000 men towards Loch Tay and Breadalbane. His army advanced in two columns along the sides of Loch Tay, plundering the territories of Sir Robert Campbell of Glenorchy and his eldest son Sir John Campbell, and the estates of Sir Mungo Campbell of Lawers. Glenorchy's losses from the whole campaign were later put at the equivalent of more than £66,000 sterling. Any castles and fortified houses which held out against the rebels were ignored: no time could be lost besieging them if Montrose wanted to surprise his enemies farther west.

The strategy worked well enough until Montrose approached Loch Dochart. Then, he found his path blocked by the guns of a Campbell castle, which was situated on a small island in the loch, overlooking the narrow track along its shore. The castle itself had once belonged to the MacNabs of Glen Dochart, and now Iain MacNab offered his services to Montrose on behalf of his elderly father, chief of the clan. Before dawn, he went down to the shore with his leading clansmen, and hailed the Campbell garrison, shouting out that they had brought important letters from the Marquis of Argyll. Not suspecting treachery, the garrison sent over a boat to convey the MacNabs back to the castle, which they then seized from the Campbells.

This subterfuge allowed Montrose to reach Crianlarich on 13 December 1644, where he probably split his forces. One column under John MacDonald of Clan Ranald, formed by his own clansmen as well as other MacDonalds from the Braes of Lochaber, apparently turned south into Glen Falloch to reach the head of Loch Lomond, and then marched through the glens to the head of Loch Fyne. The rest of Montrose's army continued west to Tyndrum and the head of Loch Awe, where it apparently divided again into two columns.

'Herschip' of Argyll

Alasdair MacDonald probably commanded the column that now advanced south along the shores of Loch Awe towards Kilmartin, while Montrose most likely led the other column towards Inveraray, although his route is not known with any certainty. Ignoring such strongholds as Inveraray Castle, Montrose's army now put all of Argyll's territories to the fire and sword. A report on the campaign, sent to Dublin and perhaps written by Alasdair MacDonald, states 'throughout all Argyll, we left neither house nor hold unburned, nor corn nor cattle, that belonged to the whole name of Campbell', while Montrose reported that he had 'laid waste the whole country of Argyll'. Grain and goods were carried off, and all the animals driven away, or mutilated and killed if that proved impracticable.

Neither account mentioned the wholesale slaughter that occurred, especially of any able-bodied Campbell man fit to carry arms, but Neil MacMhuirich was not so reticent: 'In short, all the territories of MacCailin [to give the Marquis of Argyll his Gaelic title] were spoilt and burnt on that occasion, and eight hundred, four score and fifteen men were killed in these counties without battle or skirmish having taken place in them.' It was a 'herschip', or plunder, to rival the devastation committed by King Robert the Bruce in Buchan, more than three centuries previously. Alasdair MacDonald earned himself the fearsome name of *Fear Thollaidh nan Tighean*, or Destroyer of Houses.

Withdrawal to the North

After meeting up with his other commanders at Glassary, south of Loch Awe, Montrose started to withdraw north with his army, laden with plunder. However, he was soon forced to halt on the southern shores of Loch Etive, where there were no boats, reviving his worst fears about campaigning in a country divided by sealochs and firths, 'like the teeth of a comb'. Fortunately, Campbell of Ardchattan on the far shore was married to a MacDonald, and he provided boats for the crossing, hoping no doubt to save his lands from plunder. The great herds of cattle were forced to swim across the narrow loch, but the ebbing tide carried away some animals to the coast at Dunstaffnage Castle, where they were retrieved by its Campbell garrison. Montrose then crossed the hills from the head of Loch Creran to reach Ballachulish by way of Gleann an Fhiodh. Facing the same difficulties as previously, enough boats were eventually found to allow his forces to cross Loch Leven. By now, Montrose had reached friendly country for the first time since leaving Atholl, and his ranks were joined by 150 Stewarts of Appin, but few others.

Montrose rested his men at Inverlochy, where Sir Lachlan MacLean of Duart, and several other leading MacLeans, arrived in his camp, and Angus MacDonald of Glengarry joined his own clansmen. Montrose then continued north along the Great Glen to reach Kilcumein at the head of Loch Ness towards the end of January 1645. Kilcumein would later be called Fort Augustus in honour of William Augustus, Duke of Cumberland, the victor at Culloden. It was a good enough place for Montrose to observe the movements of his enemies, since it allowed a means of escape east into Badenoch by way of the Corrieyairack Pass, or west to the sea by way of Glen Garry or Glen Moriston.

Indeed, the Covenanters were once again gathering their armies to oppose Montrose. The immediate threat came from the north where George MacKenzie, second Earl of Seaforth, had been pressed into command of a Covenanting army of around 5,000 men. Two of its regiments came from the army that had pursued Montrose through the Highlands after his victory at Aberdeen in September 1644. Otherwise, it consisted of raw recruits raised by the Earl of Sutherland from Ross and Moray, as well as contingents from the Frasers, the Rosses and the Munros. Montrose was about to march north against this army as it advanced south from Inverness along Loch Ness, when he received a message from Allan Dubh Cameron of Lochiel that the Marquis of Argyll had arrived at Inverlochy Castle with a sizeable army.

Tradition has it that the messenger was none other than Iain Lom MacDonald, renowned as the bard to the MacDonalds of Keppoch, whose magnificent Gaelic poetry chronicles the events that affected Scotland during his lifetime, ending only with the Union of Parliaments in 1707. A council of war was hastily summoned, consisting of Montrose's chief lieutenants, among whom were Alasdair MacDonald, Donald Glas MacDonald of Keppoch, Angus MacDonald of Glengarry, John MacDonald of Clan Ranald, Sir Lachlan MacLean of Duart, Murdoch MacLaine of Lochbuie, Duncan Stewart of Appin, Donald Cameron, tutor of Lochiel, Donald Robertson, tutor of Struan, and Patrick Roy MacGregor of that ilk. Given the threat to the lands of Keppoch, Lochiel, Glengarry and Clan Ranald, among others, Montrose had little choice but to attack Argyll as his first priority.

Movements of Argyll

Argyll had returned to Edinburgh in late November 1644 from his fruitless campaign against Montrose in north-east Scotland. He was then replaced by Lieutenant-General William Baillie as Commander-in-Chief of the Army of the Covenant in Scotland, while remaining in command of Argyllshire and the Isles. Argyll then returned to Inveraray, leaving Edinburgh by 13 December 1644. There he learnt soon afterwards that Montrose was even then marching west from Atholl to invade his own territories. Only a few days later Argyll was forced to escape down Loch Fyne by galley after Montrose had started to advance south from the head of Loch Awe towards Inveraray, as already recorded. Staying to defy Montrose might have been the braver course, but besieged in Inveraray Castle, Argyll could not muster the forces needed to defeat Montrose, nor could he offer help to defend his demoralised and defeated clansmen.

Meanwhile, the news of Montrose's invasion of Argyll had reached Edinburgh by 20 December 1644, when Lieutenant-General William Baillie was ordered to take action. Baillie was a professional soldier with much experience in the Thirty Years' War. He had been recalled from England after Argyll's failure to defeat Montrose's army, especially at Fyvie. But instead of pursuing Montrose through Breadalbane, William Baillie decided to follow a more southerly and safer route, marching his men west by way of Dumbarton to reach Rosneath in early January 1645. There he met Argyll, who persuaded him to return to Perth with most of his army. By then, Argyll had learnt that Montrose was retreating north. He did not want his own territories restored to him by Baillie and a Lowland army, which would effectively destroy his reputation in the Highlands after his humiliating flight from Inveraray. Instead, he would defeat the rebels himself.

However, he took the precaution of retaining 1,100 of Baillie's best infantry for the purpose, while he recalled Sir Duncan Campbell of Auchinbreck from Ulster, along with most of his regiment. The news must have pleased the Irish confederates in Kilkenny. As already noted, their main interest in supplying Alasdair MacDonald with enough forces to wage a campaign in Scotland was to achieve just such a withdrawal of the Scots army of the Covenant in Ulster, which they were still fighting.

Together with his own levies, Argyll now had around 3,000 men under his command. He marched north by way of Castle Stalker, reaching Inverlochy nine days later on 31 January 1645, while the captain of Dunstaffnage Castle was ordered to send him ammunition and other supplies by boat to Inverlochy with the utmost urgency.

Montrose's Descent upon Inverlochy

The very same morning, Montrose began his flanking march towards Inverlochy, regarded as 'one of the greatest exploits in the history of British arms', to quote John Buchan. The decision to march from Kilcumein across the mountains to Glen Spean in the depths of winter was perhaps forced upon him. By advancing directly to the south-west along the Great Glen towards Inverlochy, Montrose would have given Argyll early warning of his approach, and plenty of time to deploy his own forces. Indeed, Montrose's army could easily have been ambushed before it left the narrow confines of the Great Glen, especially along the steep shores of Loch Oich and Loch Lochy, or as it emerged at the foot of Glen Spean.

By entering Glen Tarff, and then turning south-west at Cullachy to march parallel to the Great Glen, Montrose's army was hidden, first by the long ridge of Meall a Cholumain, and then Druim Laragan, before reaching the head of Glen Buck above Aberchalder. Guards were posted to watch the army's rear at Cullachy, and its flank at Aberchalder. Montrose then marched up Glen Buck to the valley of Allt na Larach, which he then followed with his men to reach the broad summit of the pass at well over 2,000 feet, overlooking the steep slopes of Glen Turret and its headwaters to the south. Even though the winter was mild, his men struggled through deep snow, and waded waist-deep through the cold waters of rivers in full spate. Descending into Glen Turret, Montrose and his army then gained the lower ground at the head of Glen Roy, along which he marched the many miles to Keppoch at its foot, perhaps camping out overnight on the way.

Certainly by the evening of 1 February 1645, he had forded the River Spean, and then keeping to the higher ground of Leanachan at the foot of the Mamores, east of the Great Glen, he reached a position overlooking Inverlochy Castle across what became known as *Acha a' Chatha*, or the Field of Battle. He had achieved almost complete surprise. Approaching Inverlochy, he had sent ahead raiding parties, but it seems likely that this tactic was deliberate. Indeed, they had encountered Campbell scouts, who were forced to retreat before they became aware of Montrose's real strength.

By any account, marching nearly forty miles across rugged terrain in the depths of winter was a remarkable achievement, accomplished in two short days, separated by a long winter's night. Montrose perhaps only undertook it in a desperate attempt to rescue his own reputation as a military leader. Bitterly aware that he had hesitated to invade Argyll only two months earlier, Montrose may well have wanted to show Alasdair MacDonald and his other lieutenants that he could trump their own feats of arms. His retreat north to Kilcumein had drawn Argyll into a trap, deliberately or not, and now was the time to spring it.

But equally, Montrose could not have achieved what he did without the Gael, 'the men who did all the service', to quote Neil MacMhuirich, and we do not even know what contribution Alasdair MacDonald and his other lieutenants made to his plan of campaign. Tired, wet and hungry, Montrose's troops stood to arms until dawn on the morning of 2 February 1645, and it

says much for their stamina and morale that they were now to fight the
battle that gave Montrose perhaps his greatest victory.

Battle of Inverlochy

Since the Marquis of Argyll had suffered an injury in falling from his horse,
he retired for the night to his galley, lying offshore in Loch Linnhe, while
giving command of his army to Sir Duncan Campbell of Auchinbreck. Amid
some confusion, Auchinbreck drew up his forces in a battle line so that his
left wing rested on Inverlochy Castle, facing up the Great Glen. The two wings
consisted of Lowland infantry armed with muskets, with only a few cavalry.
The centre of the line was formed by the Campbells and their Highland
allies, among whom were the Lamonts of Cowal and the MacDougalls of
Dunollie, armed with muskets, swords, bows and axes, and supported by
two small cannon.

   Montrose's army faced the Campbell forces with two of the Irish regiments
making up its wings, commanded by Manus O'Cahan on the left and
Alasdair MacDonald on the right. The Highland clansmen in the centre
formed up in three separate lines, lying behind one another. The Stewarts of
Atholl and Appin, the MacDonalds of Glencoe, and the men of Lochaber
made up the front line, commanded by Montrose himself; the MacDonalds
of Clan Ranald and Glengarry, supported by the MacLean chiefs, or so it
was said, were next in line; and the third regiment of Irish troops made up
their rear.

   Accounts of the battle are confused, but it seems that Manus O'Cahan,
closely followed by Alasdair MacDonald, first charged the Lowland infantry
on the opposite wings of Argyll's army. Orders had been given for the Irish
troops not to fire their muskets until they were almost upon the enemy,
employing the tactic now known as the 'Highland charge'. After firing a
single volley, they then threw down their muskets to engage the enemy in close
hand-to-hand fighting with their swords. Such a determined attack caused
panic among the Lowland troops, who broke ranks almost immediately to
flee the battlefield. It left the Campbell forces in the centre desperately
exposed to attack on their flanks by the triumphant Irish.

   Meanwhile, the Campbell forces had already attacked in the centre, 'as
men that deserved to fight in a better cause', as Montrose later commented.
However, Montrose pressed forward his own charge in the centre with a
single volley of musket fire, coming 'immediately to push of pike, and dint of
sword, after this first firing'. The casualties inflicted upon the Campbells
suggest that fierce fighting raged for some time, until they were driven back
with such strength and fury that their front line collapsed, and the lines

behind were thrown into utter confusion. Battle turned to rout as the Campbells fled the field for the safety of Inverlochy Castle, or south towards the foot of Glen Nevis and beyond, pursued by their victorious enemies.

The losses sustained by Argyll's army at the battle of Inverlochy may well have amounted to 1,500 men, or half its total strength. Apart from those killed on the battlefield, many were cut down as they tried to escape, or drowned as they attempted to cross the River Nevis, especially where it enters the sea. Two hundred Campbells who had taken refuge in Inverlochy Castle were put to the sword, even if the lives of any Lowlanders found among them were spared. Nothing could stop the fury of Clan Donald against their hereditary enemies.

Several families among the Campbells were virtually wiped out. 'They slew my father and my husband, three fine young sons, my four brothers hewn asunder, and my nine comely foster-brothers', the widow of Duncan Campbell of Glen Feochan lamented afterwards. According to tradition, Sir Duncan Campbell of Auchinbreck was captured, and then summarily executed by Alasdair MacDonald. Many leading Campbells were killed in the battle, and many others were captured. Their lives were spared, since such 'men of quality' could be ransomed, or used in an exchange of prisoners. Other prisoners were spared as long as they were not Campbells, but only if they agreed to serve in Montrose's army.

Flight of Argyll

Watching the battle from his galley, Archibald Campbell, first Marquis of Argyll, had seen the utter defeat of his army. Now he fled along the coast to Dunstaffnage Castle, where Colla Ciotach and Alasdair MacDonald's two brothers were still held prisoner. They were brought for greater safety to Dumbarton Castle, perhaps conveyed there in Argyll's own galley, while he returned to Edinburgh on 12 February 1645, lamenting the loss of his kith and kin, but more especially his honour. Indeed, he would never again enjoy his former power and influence over the Highland clans, nor in the councils of the Covenanters.

His downfall was celebrated in a great outpouring of Gaelic poetry, especially by Iain Lom MacDonald, whose savage verses exult in the slaughter of the Campbells and their allies at Inverlochy, while lauding the heroic deeds of Clan Donald under the leadership of Alasdair macColla Ciotach MacDonald. Even if Montrose was fighting for his King, the intensity of feeling expressed by Iain Lom's poetry leaves little doubt that the Highlanders in Montrose's army were engaged in a civil war against their fellow Gaels with all the bitterness that such an internecine struggle implies.

Chapter Five

VICTORY AND DEFEAT

After resting his army for a few days after the battle of Inverlochy, Montrose now withdrew north to confront the Covenanting army under George MacKenzie, second Marquis of Seaforth. His great victory brought Montrose new recruits. Allan Dubh Cameron of Lochiel abandoned the support he had previously given the Marquis of Argyll, bringing in a hundred well-armed Camerons, while Donald MacLean of Brolas raised hundreds of MacLeans, MacNeills and MacQuarries for the Royalist cause, acting on behalf of his elder brother Sir Lachlan MacLean of Duart.

The news of Montrose's victory went before him as he advanced along the Great Glen towards Inverness, and the Covenanting army under the Earl of Seaforth scattered in panic after the flight of its own commander, leaving only a garrison at Inverness. Montrose then marched along Stratherrick and Strathnairn to the south-east of Loch Ness, before making a wide detour towards Badenoch. However, he only succeeded in raising 300 men under James Grant of Freuchie, who did not stay long with his army.

He had greater success when he marched north towards Elgin, where he was joined by Huntly's eldest son George, Lord Gordon, and his younger brother Lewis, who eventually succeeded his father as the third Marquis of Huntly. They brought with them a troop of 200 horse, essential for campaigning in the Lowlands. Several hundred more Gordons joined his army as it marched eastwards towards Aberdeen. Even so, Montrose was still hampered by the stubborn refusal of George Gordon, second Marquis of Huntly, holding out in Strathnaver, to accept his leadership of the Royalist cause in Scotland.

Montrose was now threatened by the Covenanting army in the Lowlands, which was marching north towards Aberdeen under Lieutenant-General William Baillie, and his second-in-command, Major-General John Hurry. However, before the Lowland army had even reached the town of Montrose, Aberdeen was abandoned on 7 March 1645 by its Covenanting garrison, which fled south on hearing of Montrose's approach, leaving him free to occupy the city. He installed only a small garrison, bowing to the desperate pleas of the burgesses, alarmed that the havoc wreaked on Aberdeen only a few months previously might be repeated.

Fracas in Aberdeen

Montrose then camped at Kintore with the bulk of his army on 12 March 1645, when eighty of his cavalry officers went to stay in Aberdeen for a few days' drinking and other merry-making. Among the party was Donald Farquharson, who was one of Montrose's most trusted friends and advisers. Spies promptly reported their presence to Major-General John Hurry, who rode north from the North Water of Esk with a raiding party of 160 horse from Balcarres' regiment. He calmly rode into Aberdeen after dark on the evening of 15 March 1645, after the Royalist garrison had failed to post any guards on the city-gates. Donald Farquharson and several others were killed in the fracas that followed, a number of prisoners were captured, and all the Royalists' horses were seized, before Hurry left to rejoin the Covenanting army at Montrose.

After this setback, Montrose continued his southerly advance by way of Stonehaven, Fettercairn, and Brechin, leaving Alasdair MacDonald in Aberdeen to bury Donald Farquharson with full military honours. By now, the two armies were roughly the same size, each numbering around 3,000 infantry. However, the advantage still lay with the Covenanters, who had around 600 or 700 cavalry, more than twice the number possessed by Montrose. Neither army felt itself strong enough to attack the other in pitched battle, so only minor skirmishing occurred as Montrose made a series of forced marches along the foot of the Highlands towards Dunkeld, plundering and laying waste the countryside as he advanced, while the Covenanting army under Baillie closely followed his trail.

Descent upon Dundee

Montrose was now threatened by desertions from his army, as men left to return home with their plunder, or to defend their own territories against local Covenanters. He therefore undertook a daring exploit to demonstrate he still retained the initiative, hoping to rally the flagging morale of his own men, which very nearly backfired. Reaching Dunkeld, he suddenly turned on the night of 3 April 1645, and marched on Dundee with 150 cavalry and 600 footsoldiers, thinking that Baillie with his Covenanting army had retired south of the River Tay.

Arriving at Dundee around noon on 5 April 1645, Montrose first called upon the burgh to surrender. However, he did not even wait for a reply before launching an attack against the town walls where they were being repaired. Seizing the advantage, his troops fought their way into Dundee by the West Port and the Nethergate, led by Lord Gordon and Alasdair MacDonald. By late afternoon, the town was in Royalist hands, and many of Montrose's men had taken to plundering and drinking.

It was only then that Montrose learnt that Baillie and Hurry were just a few miles away, advancing at full speed on Dundee with their cavalry from Perth, where they had been all the time. It says much for Montrose and his officers that they first rounded up nearly all their men despite their drunken state, and then withdrew from Dundee in an orderly if hard-fought retreat towards the East, as the Covenanters entered Dundee from the West. Indeed, he could have abandoned his men to their fate by fleeing for his own life.

Instead, Montrose sent 400 men ahead, while remaining behind to command a rearguard action with his cavalry, and the rest of his infantry. Fortunately for Montrose, darkness soon fell, and he and his men were able to escape without suffering the heavy losses later claimed by the Covenanters. Approaching Arbroath, they retreated north-west towards Friockheim, and then past Guthrie and Melgund Castle to the ford at Careston over the South Esk, where they were harried by the cavalry of Major-General Hurry. Eventually, they gained the safety of Glen Esk, after covering more than seventy miles in forty-eight hours without food or sleep.

Division of Forces

Montrose now divided up his forces again, sending Lord Gordon to Strathbogie in an attempt to raise more levies, while Alasdair MacDonald roamed the eastern Highlands, recruiting wherever possible, and plundering the lands of anyone who refused to co-operate in the Royalist cause. Montrose himself moved west along the fringes of the Highlands with the rest of his army, passing through Dunkeld, then along Strathbraan and through the Sma' Glen to Crieff. He then marched to Loch Earn and beyond, harried along the way by Baillie's forces. A few days later, Montrose was joined to the south of the Trossachs by Lord Aboyne, Huntly's second son, who had copied his own earlier ride north from Carlisle. By 20 April 1645, he was at Doune, from where he wrote to Charles I, recording his progress.

Now word came from Strathbogie that Lord Gordon and his Royalist forces were threatened by Major-General Hurry, who had marched north with 1,200 infantry and 160 horse to rally the Covenanters around Aberdeen. Montrose was himself hard-pressed by the rest of the Covenanting army under Baillie, but it seems that Alasdair MacDonald mounted a diversionary attack on Coupar Angus to relieve this pressure. Montrose was now forced to go north, where Hurry threatened to attack Lord Gordon and his forces, instead of staying to deal with Baillie. But the Gordons were among the strongest of Montrose's potential allies, despite his personal differences with the Marquis of Huntly. He first withdrew north from Doune, marching towards Loch Katrine in the Trossachs, and then embarked on yet another of the extraordinary route-marches across country for which he is so justly famous.

Route-March to Auldearn

Montrose and his forces first crossed the mountains north of Loch Katrine by way of Bealach a'Chonnaidh to the Braes of Balquhidder, and then marched along Loch Voil to the foot of Glen Ogle. Striking north to reach the head of Loch Tay, he then marched east into Atholl. What route Montrose followed to the east of Atholl is not clear. Our only account states that he marched down Glen Muick, which he had presumably reached from Glen Clova by crossing the Capel Mounth, but the more obvious route into Mar lies farther west, passing from Glenshee by way of Cairnwell to Braemar. However he gained Deeside, Montrose marched down the River Dee on 1 May 1645 to camp overnight at Skene. Next day, he pushed forward towards Strathbogie and Elgin. Montrose was probably joined by Alasdair MacDonald as he moved north, while his forces were further strengthened by Lord Gordon, who had previously taken refuge from Major-General Hurry's forces in Auchindoun Castle near Dufftown.

Hurry himself had been delayed at Aberdeen by a mutiny in his own forces, but by 20 April 1645, he had left for Strathbogie and the Gordon country, which he ravaged with fire and sword until 2 May 1645. Then, learning of Montrose's approach, he first fell back towards Elgin and Forres, and then marched west to Inverness at the head of only two regiments. There he was reinforced by the Covenanting forces that still remained in winter quarters at Inverness after the ineffectual campaign waged by the Marquis of Argyll the previous autumn.

Meanwhile, George MacKenzie, second Marquis of Seaforth, had briefly rallied to the Royalist cause after Montrose's victory at Inverlochy, so he was regarded with deep suspicion by the Covenanters. However, he now joined them with his own MacKenzie clansmen, together with the MacLennans, the MacRaes, and even some MacAulays of Lewis. John Gordon, thirteenth Earl of Sutherland, was also prominent among the Covenanting ranks, leading the men of Sutherland and Caithness. Joining his forces were Sir James Fraser, Lord Lovat's brother, leading the Frasers and their allies, including the Rosses, the Munros, and some MacIntoshes. From Moray came the Innses, the Dunbars, the Cummings, and the Roses of Kilravock.

Conflicting Accounts of Auldearn

According to Montrose's own brief account of the ensuing battle of Auldearn, which may well have hidden more than it revealed, he pursued Hurry all the way to Inverness, before falling back to camp at Auldearn on the night of 8 May 1645. Meanwhile, Hurry had mustered his own forces of around 4,000 men with several troops of cavalry. He marched out of Inverness on the evening of 8 May 1645, evidently hoping to surprise Montrose's army by advancing against it under the cover of darkness.

Montrose so failed to collect adequate intelligence of Hurry's movements that he might well have been taken completely by surprise on the morning of 9 May 1645. But Hurry ordered his men to discharge their muskets to clear them in the heavy rain while still some miles from Auldearn. The sound was heard by scouts lying in front of Montrose's camp, who hurried back to raise the alarm, or so it was said. It is not clear what happened next, nor how Montrose was even then able to win a resounding victory at Auldearn, since there are conflicting accounts of the battle itself.

According to Samuel Gardiner, writing in the late nineteenth century, Montrose secured his victory by superb tactics. They involved mounting a cavalry charge from a hidden position on Montrose's left flank against the Covenanting forces, which had meanwhile been drawn into battle by the infantry under Alasdair MacDonald on the opposite flank. Montrose's many biographers and other historians uncritically accepted this account until 1980, when David Stevenson argued that Gardiner's reconstruction was pure fabrication. Not a single account of the battle by contemporary sources even mentions a cavalry charge from the left flank. Indeed, when Gardiner writes, 'The thing too was so easy to do, and so advantageous, that Montrose can hardly have failed to do it', he must surely be suspected of wishful thinking, not based on the objective assessment of whatever sources were available to him.

In fact, Gardiner virtually ignored the account given by Patrick Gordon of Ruthven in favour of one written by George Wishart, Montrose's contemporary and among the most eulogistic of all his biographers. Since then, three other sources have come to light, adding greatly to our knowledge, which David Stevenson has used to give a more realistic account of the battle.

Hurry's Advance from Inverness

Hurry in his march east from Inverness most likely crossed the River Nairn at Cawdor, if not even further upstream at Cantray, rather than further downstream at Nairn, as Gardiner thought. Such a crossing at Nairn would surely have been recorded, given the size of the burgh, but not a single source mentions it. After crossing the River Nairn at Cawdor, or even Cantray, Hurry would then have advanced towards Auldearn from the south-west along the line of the old coach road, now followed by the B9101. Drawing close to Auldearn, he may well have decided to follow the low ridge of slightly higher ground lying to the north of the modern road, as suggested by some accounts.

It was behind this ridge that Gardiner placed Montrose's cavalry, and some infantry, where they could not be seen by Hurry if he had been advancing from Nairn. As it was, Montrose's army was almost certainly encamped in a steep-sided hollow around Boath House, which lies just east of the village itself, unaware of the impending attack, but hidden from view on all sides. Then, when the alarm was first raised, Alasdair MacDonald roused his own regiment of Irish troops, along with some Highlanders and Gordons. He then rushed forward to meet the enemy attack just west of Auldearn village, supported by only a few hundred men.

The village of Auldearn occupied another ridge of slightly higher ground, running north-west from Auldearn Church for several hundred yards to Castle Hill. Its houses were scattered along this ridge, especially around the church, while their gardens and other walled enclosures descended south-west towards an area of low-lying and boggy ground, drained by a tributary of the Auldearn Burn. Alasdair MacDonald managed to draw up whatever forces he had available in line of battle along this slope. Evidently, he hoped to hold off the Covenanters' advance across the boggy ground to his south-west, so giving Montrose time to rally the rest of his forces.

Attack and Counter-Attack

Hurry made no real attempt to deploy his own forces as he approached Auldearn from the west or south-west, planning instead to mount a surprise attack on Montrose's army. The vanguard of the Covenanting army consisted of a foot regiment under Sir Mungo Campbell of Lawers, while two more infantry regiments followed behind, commanded by the Earls of Lothian and Loudoun, together with several troops of horse. It was therefore Lawers' regiment that first encountered Alasdair MacDonald and his advance guard across the boggy ground to the west of Auldearn. Forced to give ground, Alasdair MacDonald was able to occupy a defensive position by retiring up the slope at his back to take cover behind the walls of the village gardens.

Alasdair MacDonald now mounted a counter-attack, after the footsoldiers of Lawers' regiment had been driven back by salvos of musket-fire. Such a charge against the enemy seemingly took Alasdair MacDonald farther to his left than previously. He was possibly aware of the danger of being outflanked by Lawers' regiment around the south end of the village. It was perhaps a deliberate manœuvre on Alasdair MacDonald's part, intended to prevent the rest of Montrose's army being revealed to the enemy. But he now faced Lothian's regiment as well, advancing against him to his right. Both these foot-regiments were flanked by troops of cavalry. Fighting desperately with great courage and skill, Alasdair MacDonald managed to extricate his forces from such an exposed position, as they were driven back to take refuge once again behind the walls of the village gardens.

Rallying of Montrose's Forces

The tide of battle now turned against the Covenanters. While Alasdair MacDonald held off the ever-increasing attacks of Hurry's forces as more and more Covenanters poured on to the field of battle, Montrose managed to gather together his own men into some semblance of order. The first to engage the enemy were a Gordon troop of 100 horse under Lord Aboyne. They wheeled south of Auldearn to attack the enemy cavalry on Alasdair's left flank, where he was most vulnerable. The ferocity of his charge scattered the Covenanters' horse, driving them from the field. Soon afterwards, Lord Gordon mounted his own charge with another troop of a hundred cavalry against the Covenanters' horse on Alasdair's right flank, wheeling north around Castle Hill to drive them from the field as well.

By now, Montrose had rallied his infantry, who started to move forward to reinforce Alasdair MacDonald and his men, who had borne the brunt of the battle for quite some time. Slowly, they began to advance upon the Covenanters' foot-regiments of Lawers and Lothian. Quite possibly, Montrose now ordered the infantry on both his wings to follow up the cavalry charges of Lords Aboyne and Gordon, attempting to encircle the enemy.

A troop of Covenanting horse commanded by Major Drummond had already caused chaos when it wheeled left into the massed ranks of Lawers' regiment, rather than right in a charge against the Royalist cavalry under Lord Aboyne. (Drummond was later shot after a court-martial which judged him guilty of treachery instead of simply acting out of confusion in the heat of battle.) Soon afterwards, Lord Gordon broke off his pursuit of the Covenanting cavalry. He had seen Lord Aboyne and his troop at a distance, mistaking them for Covenanters as they had not yet furled the enemy colours they had captured. Although the mistake was soon put right, it prompted Lord Gordon and his cavalry to return to the battlefield, where their enemy were now surrounded on all sides.

The battlefield now turned into a killing ground. The Covenanters' foot-soldiers were cut down where they stood, closely packed in rank and file. The regiments of Lawers and Lothian, which had first advanced against the Royalists, suffered great losses. So did Loudoun's regiment with the Highland levies of the MacKenzies and the Frasers, which had brought up their rear. Sir Mungo Campbell of Lawers and nine of his senior officers were killed, along with 200 soldiers from his regiment. Major-General John Hurry, the Earls of Seaforth and Sutherland, Sir James Fraser and the other commanders all managed to escape with their lives on horseback, being well-mounted. They left perhaps 2,000 of their men to die upon the battlefield, while the survivors fled for their lives.

Indeed, the death toll suffered by Hurry's forces, amounting to perhaps half his army, may well have exceeded the size of Montrose's own army at Auldearn. In contrast, only around 200 men were killed among Montrose's own forces, perhaps a tenth of their number, since it is usually accepted that his total strength at Auldearn was around 2,000 men, including 200 cavalry.

Alasdair MacDonald's Triumph at Auldearn

Far from Auldearn being a great victory, won against overwhelming odds by the brilliant tactics of James Graham, first Marquis of Montrose, it had very nearly turned into a defeat for the Royalist forces. As David Stevenson wrote:

> The battle was won by the astonishing feats of arms of the Highlanders, Irish, and the Gordons, who . . . taken by surprise by a greatly superior enemy, snatched victory when defeat seemed certain . . . The chief glory belongs to Alasdair MacColla [MacDonald] and the few hundred men under him whose epic deeds checked the first onslaught of the enemy . . . They had fought off the initial enemy attack and thus saved the rest of the army. They in turn had been saved by the charges of the Gordon cavalry, and then by the arrival of the rest of the foot under Montrose . . . All had shared in a most extraordinary victory, and their joy must have been accentuated by relief at disaster so narrowly averted.

March and Countermarch

After the victory at Auldearn, Montrose rested his men for only a day before turning to face Lieutenant-General William Baillie, who was already march-ing north against him from Perth with 2,000 foot and 120 horse. Passing through Atholl, he marched north-east through Glen Tilt into Mar, where he camped between the parishes of Coull and Tarland on 11 May 1645, two days after Montrose's victory at Auldearn. There he was reinforced by the Earl of Balcarres with two more regiments.

By then, Montrose had reached Elgin, where he remained for a few days. Meanwhile, Alasdair MacDonald had marched west into Easter Ross to take revenge against the Frasers and the MacKenzies for their support of the Covenanters, returning later to rejoin Montrose. The rival armies under Baillie and Montrose now engaged in a bewildering series of marches and counter-marches as each tried to checkmate the other in a complex game of chess, waged upon the chequerboard of the eastern Highlands.

Baillie first advanced north towards Strathbogie, where he came face-to-face with Montrose on the night of 21 May 1645, only to find the next morning that the Royalist forces had slipped away towards the west along the Deveron valley to Balvenie Castle. Shadowed by Baillie's forces, Montrose then marched south-west through Glen Rinnes into Glen Livet, and then across the hills to Abernethy. He then turned south-west along Strathspey to march into Badenoch, where he rested at Ruthven Castle. Meanwhile, Baillie withdrew to Inverness to replenish his supplies.

Montrose learnt at Ruthven that he now faced another Covenanting army, which was marching from the south towards Dunkeld under the command of the Earl of Crawford and Lindsay. Hoping to outflank the enemy forces, Montrose decided to cross the Mounth into Angus in yet another spectacular expedition. Marching up Glen Feshie and then east through the Forest of Mar towards Braemar, he then turned south, crossing the Cairnwell to reach Glen Shee and then Glen Isla.

However, Montrose abandoned his planned attack upon the Earl of Crawford and Lindsay when he learnt that Baillie had left Inverness to march east into the Garioch, devastating the Gordon lands along the way. Deserted by the Gordons in his army, who were recalled to defend their lands, lack of numbers forced him to withdraw by retracing his steps back north to Braemar. Alasdair MacDonald left him at Braemar to march along Glen Tilt to rally more support in the western Highlands. There he was reunited with his father Colla Ciotach and his two brothers, whom the Marquis of Argyll had released after six years of captivity in an exchange of prisoners.

Montrose himself now marched along the River Dee into Cromar, before he retired north to the remote castle of Corgarff in Strathdon. However, he advanced once again after learning that Baillie had moved north to attack Gordon Castle, just outside Fochabers. Marching east along Strathdon to Kildrummy, Montrose then turned north, eventually making contact with Baillie's forces, which he found occupying a strong defensive position on the north bank of the River Isla, close to the village of Old Keith.

When Baillie refused to give battle, Montrose withdrew south to Pitlurg, and then to Druminnor Castle near Rhynie, seat of Lord Forbes, thus tempting Baillie to advance against him by pretending to retreat. When the bait was taken, Montrose fell back across the eastern flanks of the Correen Hills by the Suie road, and then crossed the Howe of Alford to take up a strong position on Gallow Hill above Alford, south of the River Don.

Battle of Alford

Baillie himself approached Alford by the ford at Montgarrie on 2 July 1645. He needed a victory, since he was being hard-pressed by the Covenanting authorities, who complained about the slow progress of the war against Montrose. The opposing armies were evenly matched, since they both consisted of little more than 2,000 men, although Baillie had a slight superiority in cavalry.

Montrose placed his troops of cavalry under Lords Gordon and Aboyne at the two ends of his line, flanked by parties of Irish musketeers. His centre was formed by six-deep ranks of infantry. They consisted mostly of Gordons from Strathbogie and the Highlanders, probably under the overall command of Angus MacDonald of Glengarry. It was the only battle fought and won by Montrose in which Alasdair MacDonald was absent, although all three Irish regiments were present, if reduced in number.

The fighting itself was over quickly. Lord Gordon's cavalry charged first on the left wing, engaging the Covenanters' horse under the Earl of Balcarres in close combat. Lord Aboyne was not far behind in mounting his own cavalry charge on the right wing. Montrose then ordered his infantry to charge the enemy lines, while his cavalry attacked their rear. Their onslaught broke the Covenanting ranks, who were routed with heavy losses. The Irish carried out much of the slaughter, performing it 'with too little compassion, and too much cruelty, no quarters being granted to any whom they could reach', according to Patrick Gordon of Ruthven.

Montrose's victory was largely achieved by the Gordons, but their triumph was marred by the death of Lord George Gordon. He was shot in the back as he charged behind the enemy lines, perhaps in pursuit of Baillie. His followers showed no mercy to the defeated Covenanters whom they pursued for several miles from the field of battle. The Covenanters' losses were reported as a third of their strength, while only three others apart from Lord Gordon were killed from the Royalist ranks, or so it was said.

March to Kilsyth

By defeating the Covenanting armies under Hurry at Auldearn, and Baillie at

Alford, sent north against him, Montrose was now free to move south against the Lowlands without any danger to his rear. His determination to do so was greatly strengthened by news of the crushing defeat suffered only a fortnight earlier by the Royalist forces at Naseby. Marching south to cross the River Dee inland of Aberdeen, he was rejoined by Alasdair MacDonald at Fordoun in the Mearns. Accompanying him were much-needed reinforcements from the western Highlands, among whom were the MacDonalds of Clan Ranald, the MacLeans of Duart, and the MacDonalds of Glengarry, numbering around 1,400 men. The Robertsons of Struan, together with the Stewarts of Appin, the MacNabs and the MacGregors, all returned to his ranks around the same time.

Montrose now marched along the Highland fringe to Dunkeld. He then advanced to within eight miles of Perth, now the seat of the Covenanting regime after it had been driven by the bubonic plague from Edinburgh and Stirling. However, he lacked the strength to mount an attack, and indeed the Covenanters' cavalry forced him to fall back in some confusion on Dunkeld. He was joined there a week later by Lord Aboyne with 800 infantry and three or four hundred cavalry, together with nearly a hundred Ogilvie horsemen. Montrose's army now had around 5,000 foot under arms, strengthened by several hundred cavalry.

Montrose now felt strong enough to bypass the Covenanting stronghold of Perth, breaking out south through Glen Farg to Kinross. He then turned west by way of Crook of Devon and Rumbling Bridge, marching against the Marquis of Argyll's estates around Castle Campbell at Dollar. Although the castle itself was not sacked, the MacLeans devastated the surrounding country in full view of its garrison, which may even have included the hapless Marquis.

Montrose's army now marched past Alloa, where he accepted an invitation from the Earl of Mar to dine at Alloa House. Accompanied by his leading officers, and all his horse, he left his infantry under Alasdair MacDonald to continue its advance west towards Stirling without the protection of any cavalry. The danger of Montrose's position, and his total lack of judgment, soon became clear when news arrived just after the banquet had ended that the Covenanting forces under Baillie were rapidly approaching from the direction of Perth. Abruptly leaving his host, Montrose caught up with Alasdair MacDonald and his infantry. Crossing the River Forth above Stirling, he turned south to reach Kilsyth on 14 August 1645, where he camped with his army.

Battle of Kilsyth

When Baillie advanced against him from the north-east on the morning of 15

August 1645, Montrose had already chosen the ground on which to fight. Baillie also faced a further difficulty in that he was only in nominal command of his forces. He lacked any real authority, since he was accompanied by a committee of Covenanting noblemen, including the Marquis of Argyll, appointed by Parliament. Baillie first drew up his forces to the east of Montrose's army, so that the two battle lines faced one another across Banton Burn. However, the other leaders among the Covenanters objected, arguing that their forces would be better placed further north and west to take advantage of higher ground, overlooking Montrose's lines. After much heated debate, Baillie agreed out of sheer exasperation. He ordered his forces to face right and march past the enemy lines towards their new position, attempting to outflank Montrose's army. It was a manoeuvre fraught with danger.

The disposition of Montrose's own forces is far from clear, but it is most likely he placed the Gordon and Ogilvie cavalry on his two wings, so that the bulk of the infantry formed the centre of his line of battle. As usual, Alasdair MacDonald commanded the front ranks of the infantry, which apparently consisted of Highlanders, such as the MacDonalds of Clan Ranald and the MacLeans, as well as his own Irishmen, while two other regiments were held in reserve. In front of his main line, Montrose placed a small party of infantry among the gardens of some cottages as an outpost on his right wing, commanded according to tradition by Ewen MacLean of Treshnish. Now, he ordered forward a troop of cavalry under Nathaniel Gordon on his left wing as soon as he realised that Baillie was trying to outflank him to the north.

The battle of Kilsyth started almost as soon as Baillie embarked on his risky manoeuvre to gain the higher ground to the north, and almost immediately Baillie and Montrose lost control of their forces. Rather than holding their ground as ordered by Baillie, the cavalry regiments supported by the infantry on his left wing, which now made up the rear of his army, came into contact with the advance party of Highlanders under Ewen MacLean of Treshnish. They started to attack the Royalist position around the cottages. Equally, the cavalry regiments on Baillie's right wing, supported by a party of footsoldiers, now in the vanguard of his army, started to attack the Gordon cavalry dispatched by Montrose to guard his left wing. They thus abandoned the attempt to outflank Montrose by occupying the higher ground to the north and west, as they had been ordered to do by Baillie.

The Covenanting forces now pressed home these two attacks so fiercely that the infantry outpost held by Ewen MacLean of Treshnish, and the cavalry under Nathaniel Gordon, were both in danger of being overwhelmed. Realising the danger, and without waiting for Montrose's orders, Alasdair MacDonald launched an attack from the centre, charging against the enemy with his infantry. Clan Ranald was in the vanguard, attacking the Covenanting cavalry with his clansmen. Soon afterwards, Lord Aboyne rode with the rest of the Gordon cavalry from the rear to relieve his kinsmen on his left wing, supported by the troop of Ogilvie horse, routing Baillie's right wing. Montrose thus had little choice but to order the rest of his forces to charge the enemy, determined to take full advantage of the confusion in Baillie's ranks.

Baillie's army soon gave way as it faced the onslaught of the Highlanders under Alasdair MacDonald, and then the rest of Montrose's infantry as it charged through the disorganised ranks of the Covenanters' cavalry to engage the enemy at close quarters. Even as the bewildered Covenanters turned to face Montrose's troops, the fighting turned to carnage as they were cut down where they stood, or vainly attempted to flee the field. Baillie himself rode to his rear to rally his reserve of Fife levies, only to find that they had fled. The battle was over, apart from the slaughter. The Covenanters suffered just as great losses as previously at Inverlochy or Auldearn, losing perhaps half their original strength of 7,000 infantry, quite apart from the cavalry. Archibald Campbell, Marquis of Argyll, took horse to Queensferry, and then fled by boat to safety in Berwick.

Significantly, Montrose's victory was lauded by a bard of Clan Donald as a victory of Gaeldom over the *Goill*, referring to the Lowlanders of Scotland with their Presbyterian beliefs. Just as revealingly, he identifies the *Goill* with the men of *Alba*, using the Gaelic name for Scotland. As David Stevenson comments:

> Calling the Covenanters the men of *Alba* emphasises the sense of alienation created by the use of the word *Goill*, for *Alba* is Scotland; the poet does not, it seems, consider himself and the other Gaelic Highlanders to be 'men of Scotland', even though they are nominally fighting for the king of Scotland.

Even so, Alasdair MacDonald may well have been gratified when he was knighted by Montrose in the King's name, only a few days after the battle of Kilsyth.

Divisions within Montrose's Camp

Montrose's sixth and final victory at the battle of Kilsyth left him in control of the Scottish Lowlands, since there were no Covenanting forces left in Scotland to oppose him. As Edinburgh was barred by an outbreak of bubonic plague, he first established his headquarters in Glasgow. He then moved to the more salubrious surroundings of Bothwell to exercise his powers as the newly appointed Captain-General and Lieutenant-Governor of Scotland. There he stayed until 4 September 1645, taking submissions from prominent individuals and representatives from the burghs and shires, while giving protections to anyone who would enter into the King's peace.

Since Ayrshire still remained a Covenanting stronghold, he now dispatched Sir Alasdair MacDonald there in late August with a force of a few hundred Highlanders and half his Irishmen. But when Alasdair MacDonald returned to Bothwell at the very beginning of September, he found Montrose facing a crisis in his own camp, which was about to be deserted by all the Gordons, as well as the remaining Highlanders, including the clansmen of Clan Donald among others, if indeed they had not already left.

It is possible, but by no means certain, that they had refused to venture any farther south in a cause which lacked their whole-hearted support. After all, their rallying to the Royalist standard was only a means to an end. As already emphasised, the Irish forces raised by the Earl of Antrim under Alasdair MacDonald were largely fighting the Covenanters in Scotland in an attempt to force their withdrawal from Ulster. Equally, Alasdair MacDonald and his Highland allies were just as intent on curbing the power and influence of the Marquis of Argyll.

However, although they had largely achieved this objective, such gains could only endure, and the lands of Clan Donald could only be restored, if the Royalist cause triumphed over the Parliamentarians in England. Perhaps the Highlanders under Alasdair MacDonald realised more clearly than Montrose that Charles I was slowly losing the Civil War in England, and that it was already too late to come to his aid. Even so, it hardly seems in their warlike character to abandon such a campaign before it was well and truly lost. Equally, they must have been concerned that the Campbells still needed to be kept in check if they were not to harass their own lands, since they had evidently started to recover from their defeat at Inverlochy. More likely, Montrose's need to keep and hold territory if he was to have any credibility as the Lieutenant-Governor of Scotland clashed with the Highlanders' strategy of waging guerilla warfare on a large scale, defeating their enemies in lightning strikes and withdrawing to the safety of the Highlands before launching another and equally unexpected attack.

However, it was common enough practice for Highlanders to return home during the course of a campaign to deposit their plunder, only to reappear later, as they had done on many previous occasions. Moreover, as summer turned to autumn, and the harvest needed to be gathered, the well-being of their womenfolk and children during the months ahead may have been uppermost in their minds. Indeed, the mercenary soldiers or redshanks provided by the Highland chiefs in the late sixteenth century for service in

Ulster had only campaigned during the summer months, leaving home once the crops were sown in the spring, and returning in time for the harvest.

Montrose was thus forced to agree when the Highland chieftains requested leave of absence to travel home with their clansmen, agreeing to return within forty days with fresh recruits. Not long afterwards, he lost several hundred horsemen and perhaps as many footsoldiers from his army when Lord Aboyne withdrew from Montrose's camp with all his men and cavalry. He was recalled north to Strathbogie by his father George Gordon, second Marquis of Huntly, who had returned from Strathnaver to his estates, which needed to be protected from the Covenanters in the north.

Thus, Montrose was deprived of 2,000 Highlanders at a critical time when they were most needed, and he was defeated at Philiphaugh long before they were due to return to his camp after the forty days had elapsed. Alasdair MacDonald and the other Highland chieftains have been bitterly criticised for their desertion of Montrose in his hour of need. But it is not even certain that Montrose was aware when they left of the danger posed by the Scots army of the Covenant under Lieutenant-General David Leslie, distant kinsman of Alexander Leslie, first Earl of Leven, which was then massing against him in the north of England.

Motives of Alasdair MacDonald

Alasdair MacDonald left Montrose's camp once again on 3 September 1645 to join Sir James Lamont of that ilk, who had earlier received a commission from Montrose on 26 August to go to Argyll to raise all fencible men for the King's service. Indeed, Sir James Lamont later asserted that he requested the help of Alasdair MacDonald with some 500 or 600 men to undertake what was a Herculean task, and that Montrose willingly gave his assent. There seems no reason to doubt the truth of Lamont's claim, since Alasdair MacDonald did indeed join Sir James Lamont in Cowal, taking with him around 500 Highlanders.

It is often charged that Alasdair MacDonald never intended to return, but as David Stevenson has emphasised, the strongest argument against such an accusation has been totally overlooked in the past: when he left for Argyll, Alasdair MacDonald left behind nearly all of his Irish troops with Montrose, apart from his own bodyguard of 120 clansmen. Had Alasdair MacDonald intended to desert Montrose with no thought of return, leaving him to almost certain defeat, it is scarcely conceivable that he would have deliberately abandoned his own troops as well. He had after all commanded them to brilliant effect in a long and arduous campaign over the previous year. He must surely have realised what odium and obloquy such a cynical act of cowardice – deserting not only his best troops, but some of his closest friends and kinsmen as well – would have looked like to posterity.

March South to Philiphaugh

Montrose struck camp at Bothwell on the morning of 4 September 1645, and marched east towards Edinburgh, and then south into the Borders, only a day after Alasdair MacDonald had left for Argyll. Despite all his brave talk of invading England with 20,000 men, he now had little more than a thousand veterans of Kilsyth still remaining in his army, which consisted mostly of the Irish regiments. Another 1,000 horsemen had joined his ranks since Kilsyth, but they were mostly nobles, gentry and others, poorly trained and ill-disciplined. Even their loyalty was doubtful, since many were only present out of a sense of political expediency.

If Montrose had hoped to recruit more men to the Royalist cause as he marched south, his optimism was sorely disappointed: the plague prevented him from entering the towns, which might have proved fertile grounds for such recruitment, while the Earls of Home, Roxburgh and Traquair never honoured their promises to raise levies for the Royalist cause. Indeed the first two earls abandoned Montrose by surrendering to the Covenanting army of David Leslie as soon as it crossed into Scotland from Berwick.

Confidently expecting Montrose to retreat north into the Highlands as the only course now open to him, David Leslie marched towards Stirling, hoping to cut off his retreat. Montrose however lingered in the Borders, perhaps overcome by a sense of fate, since it seems his pride would not allow him to retreat from what he had achieved in the King's name. After advancing towards Kelso from Galashiels, he camped for two days at Stichill, and then decided to march west through the hills around St Mary's Loch into Dumfriesshire, where the dwindling ranks of his army might be strengthened by recruitment in a district more favourable to the Royalist cause. After passing through Jedburgh, he reached Selkirk on 12 September 1645.

His small army camped a mile to the west at Philiphaugh, close to the meeting of the Yarrow and Ettrick Waters, while he himself retired to Selkirk for the night. It was utter folly to separate himself from his men when he knew that a formidable army under David Leslie, consisting of 5,000 cavalry and more than a thousand foot, was even then searching him out, and rumoured to be in the vicinity.

But such folly was compounded when he refused to believe a report during the night that a troop of his own scouts had been surprised by an advance party from Leslie's army, which had marched south from Haddington along the Gala Water to Galashiels. It was only at breakfast on the morning of 13

September 1645 that he learnt that Leslie was within a mile of his own forces at Philiphaugh.

Battle of Philiphaugh

Hurrying to Philiphaugh, Montrose found his own forces in chaos, apart from the Irish, who calmly awaited his orders, 'ready to die and live with him as they had been from the beginning', or so it was said. Much of his cavalry deserted the field, leaving him with only a few hundred horsemen, which he mustered on his right wing, while the Irish foot made up his centre, guarded on their left by the slopes of Harehead Hill. Even if Montrose mounted a desperate defence against the first charge of Leslie's cavalry with his own horse, the day was already lost for the Royalist cause.

Neither his horse nor his musketeers were able to resist when Leslie's cavalry charged for the second time, although the Irish infantry stoutly stood their ground, absorbing the impact of heavy cavalry with great resolution. Leslie had divided his forces, and now his other division advanced upon Montrose's army across the Ettrick Water in a flanking movement, so that the Royalists were caught in deadly cross-fire.

Now realising he could do nothing to save his infantry, Montrose was persuaded to flee the field, perhaps acting against his better judgment, leaving the Irish troops who had fought his cause so valiantly to their fate. Surrounded by Leslie's cavalry, they were slaughtered, just as they had slaughtered their opponents at Inverlochy, Auldearn and Kilsyth. Over half of them died fighting, while many others were captured, or surrendered on promise of quarter, only to be executed afterwards. Not even the camp-followers were spared: 300 of them, 'boys, cooks, and a rabble of rascals and women with their children in their arms . . . were cut in pieces with such savage and inhuman cruelty as neither Turk nor Scithean was ever heard to have done the like'.

Many of Montrose's most loyal followers were captured, and then executed after a trial before a Covenanting tribunal, rather than Parliament. The Covenanters justified such actions by affirming that 'God, who was the just judge of the world, would not but judge righteously and keep in remembrance that sea of innocent blood which lay before his throne crying for vengeance on those bloodthirsty rebels, the butchers of so many innocent souls'.

Chapter Six

CAMPAIGNS IN THE HIGHLANDS

Montrose escaped north from his defeat at Philiphaugh with only a few close companions, attempting at the same time to regroup his scattered forces. Arriving at Druminnor Castle, he met Huntly's eldest surviving son Lord Aboyne, who conveyed a message of reconciliation from Montrose to his father at Strathbogie. As already mentioned, after his own attempt at a Royalist uprising had failed in April 1644, George Gordon, second Marquis of Huntly, had remained aloof in Strathnaver, perhaps resenting Montrose's successes over the next year-and-a-half, and jealous of his own commission as the King's Lieutenant-General in the North. No doubt, he still bore Montrose a bitter grudge for the act of treachery which had made him a prisoner in 1639. Even now Huntly refused to act as decisively as Montrose had hoped. Indeed, his lands were now threatened by a Covenanting army under John Middleton, veteran of the battle at Brig O'Dee, which the Covenanting regime had sent north to subdue the Royalists.

Montrose therefore went south to Dunkeld in late October, from where he marched west into Lennox with 1,200 foot and 300 horse. He perhaps hoped that Alasdair MacDonald would join him there with his own forces if he returned from Argyll. When Alasdair MacDonald failed to appear, Montrose marched back north to Strathbogie through the Glens of Angus a few weeks later in November. It was only then that Huntly was reluctantly persuaded by Montrose to advance with him against Inverness. But they quarrelled over the wisdom of laying siege to the town, since Huntly argued that they should first subdue the Covenanters farther north, such as the Earl of Sutherland. Montrose remained behind to besiege Inverness during what was a very severe winter, said to be the worst in living memory, while it seems Huntly returned to his own estates.

Farther north, George MacKenzie, second Earl of Seaforth, was active as well on behalf of the King, attempting to rally the northern clans, but to little effect. Only Sir James MacDonald of Sleat agreed to lend his support.

However, the situation changed abruptly in April 1646 when the Covenanters sent another force north under John Middleton to relieve Inverness. It surprised Montrose by the rapidity of its approach, forcing him into flight. Moving south-west through Strathglass, he crossed the Great Glen into Stratherrick, and eventually reached Strathspey. It was there on 2 June 1646 that he received a letter from Charles I, ordering him to disband his forces.

Surrender of Charles I

Charles I had left Oxford in disguise on 5 May 1646, realising that his cause was lost. After making his way to Newark, where the Royalist garrison was still under siege, he surrendered to the Scots army of the Covenant. By now, Montrose was his only bargaining counter as he tried to come to terms with the Covenanting regime, taking advantage of the growing divisions between the Scots and the New Model Army of Oliver Cromwell. The Covenanters for their part were alarmed that Montrose might still have sufficient resources to raise another army in the north for the King. They were therefore willing to provide Montrose and the other leaders of the Royalist forces with safe-conducts to leave the country, while offering a full pardon to his followers so that peace could be restored in the north.

Montrose agreed to the Covenanters' terms at a meeting with Middleton on 22 July 1646, held on the Water of Isla. He agreed to leave Scotland by the first of September in a vessel provided by the Covenanters. After disbanding his forces as agreed, Montrose waited for the vessel. It only appeared at the very last moment, and even then its captain refused to sail before the dead-line had expired. Fearful of a trap, Montrose hired a Norwegian sloop instead to carry him and his companions to exile in Bergen. When it anchored off the coast on the evening of 3 September 1646, Montrose rowed out to the boat, dressed as the poorly-clad servant of the Reverend James Wood, so that he left Scotland in disguise, just as he had arrived with such high hopes in 1644.

Capture of Huntly

Meanwhile, George Gordon, second Marquis of Huntly, had reversed his earlier decision to disarm his own forces, as requested by the King. After leaving Montrose to besiege Inverness, it seems Huntly had occupied the town of Banff over the winter of 1645 with his own forces, said to be 2,000 strong. However, he abandoned Banff after a force of Covenanters under Lieutenant-General David Leslie was dispatched north in the spring of 1646 to deal with him. Retreating into Badenoch, where Leslie established a garrison at Ruthven, Huntly remained at liberty until December 1646, wandering his own lands and perhaps farther west as a fugitive.

Huntly was eventually captured near Tomintoul at the farmhouse of Delnabo, but it was more than two years before he was brought to trial in Edinburgh on 16 March 1649. He was then condemned to death after being found guilty of treason. His beheading at the Mercat Cross on 22 March 1649 occurred only a few weeks after his own sovereign was executed in London. Huntly's capture fifteen months earlier had brought peace of sorts to the country, after Donald MacKay of Strathnaver, first Lord Reay, fled abroad into exile.

Lord Reay and the Royalist Cause

Lord Reay's support for Charles I had been just as ineffectual, constrained by the presence of the Earl of Sutherland as his feudal superior in the far north. Indeed, as already recounted, Lord Reay had even joined a Covenanting force of 4,000 men under George MacKenzie, second Earl of Seaforth, which had marched into Moray during the course of the First Bishops' War in the summer of 1639. However, the Covenanters had even then suspected Reay and Seaforth of Royalist sympathies, holding them briefly captive in Edinburgh Castle, before Lord Reay was allowed to return north to Strathnaver.

Even before the Civil War broke out two years later in England, Lord Reay had left the country for Denmark. He evidently hoped to bring assistance to Charles I, who had earlier offered Christian IV of Denmark the Orkney Islands in return for his help. Early in 1644, Lord Reay left Denmark with some ships laden with arms and ammunition, and landed at Newcastle, shortly before the Scots army of the Covenant laid siege to the town in February 1644. He remained there acting in its defence until 14 October 1644, when Newcastle finally fell to the Scots, and he was imprisoned in Edinburgh Castle. However, Montrose's victory at Kilsyth in August 1645 resulted in his release, and again he returned home to Strathnaver.

There Lord Reay found himself in dispute with John Gordon, thirteenth Earl of Sutherland, over the lands of Strathnaver. They had apparently been sold in 1642 in an attempt to meet Reay's debts, but they may well have been seized by his creditors after he had failed to pay up. The matter was reported to Parliament in March 1647, which authorised the dispatch of 500 troops to assist the Earl of Sutherland to regain his lands. However, Lieutenant-General David Leslie refused to allow his forces to be used for such a private expedition, and it was not until October 1647 that the Earl of Sutherland finally induced General John Middleton to provide him with troops.

Advancing with this force to Rossal on the borders of Strathnaver, the Earl of Sutherland then persuaded Donald MacKay, first Lord Reay, to agree to a settlement between them, which he eventually signed in January 1648. Not long afterwards, in the spring of 1648, Lord Reay took ship at Thurso, and sailed again into exile, dying just a year later in Copenhagen. His body was brought back to Tongue for burial in the family vault by order of Christian IV of Denmark, whom he had served with such distinction during the Thirty Years' War.

Actions of Alasdair MacDonald

As these events unfolded in the far north of Scotland after Montrose's defeat at the battle of Philiphaugh in September 1645, Alasdair MacDonald was active in Argyll against the Campbells. Archibald Campbell, first Marquis of Argyll, had already started to recover from his crushing defeat at the battle of Inverlochy in February 1645 and the 'herschip' of his territories. By July 1645, he had established himself at Kilchurn Castle at the head of Loch Awe, where he issued orders to his kinsmen to draw together their forces, and to send out spies so that they might be warned of any enemy movements on the borders of his vast fiefdom. The synod of Argyll met on the same day at Inveraray for the first time since May 1644, so that the Covenanting regime had begun to restore its control over Argyll as well.

It was evidently to thwart such a recovery that Alasdair MacDonald had left Montrose after the battle of Kilsyth to march west into Argyll for one final attempt to reclaim these territories for Clan Donald and his patron, Randal MacDonald, second Earl of Antrim. Avoiding Glasgow, and marching west past Dumbarton, Alasdair MacDonald first reached Rosneath, and then Cowal, ferrying his forces across Loch Long in boats provided by Sir James Lamont's brother Archibald. Joining together, they then marched across Cowal to Strachur on Loch Fyne, before turning south through Glendaruel to the Campbell lands of Auchinbreck at the head of Loch Riddon.

Sir James Lamont now made good his promise to raise all his friends and followers. Together, they marched with Alasdair MacDonald through Cowal, Argyll, Lorne and Kintyre for the next five weeks, without meeting any opposition.

Atrocities and Reprisals

Soon Alasdair MacDonald and his allies had 2,000 men under arms, drawn partly from the local clans hostile to the Campbells, Earls of Argyll. However, the Campbells now mounted a raid on the Lamont lands in Cowal, killing men, women and children, burning their houses, and driving off their animals. Such savage behaviour served to justify Alasdair MacDonald in putting all the Campbells they captured to the sword as a reprisal. Indeed, it is doubtful if they spared anyone, young or old, woman or child, even if they said otherwise.

Even while Alasdair MacDonald and Sir James Lamont were attacking the Campbells in the south and east, other Highland chieftains who had left Montrose before the battle of Philiphaugh were mounting their own assaults from the north and west. Already, MacDougall of Dunollie had 500 men in arms, perhaps marching with Alasdair MacDonald, while the lands of Glendochart, Glenlochy and Glenfalloch were attacked in early October 1645 by a force of 600 men, among whom were the Camerons of Lochiel and the MacDonalds of Clan Ranald, Glengarry and Glencoe.

Quite likely they were all acting in concert with one another in attacking Argyll, since the two separate forces joined up with one another in Lorne in December 1645. Sir Lachlan MacLean of Duart met Alasdair MacDonald at Kilmore, staying with him for three nights, and the two men may well have signed with the other chiefs what was later described by their enemies as 'a most cruel horrid and bloody band [pact] . . . for rooting out the name of Campbell'. Indeed, they were close to success, since the Campbells only held out in scattered strongholds by the end of 1645, many of which were running short of provisions.

Attempting a counter-attack, orders were given by the Covenanters to levy a Highland regiment under Argyll, only to meet with another setback. After Sir James Campbell of Ardkinglas had gathered together the survivors from among the Campbells, he started to march towards the Lowlands. Along the way, he recaptured the island castle of Loch Dochart from the MacNabs, and besieged Edinample Castle near the head of Loch Earn. Men loyal to the Campbells from among the Menzies, and the Stewarts of Balquhidder, joined him as well, so that he reached Callander with a force of around 1,200 men. There he was suddenly attacked and routed on 13 February 1646 by a much smaller force of Highlanders from Atholl.

Alasdair MacDonald in Argyll

By early 1646, Alasdair MacDonald had established a strong position in Argyll. He evidently held nearly all of Argyll's territories in Lorne, Knapdale and Kintyre, and then, in February 1646, he invaded Bute, so threatening Ayrshire. By then, he had probably also seized all of Islay with the help of John MacDonald, Captain of Clan Ranald, and his clansmen. Tradition has it that Alasdair MacDonald laid siege at various times to the Campbell

garrisons in their strongholds at Kilberry, Duntroon and Craignish, and later
Skipness. However, he lacked cannon to capture these castles, but he did
prevent supplies from reaching the castles of Sween, Dunstaffnage, Barcaldine
and Stalker. Indeed, he may even have succeeded in capturing Castle Sween,
but otherwise the castles of 'stone and lime' remained loyal to the Campbells.

While the Campbell forces usually fled at his approach, he apparently
routed with great loss of life what Campbell forces resisted him at the battle
of Lagganmore in Glen Euchar, west of Loch Scammadale. There, his own
forces were reinforced by the MacDougalls of Dunollie, and the MacAulays
of Ardincaple, while the Malcolms of Poltalloch were among the Campbells'
allies. The scale of the destruction may be judged by the enormous sums of
£15,000 and £30,000 Sterling which were later awarded in compensation
respectively to the Marquis of Argyll, and to other landowners throughout
Argyll, for the damage they had suffered. A collection was ordered throughout the churches of Scotland in early 1647 to relieve the distress of the
common people.

Reprisals against the Lamonts

After Sir James Campbell of Ardkinglas had suffered such a setback at
Callander in February 1646, he did not recover until May 1646, when he
landed in Cowal with a large force of Campbells from Ayrshire. Several
months earlier, Sir James Lamont and 600 men had ravaged the Campbell
lands around Strachur, killing thirty-three men, women and children,
destroying much grain, and driving off 340 cattle and horses. Now the
Lamonts retired to their castles of Toward and Ascog, where they were
besieged by Campbell forces until 1 June 1646, when the Campbells brought
up cannon.

Two days later, Sir James Lamont in Toward Castle agreed to surrender,
perhaps after learning that Charles I had ordered all his forces to disband,
and then persuaded the other garrison in Ascog Castle to give itself up as
well. However honourable, the terms of surrender were not kept by the
Campbells. They argued afterwards that Sir James Lamont had not been
fighting for the King, and so did not enter into his peace. Indeed, it seems
quite likely that the Campbells used all their legal wiles, deliberately drawing
up terms of surrender that showed Sir James Lamont still to be a rebel. The
castles of Toward and Ascog were plundered and burnt, and all the Lamont
prisoners taken to Dunoon for what was a travesty of a trial.

Sir James Lamont was held prisoner in the dungeons of Dunstaffnage
Castle for the next five years, while thirty-six gentlemen and vassals of the
name of Lamont were hanged, and then buried alive after their bodies were

cut down before they were even dead. Another hundred clansmen, together with their womenfolk and children, were slaughtered in a churchyard, and the whole district was put to the flames.

First Expedition against Alasdair MacDonald

Another Campbell campaign against Alasdair MacDonald and his allies took place in the spring of 1646, after the Marquis of Argyll had gone to Ulster. He had hoped to persuade Major-General Robert Munro to use his army against Alasdair MacDonald in Argyll, but his request was refused. Instead, Argyll was allowed to recall what remained of his own regiment, which had returned to Ulster after the battle of Inverlochy in February 1645, more than a year earlier. It seems his forces first landed on Islay under the command of Matthew Campbell of Skipness, and briefly held Dunyvaig Castle. However, they were soon repulsed by Clan Ranald, apparently returning to Ulster by the very end of May 1646. A contingent may also have landed in Kintyre, where it was equally unsuccessful, despite the glowing reports reaching London. Perhaps the only success of this Campbell campaign was the temporary raising of the siege of Skipness Castle by Sir James Campbell of Ardkinglas, before he launched his attack against the Lamonts in Cowal. However, the siege was renewed after he withdrew. Then any help that the Scots army in Ulster could give the Marquis of Argyll disappeared when it was decisively defeated in June 1646 by the Irish confederates at the battle of Benburb.

Landing by the Earl of Antrim

Ever since Alasdair MacDonald had first embarked on his expedition to Scotland in June 1644, he had hoped to receive reinforcements from Randal MacDonald, second Earl and now the first Marquis of Antrim. However, only now were his hopes realised when Randal MacDonald landed in Kintyre, accompanied by an unknown number of men. They were mostly fugitives, expelled by the Covenanters from his own estates in County Antrim. Soon afterwards, his exhilaration on returning to the ancient lands of Clan Donald, promised to him by the King, changed into bitter dismay when he learnt that the King had ordered all the forces acting in his name to be disbanded.

At first, the Earl of Antrim did not obey the King's command, entering instead into negotiations with the Covenanters to obtain better terms. He sought to guarantee the safety of himself and his men, while seeking a promise from Charles I that he would indeed be granted the lands of Kintyre as soon as they were forfeited from the Marquis of Argyll. Even after coming to terms with the Covenanters, his men refused to return to Ulster, perhaps with his secret encouragement, and he did not finally leave Kintyre until late in 1646. But any hopes that he might still recover the lands of Clan Donald for his family were now doomed to failure, especially after the Covenanters in Scotland surrendered Charles I to the English Parliament in January 1647. Even so, the Irish confederates still thought it in their interest to send more reinforcements to Alasdair MacDonald. However, their decision came far too late to prevent the collapse and eventual defeat of Alasdair MacDonald's rebellion, and the forces were never sent.

Isolation of Alasdair MacDonald

Once Charles I had ordered all his followers in Scotland to disband their forces, Alasdair MacDonald suffered a haemorrhage of support since he could no longer claim to be fighting for the Royalist cause. Already, the Lamonts were lost to his cause, and soon afterwards the MacLeans of Lochbuie withdrew as well, followed by the MacNeills, the MacMillans and the MacDougalls. Anxious to restore peace in the Highlands, the Covenanters were now willing to offer pardons to nearly all the Royalist rebels apart from Montrose and Alasdair MacDonald. By the end of 1646, George MacKenzie, Earl of Seaforth, MacDonald of Sleat, MacDonald of Glengarry, MacLean of Duart, and MacNab of MacNab, had all been pardoned, so that Alasdair MacDonald was now bereft of any allies apart from Clan Ranald.

He still retained hold of Islay and Kintyre, if not any other territories in Argyll, but he was realistic enough to try to come to terms with the Covenanters, hoping to leave the country for Spain. When his approaches were rebuffed, he prepared to fight his last campaign. The forces mounted against him were formidable. The Scots army of the Covenant had marched north from Newcastle on 30 January 1647, after receiving the arrears of pay owed to them by England. Charles I was allowed to go south after he had failed to make any concessions over the previous months. Thus strengthened by the withdrawal of its army from England, the Covenanting regime in Scotland was now able to crush the rebels still under arms. However, it acted first against the Marquis of Huntly in the north, before turning against Alasdair MacDonald in Argyll.

Rout of Alasdair MacDonald

It was only in April 1647 that Lieutenant-General David Leslie reached Dunblane after leaving John Middleton to pursue the Marquis of Huntly through the Highlands. There he spent the next month assembling his forces, which consisted of only two or three thousand men, described as 'a very small and ill-provided army'. The Campbells formed two regiments, commanded by the Marquis of Argyll and Sir James Campbell of Ardkinglas, while there were three Lowland regiments as well.

David Leslie left Dunblane on 17 May 1647, fearing an outbreak of bubonic plague, and quickly marched west, hoping to defeat Alasdair MacDonald before he could receive any reinforcements from Ireland. Reaching Inveraray on 21 May, he found Alasdair MacDonald had withdrawn into Kintyre, after laying waste the lands of Kilmartin, Kilmichael and Kilberry, along with the town of Inveraray itself. His own forces then entered Kintyre on 24 May 1647, putting Alasdair MacDonald and all his forces to flight.

According to later accounts, Alasdair MacDonald had no more than 1,500 men under arms, along with two troops of cavalry. He was evidently surprised by the speed of Leslie's approach, and perhaps he was quite unaware of the danger, just as Montrose had been taken by surprise before the battle of Philiphaugh through a lack of intelligence. Leslie had left Inveraray on 23 May 1647 on a forced march towards Tarbert, where he learnt that the passes into Kintyre were not even defended. Such a lack of foresight remains inexplicable, unless Alasdair MacDonald was convinced that David Leslie would attack him from the sea.

Leslie now pushed ahead with his cavalry, leaving his infantry to follow far behind, and crossed the narrow isthmus into Kintyre without any difficulty. Moving rapidly along the west coast, he managed to cross the narrow strip of flat-lying land just south of Clachan before Alasdair MacDonald could even rush his own forces north to hold such an easily-defended position. Leslie thus gained the wide expanse of flat ground behind Rhunahaorine Point, where his cavalry routed the forces of Alasdair MacDonald towards evening, killing up to eighty of the rebels, and capturing three of their commanders. Alasdair MacDonald himself escaped by sea, first to Gigha, and then to Islay with his father Colla Ciotach and many of his officers.

Massacre at Dunaverty Castle

The lack of any infantry prevented Leslie from following up his victory, and it was only two days later that he marched south to the fort at the head of Campbeltown Loch. The remnants of Alasdair MacDonald's forces had already fled south to seek refuge in Dunaverty Castle on the Mull of Kintyre, which was then held by Archibald Mor MacDonald of Sanda. After refusing to surrender the castle and its defenders despite the promise of quarter, he was forced to admit defeat only a few days later when the castle's water supply was captured by the Covenanters, who killed around forty of its defenders during the attack.

Even if David Leslie was still prepared to spare the garrison, and there are conflicting accounts as to what terms he offered, he was seemingly persuaded to change his mind by the religious fanaticism of a regimental chaplain, influenced by the Marquis of Argyll. The whole garrison of 300 men was put to the sword, perhaps literally, if they were not simply shot, or thrown over the cliff, tied together in pairs as local tradition would have it. Another eighty men had their lives spared when they agreed to serve in the French army, as did John MacDougall the younger of Dunollie, who was only a child at the time. Most of the victims were local men, but an incomplete list of the victims gave the names of ninety MacDougalls, half of them identified as the leading gentlemen of the clan. As a Royalist sympathiser later commented of the massacre at Dunaverty, which he had witnessed at first hand: 'Yet I shall not deny but here was cruelty enough; for to kill men in cold blood, when they have submitted to mercy, has no generosity in it at all.'

Capture of Islay

David Leslie returned to Campbeltown, where executions took place among the MacAllisters of Loup, and then marched north to Loch Tarbert to await the boats that he needed to carry his forces across the Sound of Jura. Meanwhile, Alasdair MacDonald had reached Islay after fleeing first to Gigha, pursued ineffectually by 300 men under Dougal Campbell of Inverawe, who went first to Castle Sween in an unsuccessful attempt to find boats. It was not until 19 June 1647 that David Leslie had enough boats to transport an infantry force and eighty cavalry to Gigha, and he only reached the island on 23 June 1647.

Despite the stormy weather, which nearly scattered his fleet when he ordered it to sail for Jura, he managed to get all his forces to Islay by midday on 24 June 1647, landing within four miles of Dunyvaig Castle. Capturing a party of rebels, he then learnt that Alasdair MacDonald had sailed for Ireland more than a fortnight earlier, where his arrival was reported to Dublin by 9 June 1647. He left his father Colla Ciotach and his brother to hold Dunyvaig Castle with 200 men, among whom were a hundred of his Irish troops.

Withdrawal to Ireland

Before Alasdair MacDonald left for Ireland, he did promise to return, perhaps with the 5,000 men that the Irish confederates had just agreed to raise jointly with the Earl of Antrim for service in Scotland against the

Covenanting regime. He may therefore have only intended to make a tactical withdrawal at the time. Quite how Alasdair MacDonald stood at this time with regard to the Earl of Antrim remains a mystery, but the two men may well have agreed between themselves that Alasdair MacDonald should receive Islay, while the Earl of Antrim had a better claim to Kintyre.

Certainly, on 5 May 1647 Alasdair MacDonald had given a commission to his father Colla Ciotach to act as commander-in-chief of the lands of Islay, and all his other lands in Scotland, acting under the useful title of Major-General of the King's forces in Scotland. It can only suggest that he did indeed lay claim to the island. Equally, it seems he was intending to withdraw all his forces from Kintyre when he was taken by surprise by the rapid advance of David Leslie and his cavalry on 24 May 1647, just before the battle of Rhunahaorine Point. Indeed, when David Leslie reached Campbeltown Loch two days later, he apparently found that 800 or 900 of Alasdair's men had just sailed for Ireland, where they landed in County Down. He evidently thought that nearly all of Alasdair MacDonald's forces had escaped from Kintyre. Perhaps, as David Stevenson has recently suggested, the embarkation was almost ready to proceed, or it may even have started, when Alasdair MacDonald learnt of Leslie's rapid advance into Kintyre.

The engagement at Rhunahaorine Point was thus perhaps only intended as a rearguard action, fought chiefly by the MacDougalls of Dunollie and the local men of Kintyre as a delaying tactic, while the bulk of Alasdair's forces were evacuated to Ireland. They could well have sailed by way of Islay to pick up Alasdair MacDonald and his leading commanders, since they only reached Ireland more than a week later. He left behind a few hundred men on Islay, including a hundred Irish troops, to garrison the castles of Dunyvaig and Loch Gorm, swearing to his father that he would return shortly to relieve him.

Capture and Execution of Colla Ciotach

Once David Leslie had landed on Islay, he laid siege to Dunyvaig Castle, demanding its surrender, which was refused by Colla Ciotach as its captain. It seems that Colla Ciotach now took to leaving the castle with an armed escort to speak with Sir Archibald Campbell, captain of Dunstaffnage Castle, whose friendship he had enjoyed while earlier a prisoner in his hands, without even obtaining a safe-conduct. Moreover, imposing on the friendship, he even sent out a soldier with a letter to Sir Archibald, asking for four dollars worth of aquavitae or whisky. Leslie and his officers decided to take advantage of his peculiar behaviour, but not without some stain upon their honour, as it was later observed. Colla Ciotach was made a prisoner after he had again left the security of Dunyvaig Castle on 1 July 1647 to drink with Sir Archibald Campbell.

As he was now seventy-six years of age, the odd behaviour of Colla Ciotach was perhaps due to senility, except that his idea of honourable behaviour could well have departed from the conventions of warfare as waged by a Lowland officer like David Leslie. Dunyvaig Castle held out for only a few more days of 'hard shooting' until the garrison surrendered on 5 July 1647. The terms were so generous that they had to be justified later by Leslie on the grounds that he was running short of the food and other supplies needed for a long siege. 176 men surrendered, and their lives were spared after they had sworn never again to take up arms against the kingdom of Scotland. Even the Irish among them were allowed to leave the country, provided they agreed to enter the service of the Scots regiment in France.

David Leslie was ordered by Parliament to send Colla Ciotach to Edinburgh for trial, where he arrived by ship on 7 September 1647. However, the Marquis of Argyll, fearing that Ciotach would escape with his life, manœuvred to have him sent back for trial to Argyllshire. After a trial at Dunstaffnage Castle, he was sentenced to death by the Marquis, acting as Justice-General of Argyll and the Isles, and his deputy, George Campbell of Airds. Tradition has it that he was hanged from the mast of his own galley. Two of his sons were executed around the same time, as well as several of the senior officers in Alasdair's regiment, after they had been captured.

Alasdair MacDonald in Ireland

Alasdair MacDonald survived his father for only a few brief months. Reaching Ireland early in June 1647, he found the Irish confederacy so engaged in internecine feuding that they had allowed the Protestant forces loyal to the English Parliament to take advantage of their divisions. Parliamentary troops were just about to land at Dublin to establish a bridgehead in Leinster, while Murrough O'Brien, Lord Inchiquin, had already launched an offensive further south against the Confederacy in Munster. Alasdair MacDonald could not hope to return immediately to Scotland with reinforcements, as he had promised. Instead, it was decided that his military skills would best be used in Munster, where he became Lieutenant-General of the Confederacy army, and Governor of Clonmel in County Tipperary.

Alasdair MacDonald died in battle, as no doubt this greatest of all Gaelic warriors would have wished. The summer and early autumn of 1647 were spent by the Confederacy army in Munster under the command of Lord Taaffe, who had waged an ineffective campaign against the Parliamentary army of Lord Inchiquin, while Alasdair MacDonald remained in Clonmel with his own forces. However, early in November 1647, Lord Inchiquin concentrated his forces in County Cork, and Lord Taaffe decided to give battle, hoping to restore his military reputation.

The two armies made contact with one another on 12 November 1647 near the hill of Knocknanus, where Lord Taaffe had taken up a strong position with his army of 7,000 infantry and 1,200 horse. Although he had the same number of cavalry, Lord Inchiquin was heavily outnumbered, since he had fewer than 4,000 infantry. Next day, Lord Taaffe drew up his forces in two wings without a separate centre, placing two regiments of cavalry on each wing, so that he commanded the left wing with 4,000 foot, and Alasdair MacDonald the right wing with 3,000 foot.

Lord Inchiquin took the initiative in the battle that followed, first attacking the forces under Alasdair MacDonald on the right wing, and then switching his attack to the left wing. Lord Taaffe reacted by first trying to reinforce Alasdair MacDonald on his right wing, until he suddenly realised that his own left wing was about to bear the brunt of Lord Inchiquin's attack. He ordered a general advance but it came too late, since many men on his own left wing had become demoralised after watching these confusing manoeuvres for more than two hours. They attempted a half-hearted charge in some confusion, but it failed against the determined volleys of musket fire from the enemy. Soon, they were streaming from the field in panic, and Lord Taaffe joined them after he had failed to stop their flight. By then, Alasdair MacDonald had ordered forward his men in a terrifying Highland charge, 'routing down like a Torrent impetuously upon our foot', as one of Lord Inchiquin's officers described it. Indeed, the enemy under Lord Inchiquin fled so precipitately from the field that they suffered relatively few casualties, perhaps forty or fifty men, including two of their commanders.

Even so, Alasdair MacDonald now realised the danger of his position, since the rest of the Irish army were far behind him, fleeing for their lives, and his own men had taken to plundering Lord Inchiquin's baggage train. Hastily regrouping his forces, he was returning to the field when he was attacked by Lord Inchiquin's cavalry. Alasdair MacDonald, all his senior officers, and many of his own troops were surrounded and slaughtered. Indeed, nearly half of the Irish army died with Alasdair MacDonald, since a great number found no safety in flight, and Lord Inchiquin soon controlled much of Munster.

Death of Alasdair MacDonald

Exactly how Alasdair MacDonald died is not known, but rumours soon began to circulate that he was the victim of treachery. Such legends often arose with great warriors, whose heroic deeds in the past made them seem invincible in the present: even the death of Somerled in 1164 was put down to his assassination on the eve of a lost battle. If it cannot be admitted that so great a hero was killed in a fair fight, it is natural to think he must have died by treachery.

However, tradition and legend together provide enough evidence to suggest that Alasdair MacDonald was indeed killed after surrendering to the enemy, perhaps attempting to gain quarter for his men when they were faced with utter annihilation. Several accounts point to a Major Nicholas Purdon as his killer, even if they differ in detail. One account has Alasdair parleying with the enemy, only to be stabbed treacherously in the back by an unknown soldier; another has him killed in cold blood by Purdon whilst being led a prisoner from the field; and yet a third has him killed in a fury by Purdon after a junior officer had already granted him quarter. He was little more than forty years of age.

Final Campaigns in Ireland

The death of Alasdair MacDonald at the battle of Knocknanus left only Angus MacDonald of Glengarry in the service of the Irish confederacy. He had evidently accompanied Alasdair MacDonald to Ireland in June 1647, joining the army of General Thomas Preston soon afterwards in Leinster with several hundred men. This army met almost at once with disaster, when it was routed by a Protestant army at Dungan Hill on 8 August 1647. Nearly all Glengarry's men were killed or injured, fighting to the end, but he himself escaped with his life.

The following year Angus MacDonald of Glengarry was joined in Ireland by Donald MacDonald, son of the Captain of Clan Ranald. He sailed with 300 men from Uist in a 'rigged low-country frigate . . . and a long Gaelic ship'. Invited to serve in Ireland by Randal MacDonald, first Marquis of Antrim, Donald MacDonald served in Preston's army of Leinster, alongside Angus MacDonald of Glengarry. Together, they joined a regiment under the command of Antrim's brother Alexander MacDonald, and took part in the seizure of Belfast, Knockfergus, Coleraine and Derry.

By then, however, the dispute within the Confederate ranks had become so bitter that the Marquis of Antrim eventually withdrew his regiment from Preston's army. Retreating into Wexford, the regiment was scattered by forces loyal to the opposing faction, and Angus MacDonald of Glengarry and Donald MacDonald, son of Clan Ranald, were both captured. Angus MacDonald was exiled to France in 1649, where he served Charles II, returning to Scotland in 1650, while Donald MacDonald was allowed to return home after a ransom had been paid by Antrim's wife, presumably before her death in November 1649. He arrived in the Outer Isles to find his father forfeited, after a Covenanting force of 600 men had been dispatched against him the previous year.

Legacy of Alasdair MacDonald

Perhaps even before Donald MacDonald had returned to Scotland, the Protestant invasion of Ireland under Oliver Cromwell was underway, changing for ever the political landscape of the country, especially in Ulster. The estates of Randal MacDonald, first Marquis of Antrim, were now occupied by Cromwell's army, and he only regained their possession in 1665, several years after the restoration of Charles II in 1660. By then, he had abandoned any hope of regaining the Highland territories of the MacDonalds of Dunyvaig and the Glens for his own family, and, indeed, he was greatly indebted to the MacDonald chiefs of Sleat, Glengarry and Clan Ranald for the bonds of surety which guaranteed his own debts.

Equally, when Donald MacDonald returned in 1649 to the territories of Clan Ranald in Scotland, there ended the centuries-old alliance between the septs of Clan Donald and their Gaelic-speaking compatriots in Ireland, an alliance which had repeatedly brought forces of Highland mercenaries to fight in Ireland. But if these tumultuous events brought an era to a close, it was only the start of yet another phase in Highland history. Indeed, the Highland campaigns of James Graham, first Marquis of Montrose, and the extraordinary part played in them by Alasdair MacDonald and his allies among the Highland clans, laid the foundations for the support given to the Stuart monarchy by the Jacobite clans of the Scottish Highlands, which ended in such bitter ruin on the bloody battlefield of Culloden Moor in 1746.

Chapter Seven

MONTROSE'S LAST CAMPAIGN

Even as James Graham, Marquis of Montrose, fought for Charles I in the Highlands with Alasdair MacDonald in 1644 and 1645, the Royalist cause was already lost in England. Yet it was only in May 1646 that Charles I finally surrendered to the Scots army outside Newark, hoping to get better terms from the Covenanters than he could expect to obtain from the English Parliament. By then, the uneasy alliance between the two parties to the Solemn League and Covenant of 1643 had dissolved. The English Parliament had only agreed to reform their national Church because they needed the military strength of the Scots army of the Covenant against Charles I. But the Scots had demanded that the Church of England be reformed 'according to the word of God, and the example of the best reformed churches', which they perhaps naively understood to mean their own Presbyterian church.

Even though the English Parliament abolished Episcopacy and all its trappings, the attempt to introduce a doctrinaire version of Presbyterianism in England failed in practice, opposed as it was by religious zeal and popular feeling. The only lasting result was the Westminster Confession of Faith. Shorn in 1986 of its anti-Catholic excesses, it is still held as doctrine by the Church of Scotland today. Otherwise, the attempt of the Scots to impose their own religious settlement upon England simply resulted in disarray. The English Parliament refused to accept a Church independent of its own power, not unlike Charles I, while the many 'Independents', especially in the ranks of the New Model Army, came to demand freedom of religious conscience, and the right of free assembly, which was anathema to the Scots.

Desertion of Charles I

Now held by the Scots army of the Covenant in England, Charles I still refused to sign the Solemn League and Covenant, which had superseded the National Covenant of 1638. However, as already recounted, he did order his forces in Scotland to disband. Faced with the hostility of the English Parliament, which demanded that Charles I be brought to Warwick Castle, the Scots army withdrew north to Newcastle with their royal prisoner, much to the anger of London. The Scots were now placed in a quandary: they could not allow Charles I to return to Scotland, where he might inflame anti-Covenant feeling, given that Montrose was then still at large; equally, they could hardly abandon the King to his enemies in England without a guarantee for his safety, which was not forthcoming. Moreover, the English Parliament had already voted £400,000 sterling for the arrears of pay and other expenses owed to the Scots army, which might be lost if they refused to surrender Charles I to its authority.

Worse still, the Scots were threatened with the dispatch of the New Model Army, and the outbreak of hostilities with England, should they not agree to his surrender. By January 1647, after protracted negotiations, the first instalment of the £400,000 had been raised, and the Scots Parliament simply voted that Charles I should be delivered into the hands of the English when the Scots army withdrew north from Newcastle, which it did on 30 January 1647. Charles I rode south on the very same day with 900 cavalry to take up residence at Holmby Park in Northamptonshire, hoping with undue optimism that he could now reach an agreement with the English Parliament.

No sooner had the King been abandoned than fears about his safety began to mount in Scotland, especially among the nobility. It was reinforced when soldiers from the New Model Army arrested him in June 1647. Two months later, the army itself marched into London, and started to purge Parliament of its opponents, who now appeared ready to compromise with Charles I. The outcome was a series of local revolts in England against the growing power of the New Model Army, and what became known as the 'Engagement' in Scotland.

The 'Engagement'

The secret agreement known as the 'Engagement' was signed by Charles I in December 1647 when he was held prisoner by the New Model Army at Carisbrooke Castle on the Isle of Wight. Made with an alliance of Royalist noblemen and moderate Covenanters in Scotland, it offered him military assistance in restoring at least some of his powers if he would agree to introduce Presbyterianism for a trial period of three years in England. The agreement was bitterly opposed by the more radical elements in Scotland, who refused to accept that the cause of God could be advanced by a King who had not signed the Covenants. They later came to constitute what was known as the Kirk party, led by Archibald Campbell, Marquis of Argyll.

The 'Engagement' first demanded of the English Parliament that the King be set free, the Solemn League and Covenant be fulfilled, and the New Model Army be disbanded. Such demands were not just intended to placate the religious opponents of the 'Engagement' in Scotland, but to provide a pretext for war with England as well, if they were rejected. Despite a conciliatory reply from England, which it failed even to consider, the Scots Parliament then authorised the raising of a new army. Its command was given to James Hamilton, Duke of Hamilton, rather than to such a seasoned campaigner as David Leslie. Ill-equipped and lacking any clear strategy, he invaded the north of England in July 1648, only to be utterly defeated six weeks later near Preston by Oliver Cromwell, leaving 2,000 dead, and perhaps 9,000 held prisoner.

Such a defeat was partly self-inflicted, since the 'Engagement' did not draw on the services of the Highland chiefs who had previously been in rebellion against the Covenanting regime. Twenty-four leading MacKenzies, and other followers of the Earl of Seaforth, petitioned Parliament that their chief be allowed to lead his clansmen in support of the 'Engagement', since they would not follow 'any but their native superior'. But their offer of military service was spurned for fear of alienating even the moderate Covenanters. Exactly the same reasoning prevented the release from prison of George Gordon, second Marquis of Huntly, so that the 'Engagement' was denied the service of all his followers in north-east Scotland. Only Sir James MacDonald of Sleat, and John Mor MacLeod of Dunvegan, apparently raised their clansmen in support of the 'Engagement'.

Whiggamore Raid

Since the 'Engagement' was supported by much of the nobility and the lesser gentry, as well as by many burgesses and moderate ministers, the defeat at Preston left a vacuum of political power in Scotland. It was filled by an armed group of radical Covenanters, several thousand strong, who advanced upon Edinburgh from Ayrshire and Clydesdale, and soon afterwards from Galloway as well, in what became known as the Whiggamore Raid. They were commanded by the more radical members of the nobility, such as the Earls of Loudoun, Eglinton, Leven and Cassillis, as well as Lieutenant-General David Leslie.

The rebels occupied Edinburgh, even though a detachment of 700 Covenanters sent by the Marquis of Argyll from the west to relieve Linlithgow was surprised and routed near Stirling by what remained of the forces of the 'Engagement'. Soon afterwards, the Royalist cause was reinforced by an advance guard of perhaps 4,000 Highlanders, raised by the Earl of Seaforth, and another 1,200 men from Orkney under the Earl of Morton. Civil war now threatened the country since many other Highland chiefs were now prepared to raise their own forces in a confederacy with the Royalists of north-east Scotland. But they were perhaps more intent on laying waste to the lands of the Marquis of Argyll, and indeed other parts of the kingdom, than coming to the rescue of the 'Engagement' itself.

Purge by the Kirk Party

Any attempt to restore Charles I to his throne was now lost, even in Scotland, as Oliver Cromwell threatened to invade the country if the Kirk party was not brought to power. Indeed, his forces had already started to cross the Scottish border from England. Archibald Campbell, Marquis of Argyll, and other opponents of the 'Engagement', were hastily elected to Parliament, where they effectively seized power on behalf of the Kirk party. The 'Engagement' on behalf of Charles I was thus broken off, but not before it had destroyed the broad coalition which had once existed within the ranks of the Covenanters. No longer would the nobility, apart from its more extreme members, as well as the lesser gentry, the burgesses and the clergy, join together in a common cause. Instead, religious extremism became rife in the Covenanting movement for the rest of the seventeenth century, opposed as it was by the political establishment after it had regained power under Charles II in 1660.

For the time being, however, the radical Presbyterians under the Marquis of Argyll repudiated the 'Engagement', renewed the Solemn League and Covenant with England, and passed the Act of Classes. The latter measure excluded all Royalist 'malignants' from public office, whether they had supported the 'Engagement', or the campaigns fought by Montrose. It was a triumph for the fundamentalist ministers of the Kirk party, who proceeded to purge all the holders of public office in Scotland who were suspected of backsliding, and to abolish lay patronage of the clergy.

Execution of Charles I

Much the same course was pursued by Oliver Cromwell when he went south after dining in Edinburgh with the Marquis of Argyll. He purged the English Parliament of all his opponents, who by now were reconciled to recognising Charles I as King on his own terms, thereby hoping to restore peace and order to the country. Only an extreme and quite unrepresentative minority thus prevailed in bringing Charles I to trial for his life in January 1649, charged with treason in waging war against his own Parliament. Even though he refused to accept the authority of the court, he was found guilty and condemned to death. His public beheading at Whitehall on 30 January 1649 was witnessed by a stunned but sympathetic crowd, who uttered a 'dismal and universal groan' when his head was struck from his body. Mingled indignation and grief spread throughout the country.

When Scotland learnt of the execution of Charles I, Parliament was sitting, and two days later it proclaimed his eldest surviving son as King of Great Britain, France and Ireland. It was agreed that the coronation of Charles II would only be delayed until he had given satisfaction as regards the Covenants. Such actions by the Scots were tantamount to breaking the alliance with England, which had by now declared itself a republic by abolishing the monarchy and the House of Lords.

Reaction in Scotland

The execution of Charles I almost immediately caused unrest within Scotland, especially in the northern Highlands. The support given earlier to Charles I by Donald MacKay, first Lord Reay, had come to very little, especially after he had become embroiled with John Gordon, thirteenth Earl of Sutherland, in a bitter dispute over the lands of Strathnaver. His death abroad in February 1649 made his eldest son John MacKay the second Lord Reay. An ardent Royalist like his father, he joined Sir Thomas MacKenzie of Pluscardine, younger brother of George MacKenzie, second Earl of Seaforth, who was then exiled in Holland with Charles II. Together, they seized Inverness with a troop of 700 horse, chiefly MacKays and MacKenzies, accompanied by Lewis Gordon, afterwards the third Marquis of Huntly, together with Sir Thomas Urquhart of Cromarty, and even the staunch Covenanter, Colonel John Munro of Lemlair.

The Parliament in Edinburgh reacted to the news by ordering the raising of an army, nearly 20,000 strong, which would act as a defence against any threat of invasion from England. Meanwhile, Lieutenant-General David Leslie was ordered north with whatever troops he could muster. He arrived to find that the rebels under Sir Thomas MacKenzie of Pluscardine had thrown down the walls of Inverness. They evidently intended that the town should not be garrisoned by the extremist regime of the Kirk party in Edinburgh. Their forces had then melted away into the mountains. Pursuing them into Ross with only 800 men, or so he later reported, David Leslie then learnt that the Robertsons and Stewarts in Atholl had risen in revolt farther south under the leadership of James, Lord Ogilvie, and the former Covenanter, Major-General John Middleton.

Execution of Huntly

Faced with this double threat, David Leslie offered favourable terms to the rebel leaders in the north. They accepted them for the time being after giving assurances for their future good behaviour. The Scots Parliament now decided to make an example of George Gordon, second Marquis of Huntly, who had lain in prison after his capture at Delnabo in December 1646. He was still under sentence of death, passed after his abortive uprising of 1644. Despite the opposition of his brother-in-law Archibald Campbell, first Marquis of Argyll, and other nobles in Parliament, the more extreme members of the Kirk party now determined on his execution.

They argued that 'it is clear from the Word of God that murderers should die without partiality'. Huntly was brought to judgement, found guilty of treason, and beheaded at the Mercat Cross in Edinburgh on 22 March 1649. After his execution, Parliament bestowed his estates upon Archibald Campbell, Marquis of Argyll, who was already his chief creditor, triggering a chain of events that profoundly influenced the course of Highland history over the next fifty years. Meanwhile, to secure his title to the Gordon lands, Argyll continued to buy up Huntly's debts from his other creditors.

Renewed Unrest in the North

Huntly's execution revived the Royalist revolt in the Highlands, where Sir Thomas MacKenzie of Pluscardine, encouraged by a letter from Charles II, and accompanied by John MacKay, second Lord Reay, Lieutenant-General John Middleton, and James, Lord Ogilvie, marched into Badenoch in April 1649. They were joined there by Lewis Gordon, who was now the Marquis of Huntly after his father's execution. Even if they still did not know how they could best support the Royalist cause, their anger at the execution of Charles I, and their hatred of the Kirk party, made them a formidable threat to the government.

Lieutenant-General David Leslie now moved north from Atholl to contain this new threat, while the rebels sent emissaries to negotiate with him, perhaps hoping that he would declare for the King. However, while the rebels were encamped at Balvenie Castle near Dufftown, they were taken utterly by surprise on 8 May 1649 by three troops of horse under Archibald Strachan, which David Leslie had left to guard Ross after returning south from his earlier expedition to Inverness. Only numbering 120 horse, they killed eighty of the rebels, and captured another 800, out of a total strength of more than a thousand men. John MacKay, second Lord Reay, was among the prisoners. He was now at the mercy of the Earl of Sutherland and others, determined to pursue him for their losses at his hands, said to amount to £30,000 Scots. The other leaders escaped capture, but they submitted to the government in Edinburgh after receiving the promise of a pardon.

Renewed Plans for Invasion

Meanwhile, after proclaiming him King, the Scots Parliament had sent its commissioners to negotiate with Charles II in Holland, hoping to persuade him to accept the Covenants. Although he impressed them with his personal qualities, so different from his father's, their negotiations made little progress for well over a year. Indeed, on reaching Holland in March 1649, the Parliamentary representatives found to their anger that Charles II had already appointed James Graham, Marquis of Montrose, to be Lieutenant-Governor of Scotland, and Captain-General of its forces under the Crown, just as Charles I had done.

Six weeks later, Charles II granted Montrose authority to negotiate with the crowned heads of Europe for military assistance in launching an invasion of Scotland. By such actions, Charles II perhaps just hoped to frighten the extreme Covenanting regime in Edinburgh into making concessions, but neither party was willing to abandon its principles. Even so, he clearly favoured Montrose who argued that force was the only way to establish an acceptable regime in Scotland through the destruction of the Kirk party. Otherwise, Charles II would have to come to terms with the extreme Presbyterians in Scotland, who insisted that he sign the Covenants, and sign away almost all his powers.

Montrose now visited the courts of Europe, but he only seemed to succeed in gaining the support of Queen Christina of Sweden and King Frederick of Denmark. However, he was aided by the wealthiest merchant in Gothenburg, who went under the name of Johan or Hans Maclier. Supposedly, he was none other than John MacLean, younger brother of Sir Lachlan MacLean of Duart. Arms and ammunition were obtained through his good offices, and ships procured for an expedition to Scotland, while he lent enough money to employ several hundred mercenaries.

An advance party reached Orkney in September 1649 under the command of George Hay, second Earl of Kinnoull, consisting of eighty officers and 100 Danish soldiers. Although the Earl of Kinnoull died during the following winter, he was replaced by his younger brother and heir, who took over his command. More reinforcements reached Orkney in the early spring of 1650, but at least two supply ships were wrecked during their passage. Long delayed, Montrose himself arrived at Kirkwall in March 1650. He then found to his dismay that Charles II had agreed to enter into further negotiations with the Covenanting regime.

Nevertheless, Charles II entreated Montrose to proceed vigorously with his enterprise. Perhaps he just hoped to wring some further concessions from his opponents in Scotland if Montrose were successful. But he must have realised that any such success might allow him to ignore their demands altogether if he were restored to his throne by force. Montrose was thus to be used as a pawn in a cynical struggle for power between the monarchy and the Covenanting regime. Most likely hoping to forestall any such agreement, Montrose now embarked on what proved to be his final campaign. The apocalyptic tone of his last letters may even suggest that he hoped to sacrifice his life in the service of his sovereign.

Montrose's Last Campaign

Montrose's invasion of Scotland was launched on 9 April 1650, when Lieutenant-Colonel John Hurry, himself once a Covenanting general, received his orders to sail from Orkney on the evening tide to establish a bridgehead on the mainland. A few days later, Hurry had secured the Ord of Caithness with three hundred men, and Montrose followed with the rest of his forces, landing according to tradition at John O'Groats. They numbered 1,600 men at the very most, consisting largely of footsoldiers with hardly any cavalry.

After dispatching his lieutenants to recruit more men from the MacKays of Strathnaver, Montrose marched south to Dunbeath. The castle there had been abandoned by Sir John Sinclair, who fled south to warn John Gordon, thirteenth Earl of Sutherland, of the impending danger. He had left Dunbeath Castle in the care of his wife Lady Catherine, daughter of Fraser of Lovat. She put up a spirited defence before Montrose allowed her to withdraw south with her baggage.

Despite a half-hearted attempt at resistance by the Earl of Sutherland at the Ord of Caithness, Montrose then marched slowly south along the coast. As he advanced, the Covenanting forces of the Earl of Sutherland fell back, leaving only the castles of Dunrobin, Skelbo, Skibo, and Dornoch strongly garrisoned. Reaching Strathfleet, Montrose then turned inland to reach Gruids, south of Lairg, where he hoped reinforcements would join him from Strathnaver. It is hardly surprising they were not forthcoming. The Earl of Sutherland had already established a hostile garrison in Strathnaver, while John MacKay, second Lord Reay, was still held prisoner in Edinburgh after his capture at Balvenie, less than a year earlier.

By landing in the far north of Scotland, rather than farther south at Cromarty, Inverness or Speymouth, Montrose evidently hoped that John

MacKay, second Lord Reay, would encourage his clansmen to join his enterprise on behalf of Charles II. Equally, he must have hoped that Sir Thomas MacKenzie of Pluscardine would rally to the Royalist cause, along with the other leaders of the earlier uprising in 1649. But George MacKenzie, second Earl of Seaforth, had stayed behind with Charles II in Holland, acting as his Secretary of State for Scotland, and he doubtless knew that the King was now prepared to compromise with the Covenanting regime. The MacKenzies and their allies would not join such a quixotic venture, especially as there were Covenanting garrisons at the MacKenzie strongholds at Eilean Donnan and Brahan, and another at Chanonry on the Black Isle.

Apart from Alexander Sinclair of Brims, only Robert Munro of Achness, Hugh MacKay of Dirled, and Hutcheon MacKay of Scourie, rallied to the support of Montrose. They had their own reasons since their lands were all claimed by John Gordon, thirteenth Earl of Sutherland. As a fervent supporter of the Covenant, he had benefited in 1649 when Parliament had granted him all the MacKay lands in Strathnaver. The balance of power had thus changed in the far north. Indeed, Tongue House was garrisoned by forces loyal to the Covenanting regime, but Montrose was apparently not even aware of its presence.

Battle of Carbisdale

Montrose now crossed the River Oykel to march south along its western bank towards Carbisdale, and the present-day village of Culrain. There, he was taken unawares by five troops of horse, commanded by Archibald Strachan, who had already routed the forces of Sir Thomas MacKenzie of Pluscardine at Balvenie in 1649. On learning of Montrose's invasion, David Leslie had ordered Strachan north as an advance guard with whatever forces he could muster. They amounted to just over 200 cavalry and thirty-six musketeers.

However, there were another 400 footsoldiers, raised by Colonel John Munro of Lemlair, now apparently once again supporting the Covenanting regime after the rout at Balvenie, and by David Ross of Balnagown, whose allegiance it seems was uncertain. Apparently, Montrose expected just such numbers of reinforcements to join him, while local tradition has it that the Munros at least waited to see the outcome of any encounter before declaring their allegiance.

Advancing north from Tain, Archibald Strachan learnt on the afternoon of Saturday 27 April that Montrose was moving south with his forces. Then at Kincardine, just south of Ardgay, he moved quickly north to engage Montrose on the flat ground just north of Culrain Burn, since he was unwilling to fight on the Sabbath. Aware that Montrose thought that he faced only a single troop of horse, Strachan concealed most of his cavalry in the dead ground along the shore of the Kyle of Sutherland, where it was hidden by the broom. He then revealed the rest of his cavalry, numbering a hundred horse, as it crossed Culrain Burn.

Montrose reacted by ordering his own footsoldiers to fall back to the wooded slopes behind Culrain itself, while sending forward his own cavalry to investigate the threat. But even before Montrose's infantry could gain the shelter of the woods, Strachan's troop of horse had charged, breaking Montrose's own cavalry, only forty strong, which fell back in confusion against his retreating footsoldiers. Hardly a single volley had been fired before Montrose's forces were routed, perhaps with the aid of the Munros and the Rosses, who it is said now attacked Montrose's army from the rear.

More than 400 of the Royalist troops were killed as they attempted to escape up Strathoykel, and another 450 were captured, while 200 Orcadians drowned trying to swim across the Kyle. Wounded, and with his horse shot from underneath him, Montrose himself escaped across the Kyle of Sutherland on another horse, lent to him by James Crichton of Frendraught, and fled along Strathoykel to seek refuge in Assynt.

Capture of Montrose

Three days later, accompanied only by Edward Sinclair from Orkney, Montrose was given milk and bread at a lonely shieling near Cnoc na Glas Choille, southeast of Loch Urigill, on the borders of Assynt. He was then escorted to Ardvreck Castle on the shores of Loch Assynt. There he was apparently surrendered into the hands of Christian Munro, wife of Neil MacLeod of Assynt, rather than being taken to the Reay country as he had been promised. According to one account, Neil MacLeod was even then besieging Dunbeath Castle with the Earl of Sutherland, who had earlier appointed him as sheriff-depute of Assynt.

It is hardly surprising that Neil MacLeod of Assynt was therefore prepared to hand over Montrose to the Covenanting regime, which sent Major-General Holbourne to Ardvreck on 4 May 1650 to take custody of the prisoner. Indeed, if he had alienated such a stalwart supporter of the Covenanting regime as the Earl of Sutherland by allowing Montrose to escape, there is little doubt that he and his kinsmen would have suffered. As it was, Parliament granted him the reward of £20,000 still outstanding from 1644 for the capture of Montrose, along with oatmeal worth £5,000. Meanwhile, he was appointed captain of the Earl of Sutherland's garrison in Tongue. Only after 1660 was he tried for betraying Montrose, but twice acquitted. Two years after his death, his estates passed to the Earl of Seaforth, who had bought up his debts.

Execution of Montrose

Once described by the Covenanters as 'the most bloody murderer of our nation . . . this cursed man whose scandalous carriage, pernicious counsels, and contagious company, cannot fail to dishonour and pollute all places of his familar access, and to provoke the anger of the most high God against the same', Montrose was now brought south in their hands. Taunted as he passed through the country which had seen his greatest victories, Montrose reached Dundee, before being sent south by ship to Edinburgh. Landing at Leith on Saturday 18 May, he was first brought by cart-horse to Holyrood, where he was met by the city magistrates, the town guard, and the public hangman. He was then conducted bare-headed in a bizarre procession to the Edinburgh Tolbooth, tied by cords to a chair and set high upon a horse-drawn cart, while the public hangman rode in front on the first of the five horses drawing the cart itself.

Montrose was already under sentence of death for his rebellion against the Covenanting regime in the winter of 1644–45, and it merely remained for Parliament to confirm the sentence. Although allowed to reply to the charges against him, he was sentenced to die by hanging. It was an insult to his station in life, since as a nobleman he could have expected beheading. The sentence was carried out on 21 May 1650, when he appeared on the scaffold as if dressed for a wedding in a scarlet coat with rich lace, white gloves, silk stockings, and ribboned shoes. His body was 'headed and quartered' after it was cut down from the scaffold. His head was left to decay on a spike above the Tolbooth in Edinburgh for the next ten years, while his limbs were displayed in Stirling, Glasgow, Perth, and Aberdeen.

Chapter Eight

CROMWELL AND THE HIGHLANDS

Even before he learnt of Montrose's defeat at Carbisdale, and his subsequent capture and execution, Charles II had cynically come to terms with the Covenanting regime, although he still refused to sign the Covenants. The gravest criticism of his conduct, apart from its sheer duplicity in negotiating with the Covenanting regime while Montrose was still in arms on his behalf, is that Charles II did nothing to protect Montrose if he were captured. Instead, Charles II wrote to him, ordering him to disband his forces, perhaps reassured by the vague promise of a safe-conduct from the Marquis of Argyll which would allow Montrose to leave the country.

Then, when rumours of Montrose's defeat reached him, Charles II apparently wrote another letter, disowning Montrose's actions in invading Scotland, and denying any responsibilty for them. It was only to be delivered to the Scots Parliament if Montrose was *not* captured. Seemingly, the letter did not reach Scotland until after Montrose's execution, and it certainly was not revealed to Parliament, since its existence is still a matter of hearsay.

Charles II was now placed in such a weak position that expediency forced him into accepting all the demands made of him by the Covenanting regime. Setting sail for Scotland, he signed the Covenants only at the very last moment, when his ship was anchored off Speymouth on 23 June 1650. The next day, he landed at last in Scotland to great joy among the Scottish people. Even so, the Kirk party still remained suspicious of his real intentions as it stripped him of all his powers, leaving him to reign simply as a figurehead.

Invasion by Oliver Cromwell

Long before Archibald Campbell, Marquis of Argyll, crowned Charles II at Scone on New Year's Day 1651, more than six months later, the King's arrival in Scotland provoked Oliver Cromwell to invade the country with an army of 16,000 men. Crossing the border just a month after Charles II had landed, it encountered a wilderness of scorched earth as it marched to Musselburgh and then around Edinburgh to Queensferry. Deprived of supplies, Cromwell then withdrew his forces to Dunbar, spending the next few weeks probing the Scottish defences.

By the end of August, Cromwell advanced again towards Edinburgh, only to fall back once more to a defensive position at Dunbar. His tactical retreat was followed by the whole of the Scottish army under David Leslie. More than 20,000 strong, it established a powerful position on Doon Hill, where it commanded the road to Berwick along the coast south of Dunbar. Another detachment blocked the road itself farther south at Cockburnspath. If Cromwell now tried to withdraw south from Dunbar, he would be delayed for long enough at Cockburnspath to allow the Scots army to fall upon his flank and rear.

But David Leslie was persuaded by the Presbyterian ministers in his camp to abandon his command of the high ground on 2 September, moving his forces so that they straddled the road south of Dunbar at Broxburn. When Cromwell suddenly attacked at dawn on 3 September 1650, the Scots army was taken by surprise. Utterly routed by an assault on their right wing, 4,000 Scots were killed, and another 10,000 taken prisoner. Leslie retreated to Stirling with the remnants of his army, determined to defend Scotland north of the Forth, while Cromwell occupied Edinburgh.

The disaster at Dunbar caused widespread opposition to mount in Scotland against the regime of the Kirk party. It had not only purged the army of 'malignants' before the battle, thus depriving David Leslie of his most experienced officers, but it had also interfered in military matters by dictating the tactics that seemingly led to the defeat itself. Urgently attempting to raise new levies to defend the country, the Kirk party now agreed that its extremist officers should be allowed to command a separate army in the west. Royalists reacted furiously by demanding that they too should be allowed to defend their country against Cromwell, who incidentally had helped the religious extremists of the Kirk party to power.

Failure of the 'Start'

Charles II himself took a part when the Kirk party ordered his own household in Perth to be purged. No longer prepared to act just as a figurehead, he now became involved in a plot to seize power. Perth was to be infiltrated by Highlanders from Atholl, mostly Robertsons and Stewarts, where they would be joined by John Murray, second Earl of Atholl, and other Royalists. Another Royalist rendezvous was planned in Angus, where the earls of

Huntly and Airlie, the Earl Marischal, Lord Ogilvie, and Lieutenant-General John Middleton would join forces, while it was planned that Lord Dudhope would seize Dundee.

The uprising on behalf of the King came to nothing when Charles II revealed the plot to his English advisers, who persuaded him to abandon such a rash undertaking. He first agreed, and then had second thoughts, before he suddenly fled Perth on 4 October 1650 in the farcical incident known as the 'Start'. Meeting up with Lord Dudhope in Angus, he went first to Cortachy Castle, held by James Ogilvie, Earl of Airlie, and then took refuge for the night in Glen Clova. Next day, Charles II was persuaded to return to Perth, but the Royalist forces already gathered in arms would not disband unless they were given an indemnity for their actions, which had already caused the deaths of several Covenanters. At first, the Parliamentary Committee of Estates would only show leniency to the forces under the Earl of Atholl, sending David Leslie north on 24 October with 3,000 cavalry to disperse the Royalist forces in Angus, after they had attacked an earlier detachment.

By then, however, the Royalists were acting in concert, and they presented David Leslie with what became known as the 'Northern Band'. It was signed among others by Lewis Gordon, third Marquis of Huntly; John Murray, second Earl of Atholl; George MacKenzie, second Earl of Seaforth; Lieutenant-General John Middleton; Major-General Sir George Munro; and Sir Thomas MacKenzie of Pluscardine. Giving assurances of their good faith and intentions, they all stressed that they wished to fight as Scotsmen against the English invaders under Oliver Cromwell, fearing that Cromwell would 'reduce the whole [of Scotland] to a Province, except the Lord in his mercy prevent it, by joining his Majesty's subjects in a band of unity, which is the only mean[s] (in our Judgement) to preserve Religion, King & Kingdom'. After receiving an act of indemnity for their actions, they then disbanded their forces after signing a treaty with David Leslie at Strathbogie on 4 November 1650.

End of 'Godly Rule'

By now, the Kirk party was bitterly divided against itself, since the religious extremists in the west had in effect disowned the King, in whose name the Kirk party in Edinburgh claimed to be acting. When the Parliamentary Committee of Estates tried to end this schism by bringing the western army under its own control, its actions were forestalled by Oliver Cromwell. After two months spent occupying Edinburgh, and briefly Glasgow, he moved west in late November, where much of the English cavalry occupied Hamilton

under the command of Major-General John Lambert. The western army of
the Covenant now attacked the English garrison in Hamilton on 1 December
1650, unaware that the garrison itself had been strengthened. Its forces were
completely routed, and thereafter the religious extremists in the west ceased
to exist as a political or military force.

Soon afterwards, the Kirk party agreed after bitter debate that all those
willing to fight against the English should be allowed to do so. It thus abandoned the deeply held tenet of the religious fanatics that only the godly could
fight in the cause of true religion. Among those appointed as officers to raise
new levies were such Highland chieftains as Kenneth MacKenzie, heir to the
Earl of Seaforth; Sir James MacDonald of Sleat; Alastair MacDonald, tutor
of Keppoch; John MacDonald, Captain of Clan Ranald; Ewan Cameron of
Lochiel; MacIntosh of MacIntosh; Roderick MacLeod of Talisker, tutor of
MacLeod of Dunvegan; the chief of the MacPhersons; and the tutor to
Hector MacLean of Duart.

Although the Marquis of Argyll crowned Charles II only a fortnight later
at Scone as its leading member, the days of the Kirk party were numbered, as
ever more Royalists and other 'malignants' were first admitted to the ranks
of the army, and then into Parliament itself. When Parliament eventually
repealed the Act of Classes on 4 June 1651, the experiment of godly rule by
the Kirk party was over. Royalists now dominated its proceedings, and Charles
II had come into his own.

Battle of Inverkeithing

The country was now united under the Royalist standard, apart from the
extremists in the Kirk party, but it was still unable to put an army into the field
strong enough to defeat the English forces of occupation. But fortunately for
the Scots, they had received a temporary reprieve in February, when Cromwell
fell ill. He did not recover his health until June 1951. By then, the Scots army
had mustered at Stirling, from where it advanced against Cromwell on 28
June, only to withdraw a few days later when faced by the enemy.

Cromwell then moved farther west towards Glasgow after some skirmishes
around Stirling, while some cavalry went north to reconnoitre Menteith,
as if to cross the upper reaches of the River Forth. Indeed, they perhaps
reached as far as Aberfoyle. Meanwhile, the Scots army had trailed behind
Cromwell's forces as far west as Kilsyth. Cromwell now started to march
rapidly back towards Linlithgow, hoping to seize the initiative against
Charles II and the Scots army. Very likely, he was aware that the Scots had
withdrawn ten regiments of cavalry from Fife to strengthen their army at
Stirling, leaving the county undefended. He now started to ferry his troops

by boat across the Firth of Forth at Queensferry on 17 July 1651 under the command of Major-General John Lambert.

Taken by surprise, the Scots did not react for three days, leaving Lambert enough time to land four or five thousand troops in Fife before he was challenged. Even when around 4,000 Scots did appear at Inverkeithing on 20 July 1651, they were routed by the English army with very heavy casualties. Perhaps half their number were killed, after the Scots cavalry had buckled under the English onslaught, leaving the Scots footsoldiers without any means of defence. Among the dead were 700 Buchanans, and a contingent of 800 MacLeans under their young chief Sir Hector MacLean of Duart. They died virtually to a man, after fighting heriocally against overwhelming odds to defend their chief.

Invasion of England

The Scots army under David Leslie reacted to the defeat at Inverkeithing by marching into Fife, leaving only a small garrison to defend Stirling Castle. Meanwhile, the bulk of Cromwell's forces advanced from Linlithgow towards Bannockburn. But once Cromwell was confident that the Scots army had indeed moved into Fife, he marched his forces back towards Edinburgh. Cromwell now set about ferrying his own army into Fife, where he had an army of 14,000 men by the end of July. He then marched north towards Perth, which surrendered on 2 August 1651.

The Scots army was now outflanked, cut off from all supplies and reinforcements from the north, as Cromwell had doubtless intended. They had little choice except to stay in Stirling, where they risked being attacked or starved into submission, or to march south into England, as indeed Charles II wanted. But it was perhaps more a strategy of despair that drove the Scots army south under Charles II, now numbering little more than 12,000 men.

Battle of Worcester

Three weeks later, the Scots army had reached Worcester, raising hardly any reinforcements from the English Royalists as Charles II had hoped. Nearly a week later, Cromwell arrived outside the walls of the town, bringing the English army to more than 30,000 men. The battle of Worcester was fought on 3 September 1651 when Cromwell first mounted a general assault against its walls. They were soon breached, and the Scots were utterly routed after fierce fighting within the town itself, leaving more than 2,000 dead, and another 10,000 taken as prisoners.

Among the Highlanders present, the MacLeods of Dunvegan under their chief Rory MacLeod suffered the most devastating losses with 700 dead out of a thousand men. The clan's fighting strength seemingly took more than a generation to recover. Other clansmen who fought for Charles II at Worcester included MacKenzies, MacKays, Frasers, Farquharsons, and MacGregors, as well as the MacKinnons under their chief Lachlan, and the MacNabs under their chief Iain, who it is said was killed. Hardly any Scots escaped back to Scotland, although some reached Ireland. Nearly all the Royalist prisoners were transported to the plantations in Barbados. Charles II managed to escape from the rout with a few friends, and eventually found his way to France, where he lived in exile until 1660.

While many Highland clans rallied to Charles II under their chiefs, it is noteworthy that several other clans from the west were absent at Worcester, as David Stevenson has emphasised. Despite clan traditions to the contrary, they did not form any part of the Scots army. Why they did not rally to the King's aid, as they had done earlier in support of the Royalist campaigns under Montrose, remains a mystery. Yet it is perhaps no coincidence that Archibald Campbell, Marquis of Argyll, was censored by Parliament in April 1651 for failing to raise men from Lochaber. Until they left, none of the neighbouring chiefs were willing to send men to Stirling, fearing that their lands would be plundered in their absence.

Since the Camerons of Lochiel held their lands under the feudal superiority of the Marquis of Argyll, it seems quite likely that they refused to enter his service on behalf of the King. Ewan Cameron of Lochiel apparently had his own quarrels with his neighbours. It was probably in 1651 that he invaded the lands of Angus MacDonald of Glengarry to force a payment owed to him as feudal superior, while he mounted another expedition against the MacDonalds of Keppoch, who had not paid him interest on a mortgage. It is therefore hardly surprising that neither clan, nor their close allies, the MacDonalds of Clan Ranald, supported Charles II at Worcester.

Monck's Occupation of Scotland

Even before his victory at the battle of Worcester in September 1651, Oliver Cromwell left behind Major-General George Monck with an army of 5,000 men to complete his conquest of Scotland. Stirling Castle surrendered on 13 August, while Dundee was stormed with fierce fighting on 1 September, which left 800 Scots dead, including women and children. Aberdeen was briefly occupied early in September, but it was not until the end of 1651 that nearly all of Scotland had finally been subdued, apart from the Highlands. But already, English troops had marched north into the lowland districts of Ross, Sutherland and Caithness, after establishing a garrison at Inverness.

By then, Lewis Gordon, third Marquis of Huntly, and Alexander Lindsay, Earl of Balcarres, had submitted to English rule. Only a few isolated strongholds were left under siege, such as the castles of Dumbarton, Brodick, and Dunnottar, where the crown jewels of Scotland were hidden. After they too had surrendered early in 1652, only Archibald Campbell, Marquis of Argyll, remained outside the peace imposed by England. Excusing himself as his wife was ill, and opposed to the venture itself, he had not accompanied Charles II south to the Royalist defeat at Worcester.

Afterwards, Argyll retired to Inveraray Castle for nearly a year, until illness forced him to come to terms with the English authorities in August 1652. It was a fateful action that would cost him his head in 1661. Meanwhile, he surrendered five of his strongholds to English garrisons, including Dunstaffnage and Tarbert Castles. Meanwhile, military expeditions were mounted against the western Highlands in a three-pronged attack from Inverness, Perth and Ayr. It achieved little against the opposition of Angus MacDonald of Glengarry, afterwards Lord MacDonnell and Aros. Even so, apart from the western Highlands, the whole country was now conquered, and ruled from London.

Prelude to Glencairn's Rebellion

Argyll's submission to English rule may well have encouraged his hereditary enemies in the Highlands to raise the prospect of another Royalist rebellion. Apparently acting with the support of several other chieftains, the initiative first came in 1652 from Angus MacDonald of Glengarry. Charles II responded by appointing Lieutenant-General John Middleton to be commander-in-chief of his forces in Scotland, even though he was still exiled at St Germain near Paris. Thus encouraged, Angus MacDonald of Glengarry summoned several chiefs to meet him at Strathglass in January 1653, intending to discuss the tactics for a Royalist uprising under the pretext of reconciling a feud between the MacDonalds and the Chisholms. But few chiefs were willing to declare themselves openly, especially as Sir James MacDonald of Sleat and Archibald Campbell, Marquis of Argyll, were evidently reporting their movements to the English authorities.

Even so, sporadic attacks were mounted against the occupying forces as the uprising slowly gathered strength during the early months of 1653, encouraged by the outbreak of a naval war between England and Holland in May 1652. Kenneth MacKenzie, now the third Earl of Seaforth after the death of his father in 1651, held a council of war at Glenelg towards the end of April 1653, and numerous other meetings occurred throughout the next two months. They culminated on 13 June 1653 when William Cunningham, Earl of Glencairn, summoned all the leading Royalist sympathisers in the

Highlands to a meeting in Lochaber on 1 July 1653. They agreed that the Earl of Glencairn should command the Royalist forces in Scotland in the absence of Middleton, who was still detained abroad. Although Charles II approved Glencairn's appointment, the decision was bitterly opposed by Alexander Lindsay, Earl of Balcarres, who thought he should have command. The quarrel continued between the two men, greatly weakening the Royalist cause, until Balcarres left Scotland in the spring of 1654.

Glencairn at first adopted the strategy of avoiding any direct engagement with the English forces of occupation. Instead, he launched guerilla attacks where they were least expected, while his own forces extorted men, money and supplies from the countryside. Only in September 1653 did the Royalists succeed in mounting what could in any sense be regarded as a sustained campaign. By then, Archibald Campbell, Lord Lorne, and afterwards the ninth Earl of Argyll, had defied his father and defected to the Royalists in July, together with some other Campbell lairds.

Role of Archibald Campbell, Lord Lorne

The presence of Archibald Campbell, Lord Lorne, set up tensions within the Royalist camp, especially as he was soon drawn into a plot to oust Glencairn as commander-in-chief, after Balcarres had written to Charles II, along with several others, criticising his leadership. When Glencairn learnt of Lorne's involvement, he sent Angus MacDonald of Glengarry to arrest him, even though he must have been aware of the hostility between the two men. Indeed, when they met in September, Glengarry had to be restrained from challenging Lord Lorne to a duel, and attacking his Campbell forces. Even so, Archibald Campbell, Lord Lorne, penetrated deep into Argyllshire during the same month, accompanied by Lord Kenmore. But apart from subduing Kintyre, he achieved very little during several weeks of campaigning. Indeed, the expedition itself faltered when he quarrelled with Lord Kenmore over the wisdom of attacking the Lowland colonists in Kintyre, including some extreme Presbyterians, who had recently settled there under the protection of the Marquis of Argyll.

Meanwhile, the English army had mounted its own expedition to secure the Isle of Lewis. It was intended partly as a reprisal against Kenneth MacKenzie, third Earl of Seaforth, who had sided with the Royalist cause earlier in the year, but more importantly as an attempt to prevent any invasion of the Western and Northern Isles. It quickly reduced Lewis to obedience with very little resistance, and then sailed to Mull, where Duart Castle was captured with the help of the Marquis of Argyll. Only when its supply ships were wrecked in a storm, and the men forced to return overland from Mull, did the expedition nearly turn into a disaster. It was narrowly averted when the Marquis of Argyll conducted the English troops in person to the head of Loch Goil, where he found enough boats to transport them safely back to Dumbarton.

Divisions within the Royalist Camp

By December 1653, the Royalist forces had largely withdrawn into Badenoch, accompanied by their commanders, including the Earl of Glencairn, Angus MacDonald of Glengarry, Archibald Campbell, Lord Lorne, Ewan Cameron of Lochiel, and Lord Kenmore. Although the lands there had once belonged to Lewis Gordon, third Marquis of Huntly, they had been forfeited after the execution of his father in 1649, and given to the Marquis of Argyll for payment of his debts. Archibald Campbell, Lord Lorne, therefore demanded that he should be given command of any men raised in Badenoch for the Royalist cause. When this was refused, Lord Lorne stormed out of the Royalist camp, threatening to betray Glencairn to the governor of Ruthven Castle. He was apprehended by Angus MacDonald of Glengarry and Ewan Cameron of Lochiel, and the quarrel was resolved, but all the Campbells under Lord Lorne deserted the Royalist cause within a fortnight, returning to their own lands.

Quite possibly, Glencairn made matters worse around this time by writing to Charles II, urging him to declare the Marquis of Argyll a traitor for helping the English to capture Duart Castle. If this were done, he suggested, letters could be written to certain other Highland chieftains, 'assuring them that his Majesty will deliver them from under those bonds and yokes which Argyll has purchased over their heads'. If they would engage against him, Charles II should cancel their debts to Argyll, and remove his feudal superiority over them. But Glencairn's poor relations with the Highlanders were revealed when he also advised the King not to believe any paper unless it was signed by Angus MacDonald of Glengarry. He was evidently the only Highland chieftain who had his full trust and confidence. Yet despite such disunity, the Royalist forces under the Earl of Glencairn were still strong enough to plunder the Lowlands of Moray and Nairn in January 1654, while the English commander reported an upsurge in Royalist activity. By now, there were perhaps 5,000 men under arms in the Royalist cause, although estimates varied widely, facing an English army of occupation almost three times as large.

Arrival of John Middleton

After Lord Lorne had abandoned his command, it was given to James Graham, second Marquis of Montrose. He had succeeded his illustrious father, and returned to Scotland. Lieutenant-General John Middleton finally landed at Tarbat Ness at the end of February 1654 to take over his command from the Earl of Glencairn. He brought with him much-needed supplies of ammunition and an array of senior officers. Among them was Sir George Munro, whom he appointed as his second-in-command, much to Glencairn's anger.

The Royalists now renewed their efforts on behalf of Charles II, which even spread to the Lowlands late in March 1654, when there was a brief uprising in Dumfries and Galloway. Yet there was still dissension within the Royalist camp, especially between the Highland chieftains and the Lowland officers and noblemen in its leadership. Even before the uprising had got underway, it was reported in July 1653 to the English that:

> the greatest design the Lowland Lords have, is to make themselves so strong as is possible of Lowland men [and] strangers that they may thereby not only secure themselves from the barbarous cruelty and treachery of the Highlanders but likewise may keep them in awe.

Now, Sir George Munro denounced the Highlanders serving under Glencairn as 'a pack of thieves and robbers', and especially the clansmen under Angus MacDonald of Glengarry. It provoked a duel between the two men. Sir George Munro was wounded by Glencairn, who then withdrew the troops still under his command from the main body of the Royalist army. Not long afterwards, Angus MacDonald of Glengarry had to be prevented from fighting a duel with John Murray, Earl of Atholl, who claimed precedence over him according to his title. But such internal squabbling among the Royalists was soon overtaken by a much greater threat when Major-General George Monck arrived back in Scotland on 22 April 1654 to take up command of civil government and military authority as its Governor.

Governorship of Monck

Monck's first task in Scotland was constitutional, since England, Scotland and Ireland had now been declared a Commonwealth which had Oliver Cromwell as its Lord Protector, and the three countries united under a single Parliament at Westminster. One of his first acts was the proclamation of an Act of Pardon and Grace. It determined who should be pardoned among the Scottish nobility and gentry for supporting the Royalist cause, but more importantly who should be denied any such leniency. Even apart from those engaged in the current uprising, twenty-four persons were named who were to suffer the confiscation of their estates, along with another seventy-three who were to be fined by amounts up to £15,000. Thus, Monck set about the pacification of Scotland with punitive measures of 'rigour and ruin', as they were described at the time.

The same resolution was shown by Monck when it came to military matters. He first used his influence in London to strengthen his own armed forces before setting out on a determined campaign to reduce the Royalist rebels to obedience. He first sealed off the passes into the Lowlands along the Highland line, marching to Stirling on 10 May 1654 from his headquarters at Dalkeith, and then to Cardross on the Firth of Clyde. He then doubled back to Kilsyth, where he remained until 25 May 1654. There, he conferred with the Marquis of Argyll, who had earlier requested that his own country should be garrisoned with English troops for his own safety. Now he agreed to collaborate with Monck, who afterwards allowed him to raise a hundred armed men for his own defence.

Monck then marched north around the Campsie Fells to Loch Lomond, where he ordered all the boats destroyed. Leaving four troops of cavalry near Glasgow to prevent any Royalist incursion from the west, he then returned to Stirling, and marched north to Perth, which he reached on 2 June 1654. A week later, he marched north into the Highlands on 9 June 1654, following the course of the River Tay. On reaching the mouth of Loch Tay by 12 June, he secured the surrender of a Royalist garrison, which occupied a castle on Priory Island. He was still in the district on 14 June 1654 when he received word that a rendezvous had been called for the Royalist forces under Lieutenant-General John Middleton near Loch Ness.

Monck's Highland Campaign

Although Middleton had landed in Scotland more than three months earlier, he had spent much of the time since then in Caithness and Sutherland. Monck had reacted to the news of his arrival in Scotland by sending north one Colonel Morgan as his lieutenant, but now the Royalist forces had slipped south past Morgan's camp at Dornoch. Morgan pursued Middleton south, passing through Inverness on 14 June 1654. He then encountered a detachment of Royalist forces, 600 strong, which he routed near the head of Loch Ness. Meanwhile, Monck had marched north from Loch Tay with his own forces to Ruthven Castle in Badenoch, where he learnt that Middleton was now moving south along the Great Glen towards Lochaber.

Leaving Ruthven on 20 June 1654, Monck marched past Cluny and Glenroy towards Inverlochy, where a 1,000-strong detachment of pro-Cromwell troops had landed from Ireland to establish a garrison just a week earlier. Meeting up with its commander and the Marquis of Argyll at the head of Loch Lochy on 23 June 1654, he learnt that Ewan Cameron of Lochiel had attacked a detachment from the garrison at Achdaleiu, and sixty or seventy soldiers had been killed. Now convinced that Middleton had moved west into Kintail, Monck marched north-east along the Great Glen to Glenmoriston on the next day, and then west towards Glenshiel and the MacKenzie stronghold of Eilean Donnan Castle on Lochalsh.

There he learnt that Middleton's horse had crossed over the pass of Mam Ratagan into Glenelg. However, as his supplies were now running low, he decided on 29 June 1654 to return to Inverness, where they could be replenished. Marching through the mountains to Glen Strathfarrar, where he met Colonel Morgan on 1 July 1654, he had reached Dunain just outside Inverness two days later. He was then told that Middleton had broken out south with 4,000 horse and foot into Atholl, instead of slipping north towards Sutherland and Caithness as he had expected.

Ordering all his forces south, Monck started off in pursuit, reaching Ruthven on 7 July 1654, while Morgan was ordered to Braemar. By then, Middleton had reached Dunkeld, apparently heading for Loch Lomond, or so it was reported. Monck marched south to Weem Castle near Aberfeldy, which he had previously garrisoned, reaching it on 10 July 1654. While taking in supplies, a detachment of his forces then encountered a larger body of troops under John Murray, second Earl of Atholl. Not only did Atholl escape from the ensuing skirmish, but he was able to alert Middleton to the danger.

Then, on learning that Middleton had turned north towards the head of Loch Earn, Monck gave chase on 12 July 1654, marching west towards Finlarig at the head of Loch Tay, hoping to cut the Royalists off. But, on reaching Lawers, he found that Middleton had passed through Finlarig just a day earlier. He now pursued the Royalist forces under Middleton west through Glen Dochart and Strath Fillan to Glen Lochy, reaching the foot of Glen Orchy on the evening of 14 July 1654. There his scouts reported that the Royalist army was only five miles away in Glen Strae, north of Loch Awe. Sending out parties against the Royalists, they scattered, leaving behind some baggage horses and provisions. The main body of Middleton's army now struck out north-east towards the Moor of Rannoch, evidently heading for Badenoch.

Rout at Dalnaspidal

Since Colonel Morgan was even now at Ruthven, the Royalists were caught in a trap. Monck himself moved east in short marches, first to Strath Fillan, then to Glen Dochart, and finally to Kinnell at the head of Loch Tay, which he reached on 19 July 1654, intending to cut off Middleton if he should turn south. But by sending out scouting parties to harass the Royalists in their rear, he drove them towards Morgan's forces, which had now moved south from Badenoch across the Drumochter Pass into Glen Garry. Although aware of the English forces in his rear, Middleton neglected to send out scouts in front, while his 800 cavalry were far in advance of his 1,200 footsoldiers, who lagged behind by several miles.

Yet it seems that Morgan's forces were equally surprised when Middleton's cavalry suddenly appeared at Dalnaspidal near the foot of Loch Garry on the evening of 19 July 1654. Even so, Middleton's cavalry was soon routed and, faced with the difficulty of escaping back along the steep sides of Loch Garry, many Royalists simply dismounted and took to their heels, fleeing in several different directions. They left behind over 300 horses and several portmanteaux containing valuable papers. The English forces then dispersed the Royalist infantry, which fled across country to the safety of Lochaber. Badly wounded, or so it was reported, Lieutenant-General John Middleton managed to escape on foot, reaching Sutherland a week later, but even so the Royalist cause was lost.

Denial of the Countryside

Monck now adopted the traditional strategy of denying the Royalists their ability to live off the countryside, while offering generous terms to their leaders if they would submit to English rule. Already, while marching through the Highlands in pursuit of Middleton and his Royalist forces, he had burnt and plundered the lands of the Camerons of Lochiel, the MacKenzies of Kintail, and the MacDonalds of Glengarry. After returning to Stirling, he then marched into the Highlands once again at the beginning of August, devastating the lands around Aberfoyle and Loch Lomond, which had supported the Royalist forces over the previous winter. As the Royalists had already pursued much the same tactics, widespread devastation was caused throughout the Highlands.

Colonel Morgan had meanwhile marched north into Caithness in pursuit of Middleton, laying waste to the lands through which he passed. Two frigates patrolled the coast north of Inverness to prevent the landing of any supplies or reinforcements. Middleton himself was reported to have only 200 horse and 600 foot at his command. He was forced to flee into the western Highlands, hoping to seek refuge at the MacKenzie stronghold of Eilean Donnan, only to be pursued there by a detachment of Morgan's troops. He left Tongue House to be burnt, perhaps by Morgan's forces, if it was not put to the flames by John MacKay, second Lord Reay, to prevent it falling into the hands of the enemy.

Capitulation of Royalist Leaders

Monck's actions were harsh enough to persuade several of the Royalist leaders to capitulate. The first to do so was John Murray, Earl of Atholl, followed by William Cunningham, Earl of Glencairn, and then by Lord Kenmore and James Graham, second Marquis of Montrose. They had all surrendered by the end of September 1654. They were offered terms of great leniency, as they were allowed to keep their estates. Even if they had to find substantial securities for their good conduct in the future, they were absolved from paying any fines previously imposed under the Act of Pardon and Grace. Indeed, some Royalists actually benefited financially from their rebellion, compared with their more law-abiding countrymen.

More submissions were taken during the autumn of 1654, but they were mostly from Lowlanders of second rank in the Royalist leadership. Their defection left a hard core of support only among the Highland chieftains, but even they were unable to persuade their clansmen to rally once again to the Royalist cause. Monck complained with justified irritation that they refused to abandon the Royalist cause, long after it had been lost. Meanwhile, Archibald Campbell, Marquis of Argyll, eventually took up arms against his son Lord Lorne at the end of October 1654. Lorne had embarrassed his father greatly in September, when he had mounted an armed raid on Inveraray, seizing a quantity of provisions intended to supply the English garrison soon to be established there. Now the Marquis of Argyll drove Lord Lorne from Argyllshire, earning Monck's support, even as he evaded his own creditors.

Submission of the Highland Chieftains

Such reverses, and the failure of a general rendezvous at the end of November 1654, now induced Kenneth MacKenzie, third Earl of Seaforth, to enter into negotiations with Monck. He too was granted generous terms, later extended to the other Highland chieftains, since he and his clansmen were permitted to carry arms for their own defence. Seaforth's submission in January 1655 was followed by negotiations with Lieutenant-General John Middleton, who seemed ready to accept terms when the negotiations collapsed at the last moment.

Soon afterwards, the submission of the other Highland chieftains, who still had not made their peace with the English authorities, was delayed by the brief success of Penruddock's uprising in England. Negotiations were resumed when the rising itself was quickly suppressed. Rory MacLeod of Dunvegan was the first to submit at the urging of his brother-in-law, Sir James Campbell of Lawers. His defection seemingly convinced Middleton that the Royalist cause was now lost, especially as he had sought refuge at Dunvegan Castle. He wrote from Dunvegan urging John MacKay, second Lord Reay, to seek terms as well, before he took ship in April 1655 for the Continent, where he joined Charles II in exile.

Meanwhile, the Marquis of Agyll was active in persuading his eldest son Archibald Campbell, Lord Lorne, and through him, Ewan Cameron of Lochiel, to come to terms. They had all submitted by the end of May 1655, signing articles of agreement with the government, but it was not until June 1655 that Angus MacDonald of Glengarry finally agreed terms, even though he was briefly imprisoned by the English in February 1656, after failing to find caution for his good behaviour. Lochiel was even promised up to £500 sterling to settle the debts he owed William MacIntosh of Torcastle, together with arbitration to settle once and for all the dispute between the two men.

Pacification of the Highlands

Monck now established a measure of law and order in the Highlands which had not been seen for centuries, enforcing it with the active co-operation of the clan chiefs. By offering them treaties of surrender to sign, Monck had implicitly recognised their own authority over their clansmen, so bolstering their own positions of power. Indeed, the securities required of them made them responsible for the good behaviour not just of themselves, but of their clansmen as well. Given the right to bear arms in their own self-defence, the clan chiefs and their clansmen were thus to police the Highlands on behalf of the Commonwealth government in Edinburgh, now established as a Council of State. Ewan Cameron of Lochiel even resorted to a highly ingenious way of increasing his own following by offering his protection to anyone found carrying arms illegally, providing they were willing to take his name. The result was that 'in a short time, his name became so numerous as to spread over a great part of the Highlands'.

Even so, Monck planted large and small garrisons throughout the Highlands to keep the peace, requisitioning castles and country houses for the purpose. As well as building citadels at Ayr, Perth and Inverness to guard the periphery of the Highlands, and many other smaller forts elsewhere, he greatly strengthened the garrison at Inverlochy in the heart of Lochaber, where a substantial fortification was erected, beginning in 1654. Indeed, its construction was said to have cost £100,000. Even though Ewan Cameron of Lochiel opposed its establishment at first, he came to enjoy friendly relations not just with its governor, Colonel John Hill, but indeed with Major-General George Monck himself, whom he regarded as his 'friend and protector'. Moreover, he gained lucrative contracts to supply the garrison with timber, fuel and provisions, while he was even granted a commission in 1659 against the MacDonalds of Glengarry, who had risen in arms, robbing and plundering. Such service on behalf of the English was rewarded when Glengarry's lands were forfeited and granted to Argyll, who then gave them to Lochiel.

Lochaber was established as a separate district with its own jurisdiction to administer the rule of law. The peace that Monck established in the Highlands would last for the next twenty-five years with hardly any outbreaks of violence on a large scale. Indeed, it was said in 1655 that 'a man may ride all over Scotland with £100 in his pocket, which he could not have done these five hundred years'. But after the restoration of Charles II, it would be an uneasy peace, imposed by a weak and inefficient government, and marked by renewed inter-clan feuds, mostly over conflicting claims to land, and often aggravated by increasing burdens of debt. Whatever benefits Monck had brought the Highlands as far as good government and the rule of law were concerned, his actions eroded the traditions once enjoyed by the Highland chieftains, certainly before they were forced to submit to the Statutes of Iona, and which they hoped might be restored in some measure when Charles II returned to the throne in 1660.

Chapter Nine

RESTORATION AND REACTION

Charles II was finally restored to the throne in 1660. Oliver Cromwell had died two years earlier, and had been succeeded by his feeble and lacklustre son Richard as the Protector of the Commonwealth. The following year, the republican regime in England collapsed in incipient anarchy, and the army intervened under Major-General George Monck. After secret negotiations with Charles II, he marched south to London in January 1660 to recall the Long Parliament, which then dissolved itself. Following free elections, the new Parliament restored Charles II to his throne amid great rejoicing in May 1660. But 'they had called home a King without a Treaty', despite the Declaration of Breda, which promised a general amnesty and complete freedom of conscience to all the King's subjects. The restoration of the monarchy in England, but only of the sovereign in Scotland where Charles II had already been crowned in 1651, was quickly followed in Scotland by an aristocratic reaction to the political and religious traumas of the past two decades.

It reached its climax in the state funeral of great solemnity and magnificence given to James Graham, first Marquis of Montrose. His dismembered body had remained buried in an unsanctified grave at the place of his execution in 1650, while his limbs were displayed at various localities throughout the country. After his severed head was removed from its spike above the Tolbooth, and his limbs retrieved from Stirling, Glasgow, Perth and Aberdeen, all his remains were taken to the abbey chapel of Holyroodhouse on 7 January 1661 to lie in state. They remained there until 14 May, when they were buried with the 'greatest solemnity and magnificence' in St Giles Cathedral. Exactly the opposite fate was suffered by Oliver Cromwell, whose body was taken from its grave in Westminster Abbey and formally executed.

The Restoration Settlement

These obsequies given to Montrose may well have triggered the conservative reaction in Scotland by making him a martyr to the Royalist cause. But

129

equally, the stirrings of religious extremism in opposition to Charles II threatened the country with renewed conflict, giving fresh impetus to Royalist sentiment. The Privy Council was restored, and Officers of State appointed without regard to the Scots Parliament. Afterwards Charles II ruled Scotland largely by decree, just as his grandfather James VI had done before him with 'strokes of a pen'. The aristocracy was restored to its former position of power and influence, and its members were rewarded with the profits of high office.

It was not before time as far as they were concerned, since nearly all the nobility and many of the landed gentry faced financial ruin in 1660. Already heavily indebted before 1638, they had maintained and equipped armies for almost two decades of warfare, largely at their own expense, or indirectly through loans and taxes. Once Oliver Cromwell had conquered Scotland, they were subject to savage laws of debt. As Robert Baillie lamented in 1658: 'Our noble families are almost gone; Lennox has little in Scotland unsold; Hamilton's estate . . . is sold; Argyll can pay little annual rent for seven or eight hundred thousand merks [of debt], and he is no more drowned in debt than public hatred, almost of all, both Scotland and England; the Gordons are gone; the Douglasses little better; many of our chief families are crashing; nor is there any appearance of any human relief.'

Even so, when Charles II summoned a Parliament to meet in Edinburgh in January 1661 under Lieutenant-General John Middleton as his Lord High Commissioner, newly ennobled as the Earl of Middleton, he perhaps hardly expected it to adopt policies so agreeable to his own absolutist views. Indeed, it was commented that 'never was there a Parliament so frantic for the King'. The mood of hysteria, which now seemingly swept the country, allowed the Parliament in Edinburgh to restore the old order by annulling all the acts passed since the visit of Charles I in 1633. It effectively destroyed at a single stroke all the advances made since the National Covenant in 1638, and the earlier legislation that had prompted its signing, as well as the subsequent Acts of Parliament which had curbed the King's powers.

Although Charles II had promised to maintain the Presbyterian religion, bishops were restored to the Church of Scotland after James Sharp, Minister at Crail, had gone to London to represent the interests of moderate Presbyterians. But he changed sides, returning as the Archbishop of St Andrews. He rode into St Andrews, accompanied by 600 soldiers. Although denounced by strict Presbyterians as a traitor and a cruel and odious man, James Sharp may well have simply reflected the popular feeling in the country, where even a leading Presbyterian was forced to admit there was 'no love for Presbyterian government'.

The new settlement found no favour south of the Tay. However, farther north, the Synod of Aberdeen sent an address to Charles II, expressing its deep sorrow and regret for the nation's guilt. They requested that the Church of Scotland should be governed according to the word of God and the practice of the primitive Church, in such a manner as was consistent with royal authority and conducive to godliness, unity, peace and order. The General Assembly was suppressed as being incompatible with Episcopacy. However, Charles II did not repeat the mistake of his father, appointing only two bishops to the Privy Council. Even so, bishops took their former place in Parliament as the first of the Three Estates. Moreover, kirk sessions and presbyteries (although shorn of their elders) were preserved, but only if their meetings were authorised by the appropriate bishop, while provincial synods were abolished. Any other form of ecclesiastical meeting was condemned as seditious. No attempt was made to bring back the liturgy so favoured by James VI and Charles I.

Even so, it was the power of patronage, given back to the aristocracy as the proprietors of great estates, which caused the most offence. It was first declared that all those ministers who had entered their parishes since 1649 had no absolute right to 'their places, benefices, and kirks'. Such ministers were first required to be 'presented' by their lay patrons to their parishes, before they could be inducted into their livings by the bishop of the appropriate diocese. This requirement was later extended to all the ministers of the restored Church.

The crisis came in 1663 when the Privy Council ordered the expulsion of all those ministers who had refused to comply with the law. Nearly a third of their number were expelled from their livings by the regime under the Earl of Middleton. There were then around 900 parishes in Scotland, but ninety-six were vacant at the time. Records show that 274 ministers were actually expelled. However, among the moderate Presbyterians known as the Resolutioners, which numbered around 600 clergy, only around forty refused to conform. The numbers of ejected clergy were further reduced by the indulgences of 1669 and 1672, which were accepted by around 120 ministers.

The expulsions occurred mostly in the south of the country, and especially in the western counties, where 135 ministers lost their livings in the synods of Glasgow, Ayr, Dumfries and Galloway. North of the River Forth, few ministers were ejected except in Fife and the other lowland districts as far north as Easter Ross. The Highlands were hardly affected at all, apart from Argyllshire and the Campbell lands of Breadalbane. Indeed, Episcopalianism flourished in the Gaelic-speaking Highlands after the Restoration, where a succession of Protestant ministers was established in every parish apart from Kilmonivaig in Lochaber. Indeed, it is said that there were only four clergymen in the synods of Aberdeen, Banff, Moray, Ross and Caithness who 'conformed to Presbyterianism' in 1690.

The ejected ministers were often followed by their parishioners, who took to worshipping in the illegal meetings known as 'conventicles', held in private houses and remote steadings, or outdoors in the open fields. Such disobedience acquired a momentum of its own, especially in the Lowlands of Scotland south of the Firth of Tay, after the government resorted first to coercion and then to persecution in trying to suppress what was essentially a political movement. The Privy Council was even forced to commission the old prison on the Bass Rock to hold the more intractable offenders.

Favour and Retribution

When Charles II was restored to his throne in 1660, the Highland chieftains who had fought on his behalf expected their reward, but for the most part they were disappointed. Charles II rewarded only Angus MacDonald of Glengarry by elevating him to the peerage under the grandiose title of Aeneas, Lord MacDonnell and Aros, thus recognising him as the most steadfast of all his supporters in the Highlands. Yet the title fell far short of his claim to be made Earl of Ross as the principal man and chief of Clan Donald. Indeed, the government evidently feared that he saw himself as a latter-day Lord of the Isles. However, any such claim to be the head of Clan Donald was hotly disputed by Sir James MacDonald of Sleat, whose Protestant sympathies had persuaded him to collaborate with the Cromwellian regime in Scotland, despite his earlier commitment to the Royalist cause. As regards the other Highland chieftains, there were several who had collaborated with the English forces of occupation after 1655, such as Ewan Cameron of Lochiel. He had profited greatly from the patronage of the English, particularly in pursuing his disputes with the MacDonalds of Glengarry, and with the MacIntoshes, who complained bitterly about his actions.

Equally, Archibald Campbell, eighth Earl and Marquis of Argyll, had been instrumental in bringing about the return of Charles II to Scotland in 1650, and indeed had crowned him King after his father's execution. But his enemies were now determined to bring about his destruction. Despite the warnings of his friends, he visited Charles II in London, only to be arrested. After five months held prisoner in the Tower of London, he was sent back to Edinburgh by ship to face trial for treason before the Scots Parliament.

Argyll's prosecution was undertaken by the Earl of Middleton, who hoped to benefit personally from the forfeiture of Argyll's estates, should he be found guilty. Although he was exonerated for any part in the regicide of Charles I, and had already been pardoned for his earlier conduct by the Act of Indemnity of 1651, the intervention of Major-General George Monck, now Duke of Albemarle, sealed Argyll's fate. Found guilty of collaborating with the English after Cromwell's occupation of Scotland in 1652, Argyll was beheaded by the guillotine known as the Maiden at the Mercat Cross in Edinburgh on 27 May 1661. Iain Lom exulted at the death of the arch-enemy of Clan Donald.

There was perhaps a grim justice to Argyll's execution, since his severed head was placed on top of the Tolbooth. It came to occupy the very same resting-place as the head of James Graham, first Marquis of Montrose, placed there earlier after his execution in 1650 by the Covenanting regime. Three other Covenanters suffered the same fate as Argyll, including the intemperate James Guthrie, who had earned the King's displeasure by his fiery sermons, and the fanatical Archibald Johnston of Warriston, who had originally drawn up the National Covenant of 1638.

Charges against Lord Lorne

The execution of Archibald Campbell, eighth Earl and Marquis of Argyll, also threatened his elder son Archibald, Lord Lorne, despite his acting resolutely in the King's interest before 1660. Indeed, he had still continued to intrigue with Charles II after submitting to the English in 1655. However, his efforts to convince Charles II that his father's trial and execution were a travesty of justice so annoyed the Scots Parliament that he was committed for trial in 1662 on a trumped-up charge. Sentenced to death, he only escaped execution by the express command of Charles II.

Lord Lorne remained in prison until 1663, when the Earl of Middleton fell from power as Lord High Commissioner. John Maitland, second Earl of Lauderdale, acting as the Secretary of the Privy Council, replaced him with John Leslie, seventh Earl of Rothes. It was also under Lauderdale's patronage that Lord Lorne was restored to his grandfather's title as the ninth Earl of Argyll, together with his lands and offices, and made a Lord of the Privy Council. He thus regained the power previously exercised by his ancestors in Argyll, and elsewhere throughout the Highlands. Indeed, it was widely accepted that only the Campbells, earls of Argyll, had the power to keep the peace in the Highlands. As Lord Lorne emphasised in pleading for his father's life, his family had brought to justice 'many notorious malefactors and cruel oppressors', who could only be seized from their 'strongholds and inaccessible places, otherways hardly to be overtaken without great blood-shed and expense', amid 'the horror of rocks, woods and mountains'.

Actions of the Privy Council

While Monck's regime before 1660 had reduced the Highlands to some semblance of order, the restoration of Charles II saw a return to widespread disorder. It was exacerbated by the withdrawal of the English garrisons at Inverlochy, Stornoway, Dunstaffnage and Inverness, where the forts were demolished. Moreover, the separate jurisdiction of Lochaber was abolished. Early in 1661, alarmed by the 'thefts, robberies, murders, depredations, spuilzies [despoliations], and other heinous crimes', committed daily by 'loose and lawless persons in the Highlands', the Privy Council determined to revive the 'good and ancient custom of charging the landlords and chieftains of clans to find caution yearly in the Books of the Council'.

More than 100 such persons were first summoned to appear before the Privy Council on 1 October 1661, but only six appeared. Faced with this affront to its dignity, the Privy Council apparently did little until late in 1664, when all the landlords and chieftains listed in 1661 were again summoned to appear before it on the first Thursday of the following June, and thereafter annually on the same day. To enforce this injunction, it was intended that garrisons of forty musketeers were to be stationed at Inverlochy, Ruthven, and Braemar, supplied with fire and bedding by the local landowners. However, this plan was never put into effect, except briefly at Ruthven.

The intervening years were marked by widespread outbreaks of robbery and indeed violence. They were committed by 'caterans and broken men', who lived outside the norms of organised society, plundering, sorning, and blackmailing by forcibly exacting food and shelter and extorting protection money from their victims. It is however a moot point whether such endemic lawlessness was not greatly exaggerated to justify military intervention in the Highlands. The Privy Council learnt that Kintyre was so infested with 'vagabonds and thieves', some from Ireland, and others from the Hebrides, that the 'whole inhabitants of the said isle are abused by them and in fear of their lives continually'. Elsewhere, it was reported that 'the bounds of Lochaber and other parts adjacent are so pestered with thieves that no gentleman, tenant, or inhabitant dare assure themselves of anything belonging to them'.

Indeed, among the worst offenders were the MacDonalds of Keppoch, and their close neighbours, the Camerons of Lochiel, as well as the MacDonalds of Glencoe, and the 'broken men' of Clan Gregor. Indeed, according to Alasdair Ruadh MacDonald of Inverlair, sixty clansmen of Alexander MacDonald of Keppoch, accompanied by their young chief and 'armed with swords, hagbuts, pistols, dirks, forks, and [other] forbidden weapons', had invaded his lands in a 'most riotous and barbarous manner'. Moreover, they 'hunted and pursued him and his servants for their lives, so that they were forced to abandon their own country and shelter themselves among strangers'.

The Keppoch Murders

Alasdair Ruadh MacDonald of Inverlair, a distant kinsman to the MacDonalds of Clan Ranald, had long been settled with his family in Keppoch. Once holding his lands of Inverlair from the MacDonalds of Keppoch, he had angered the young chief of Keppoch by taking a lease from George Gordon, ninth Earl and fourth Marquis of Huntly, now restored to the title forfeited by his grandfather when he was executed in 1649, following his father's death in 1653. Huntly would soon be granted a charter to all his estates, including the lordships of Badenoch and Lochaber, once held by Archibald Campbell, Marquis of Campbell, which had fallen to the Crown after his execution in 1661.

Even though the MacDonalds of Keppoch had served the Royalist cause with distinction, they were not rewarded with a charter from Charles II to their lands, which they doubtless expected. Instead, the feudal superiority long exercised over them by the Earls of Huntly was renewed. To make matters worse, the MacDonalds of Keppoch were divided among themselves. Their new chief Alexander MacDonald had only recently come of age. During his long minority since 1649, the affairs of the clan had been directed by his uncle and tutor Alasdair Buidhe MacDonald, while Alexander himself was fostered by Sir James MacDonald of Sleat.

Then, in the early hours of 5 September 1663, Alexander MacDonald of Keppoch and his brother Ranald were murdered. They were probably the victims of a conspiracy between the MacDonalds of Inverlair and their uncle Alasdair Buidhe MacDonald, who may well have deeply resented surrendering his powers as tutor to his young nephew. The murderers, who probably included two of Alasdair's sons as well as Inverlair, broke into the 'house of Keppoch, armed with swords, dirks and other weapons', which they used to inflict ghastly wounds upon Alexander MacDonald and his brother Ranald. The poet Iain Lom visited the bloody scene next morning, and furiously denounced the murderers in his poem *Mort na Ceapaich*. But his passionate appeals for justice were largely ignored, and indeed there was surprisingly little outcry against the murderers. Even an appeal to Aeneas, Lord MacDonnell and Aros, chief of Glengarry, went unanswered. He had his own financial interests to consider as wadsetter to the murdered chief of Keppoch, whom he owed money from a redeemable mortgage on his land.

Commission against Inverlair

Two years were to pass before a commission of fire and sword was finally granted by the Privy Council to Sir James MacDonald of Sleat, allowing him to seek out the murderers of his foster-son. Fifty clansmen under Sleat's brother Archibald MacDonald laid siege to the house of Inverlair, which they put to the flames. Although Alasdair Buidhe MacDonald's two sons had fled the country, Alasdair Ruadh MacDonald of Inverlair was killed with six of his accomplices, attempting to escape. Tradition has it that Iain Lom severed their heads, and after washing them in the Well of the Heads near Invergarry, presented them to the chief of Glengarry as a rebuke to his own lack of action.

Even though the Privy Council commended Sir James MacDonald of Sleat for the 'good service done his Majesty', Alasdair Buidhe MacDonald assumed the chiefship of the MacDonalds of Keppoch after Alexander's murder, so gaining what he wanted from the act of violence. Then, after his death around 1669, the chiefship passed to his own son Archibald and his descendants, who were now the senior line of the family.

Feud of MacIntosh with Lochiel

Parliament in 1661 triggered another feud in Lochaber when it granted the lands of Glenloy and Locharkaig to Lachlan MacIntosh of Torcastle, Captain of Clan Chattan. His claim was opposed forcibly by Ewan Cameron of Lochiel, whose forebears had occupied these lands 'past memory of man'. But the MacIntoshes had almost as long-standing a claim to Glenloy and Locharkaig, dating back to a charter of 1443 if not even earlier, which they too claimed had once belonged to their distant ancestors. Indeed, it was said the feud between the two clans was an 'original and very ancient hatred, which had lasted with great fierceness and cruelty between their ancestors for the space of three hundred and sixty years'.

Faced with losing his ancient patrimony, Ewan Cameron of Lochiel was accused by Lachlan MacIntosh of Torcastle in 1663 of 'shaking off all reverence and regard to his Majesty's authority and laws . . . [and] beating, abusing, and apprehending as captives such officers and messengers as were sent among them by the petitioner for putting the law into execution'. After vainly attempting to exert his rights, Lachlan MacIntosh of Torcastle was persuaded to negotiate with Ewan Cameron of Lochiel in an attempt to end their feud. But in 1664, when they both appeared at the appointed place, they were each accompanied by their own armed retinues.

James Fraser, minister of Wardlaw, described the scene:

Mackintosh, his men, about 500 in rank and file, lay on the east side of the river [Ness] at Haughs; Lochiel's men 300, about Tomnifirich. Earth, water, air, rebounded at the sound of bagpipes' martial music. At the sound of a trumpet the meeting sits at some distance, and my Lord

Bishop of Moray and the Laird Robert Cumming of Altyre, as arbitrators and trenchermen passed betwixt them, and at last, the third day being Thursday, matters were brought to an accommodation and agreement, that it prevented litigation and cost in law.

Ewan Cameron of Lochiel agreed to buy the lands under dispute, only to renege on his agreement when MacIntosh's forces had dispersed.

Final Settlement of Feud

The dispute was then referred to the Privy Council. It determined that MacIntosh should sell his proprietory interest in Glenloy and Locharkaig to Ewan Cameron of Lochiel for the sum of 72,000 merks. But he refused, deciding instead on another show of force. Marching to the head of Locharkaig with 1,500 clansmen in September 1665, Lachlan MacIntosh came face-to-face with 900 Camerons, strengthened by another 300 men from Clan Gregor and the MacDonalds of Glencoe. His position as the Captain of Clan Chattan was already fatally weakened by the defection of the MacPhersons, who had insisted on being recognised as a separate clan. They refused to fight if a settlement could be reached peacefully, however unfavourable to Clan Chattan, given that the MacIntoshes had already failed to settle the disputed lands of Glenloy and Locharkaig through the use of force. Indeed, they had been held for generations by the Camerons of Lochiel.

Then John Campbell of Glenorchy, the future Earl of Breadalbane, arrived on the scene with a force of two or three hundred men. Armed with the full authority of Archibald Campbell, ninth Earl of Argyll, acting as Justice-General of Argyllshire, he avoided conflict by declaring that he would act impartially against whichever chief refused to settle. Lachlan MacIntosh of Torcastle was forced to accept only three quarters of what he had been offered only a month previously, augmented by the trifling sum of 500 merks. Although he was reluctant to accept, the leading gentry of Clan Chattan decided they were no longer prepared to 'venture their lives in this quarrel'. The ritual exchange of swords between Ewan Cameron of Lochiel and Lachlan MacIntosh of Torcastle on 25 September 1665 brought their ancient quarrel to its final conclusion.

In reality, however, Ewan Cameron of Lochiel was quite unable to find the money required, since he defaulted after paying the first instalment. It was left to the Earl of Argyll to advance Lochiel the agreed price, despite the burden of his own debts. Lochiel had to concede in return that he held his lands under the feudal superiority of Argyll. Moreover, he lost possession of Ardnamurchan and Sunart, which he had held from Argyll on wadset, while he was forced to surrender his own feudal superiority over Glengarry's lands in Knoydart. Finally, Glengarry also lost his wadset over the MacDonalds of Keppoch. It was immediately redeemed by Lachlan MacIntosh of Torcastle after he received the first payment of the purchase price from Argyll. Such were the complexities of the financial transactions among the Highland proprietors.

Highland Caterans

Yet the resolution of such feuds did not end the lawlessness of the Highlands. It continued to concern the Privy Council for the next twenty years, until more serious matters intervened. In fact, arguments between Highland magnates were among the least of its problems. An even greater threat to law and order were the bands of robbers and caterans, who often engaged in cattle-raiding, among other crimes. Among the most notorious was Donald MacDonald, the 'Halket Stirk' or 'Spotted Bullock', who was captured by the Laird of Grant late in 1660. But as his captive was a leading clansman among the MacDonalds of Keppoch, Grant feared the anger of his MacDonald kinsmen, should his prisoner suffer the full penalty of the law. Instead, Donald MacDonald was released on the security of £12,000 Scots, advanced by his namesake Donald MacDonald, heir to Sir James MacDonald of Sleat. Thereafter, the 'Halket Stirk' simply resumed his lawless career, seizing lands in Rannoch from Sir Alexander Menzies of Weem in 1670 at the head of an armed party, among whom were his own clansmen and a contingent of MacGregors. Most likely, they were resisting eviction by Menzies as their landlord. However, Donald MacDonald of Sleat was judged responsible, and he was summoned to Edinburgh, and briefly imprisoned, together with five other landowners who also had links with Lochaber. The incident was eventually resolved in 1672 after Aeneas, Lord MacDonnell and Aros, had accepted responsibility for the conduct of the 'Halket Stirk' – who simply resumed his lawless ways. His sons were still active in the 1690s.

Another notorious outlaw was Patrick Roy MacGregor, whose actions were even more savage than those of his more famous namesake Rob Roy MacGregor in the early years of the eighteenth century. Disappointed in the promise made to him in 1645 by James Graham, Marquis of Montrose, that Clan Gregor would be restored to their former lands of Glenlyon, Rannoch and Glenorchy, Patrick Roy MacGregor now terrorised the North-East, and especially Strathspey. He was eventually captured while attempting to extort blackmail or protection money from the burgh of Keith. He was first put to torture by the boot 'for the discovery of the many herschips [acts of plunder], thefts, slaughters and murders' he had committed. He was found guilty of such acts with his accomplice Patrick Drummond, and they were sentenced to death by hanging, but only after their right hands had been cut off.

Their execution was postponed several times by the Privy Council, perhaps at the urging of the Earl of Aboyne, tutor to his grand-nephew George Gordon, fourth Marquis of Huntly. It was suspected that the noble house of Huntly had employed Patrick Roy MacGregor as the head of its covert operations in launching illicit raids against its opponents. Indeed, Patrick Roy MacGregor had hanged some gentlemen whom he had kidnapped, apparently to satisfy the Earl of Aboyne, and not just because they had acted as witnesses against him. Soon after the final date for his execution was set, Patrick Roy MacGregor escaped from prison, only to be recaptured in 1668, when he was finally 'justified by the law'.

Commission of the Earl of Atholl

Faced with such endemic disorder, the Privy Council eventually gave a commission in 1667 to John Murray, second Earl of Atholl, with powers to apprehend by force all known lawbreakers. Already, Archibald Campbell, ninth Earl of Argyll, had been permitted to raise a watch of sixty men in Argyll for one year to defend his own country from robbers. Now, Atholl was given powers to raise an armed force of 150 men as an Independent Company. They would keep a constant watch in the shires where lawlessness was rife, guarding the passes into the Lowlands around the fringes of the Highlands, stretching from Inverness in the north to Dumbarton in the south, as well as patrolling the braes. Atholl was granted £24,000 Scots for his expenses in undertaking this commission.

Other watches were established for Banff with twenty-four men, for Cowal with twenty men under the command of James Graham, second Marquis of Montrose, and for the shires of Stirling and Dumbarton with sixty men. Argyll's own commission was extended, while further north Kenneth MacKenzie, third Earl of Seaforth, received a similar commission to Atholl's. The Privy Council thus formalised a practice apparently put into effect from the very beginning of the Restoration regime, deploying such Independent Companies for pacifying the Highlands. Later they would be known from their drab garb as the Black Watch. Already, the Privy Council had authorised the quartering of regular troops on all landowners who had failed to pay excise and other duties in Argyll, Inverness, Ross, Caithness and Sutherland.

Although it was reported to the Privy Council in February 1668 that the Highlands were 'kept quiet and free of all depredations', Atholl fell from favour early in 1669. Indeed, he was suspected of employing dubious methods to keep the peace, since it was said that 'the thieves were only quiet because they were employed to keep the rest from stealing; and for that had great liberties allowed them'. Indeed, the policy of making such Highland magnates as Atholl legally responsible for paying compensation to the victims of lawlessness was counter-productive. They simply failed to complain of their losses for fear of arousing the anger of such magnates, who were often their own landlords.

Sir James Campbell of Lawers was appointed in Atholl's place, and his commission renewed every year until 1674. Although a kinsman to the Earl of Argyll, he was recommended to the Privy Council since 'he has no dependence but upon the King's favour and the Council countenancing him, for all the great men of the Highlands hate him, especially his chief'. Not only was he paid £36,000 Scots each year for his services, but he was also given a bounty of £240 Scots for every notorious criminal he apprehended. He was also directed by the Privy Council to take bonds of surety from the clan chiefs and their leading gentry to ensure that they would pay all the taxes they owed the government, as well as honouring their promises to keep the peace. It seems that this action was needed, since a contingent of footsoldiers had met with armed resistance when sent into Lochaber to collect arrears of taxes in January 1669.

Two years later, in 1671, Lawers was ordered to evict the 'Halket Stirk' from the estates of Sir Alexander Menzies of Weem. A company of regular troops over 200 strong was dispatched at the same time to Lochaber to prevent any further disorder, but they were given as their main priority the collection of excise and other taxes from recalcitrant landowners as they marched from Stirling to Inverlochy. Eventually, in 1674, Lawers relinquished his command for financial reasons, when he was replaced by Major George Grant, Deputy-Governor of Dumbarton Castle, who held the position for the next three years. After his finances had recovered, Lawers then received back his original commission, now acting along with Aeneas, Lord MacDonnell and Aros, chief of Glengarry, in command of the Independent Company.

Regime of Lauderdale

The repressive regime now being enforced in the Highlands was partly a consequence of the religious unrest that had broken out in the Lowlands. It reached its first crisis point in 1666, when 900 men, badly armed but convinced that the 'horses and chariots of Israel' would fight for the Lord, advanced on Edinburgh from south-west Scotland. They were met at Rullion Green in the Pentland Hills by a superior force under General Sir Thomas Dalyell, who killed fifty of their number in a sharply fought skirmish.

Another thirty-six were hanged as an example, while others were transported to the plantations in Barbados. The reaction to such cruelties, and to the persecution of other suspects, forced the resignation of John Leslie, seventh Earl of Rothes, and led to the rise to supreme power in Scotland of John Maitland, second Earl of Lauderdale and a close confidant of Charles II. Maitland became Secretary of State for Scotland in 1667.

The uprising itself occurred while England was fighting a naval war over trading privileges with the Dutch republic, and its allies of France and Denmark, and this may well explain why it was repressed so savagely. It was even feared that Scotland might be invaded in 1667, when Argyll warned the regime: 'If, as God forbid, we should see an invasion, I fear the disorders [in the Highlands] would prove as great a retardment to his Majesty's affairs, as the fanatics [namely, the conventiclers].' To prove his own loyalty to the regime, which his Presbyterian views made suspect, Argyll even mounted an expedition into Kintyre, intending to root out any Covenanters among the Lowland colony settled there by his father.

Since religious dissent in the Lowlands was regarded by the Restoration regime as a far greater and more dangerous threat to its stability, challenging its very existence, it was inevitable that its priority was to contain the endemic lawlessness of the Highlands without committing too many resources. Apart from the commissions granted to the Earl of Atholl, and afterwards Sir James Campbell of Lawers, the Privy Council under Lauderdale now attempted other measures to pacify the Highlands. It took to reiterating the various acts of Parliament passed during the reign of James VI, insisting however futilely on the rigorous enforcement of all such acts to secure the peace of the Highlands. To secure their compliance, landlords and chiefs of the Highland clans were required to find caution from Lowlanders for the good conduct of their tenants and other dependants, and indeed for themselves. Later, they had to give bands of surety that they would pay the taxes they owed to the Government. Often such Highland chiefs dared not even show themselves in Edinburgh for fear of being arrested by their creditors, needing safe-conducts before they would appear each year before the Privy Council. Other chiefs, such as Ewan Cameron of Lochiel, complained that they could not find Lowlanders to give them caution, such was their reputation.

It was also forbidden for chiefs to travel through the Highlands accompanied by anyone except their own retinues of household servants. Evidently, it was feared that thieves and other 'broken men' often concealed themselves by posing as the members of such retinues, and it was even suspected that Highland chieftains aided and abetted them, particularly if they themselves profited from their activities. The difficulty faced by the regime in containing such disorder was compounded by the growth in cattle-droving as the market for exporting cattle to England expanded rapidly after 1660. Not only did the greater numbers of cattle passing through the Highlands offer a tempting quarry for caterans, but they could also disguise their own movements by claiming to be drovers going about their legitimate business. The Privy Council was evidently aware of this problem since it attempted to introduce a system for licensing all drovers in the 1670s.

The years of violence and disorder in the Highlands eventually reached a climax in the late 1670s, when Archibald Campbell, ninth Earl of Argyll, and his kinsman John Campbell of Glenorchy, embarked on a policy of territorial aggrandisement against the MacLeans of Duart and the Sinclairs, earls of Caithness. Such Highland feuds had often been driven in the past by competing claims over the ownership of land, when estates forfeited by the rebellious chieftains of Highland clans had been granted by charter to new landowners. They often only gained possession of such estates if they were originally held by clans which became divided among themselves, or which lacked heirs in the male line, so that their families were verging on extinction. But now another factor entered the complex tangle of Highland politics, namely debt.

Expenses under the Statutes of Iona

The policy of finding financial caution for their own good conduct had long been placed upon Highland landowners and clan chiefs, and latterly for the good conduct of their tenants and other dependants. They had also been summoned to appear each year before the Privy Council in Edinburgh by an Act of James VI, passed in 1594. Such an appearance every year before the Privy Council was also required by the 'Gentlemen of the Isles' under the Statutes of Iona in 1609, and under further enactments of the Privy Council in 1616. The requirement was later extended to other Highland landlords. Indeed, as already recounted, the Privy Council had renewed such a policy in 1661, although to little effect.

Such policies brought added expense to Highland landlords and clan chiefs, which they could often ill-afford. For example, in 1614, MacLean of Duart, MacDonald of Sleat, and MacLeod of Dunvegan had each to find 10,000 merks in security for keeping the peace, and another 3,000 merks that they would appear each year before the Privy Council. Lesser amounts were required of MacKinnon of Strathordle and MacLean of Lochbuie. Such sums were also surety that they would pay whatever they owed the government by way of feu duties and other taxes.

They also had the heavy expense of appearing each year before the Privy Council in Edinburgh. As Sir Rory MacLeod of Dunvegan complained to

James VI in 1622, he had to reside in the Lowlands for the better part of half a year, neglecting his estates. He was thus unable to 'defray my debts and pay my creditors that I may be free'. Further expenses were incurred in educating a chief's eldest son, or daughter if he had no sons, in the Lowlands, as stipulated by the Statutes of Iona. One-and-a-half-years' board in Edinburgh for his eldest son under the tutorship of Martin Martin, together with the employment of a servant, cost Iain Breac MacLeod of Dunvegan the sum of £720 Scots in 1690.

Closer contact with the government also meant that Highland chieftains often used lawyers to represent their interests, so incurring large bills for legal expenses. John MacLeod of Dunvegan owed £3,632 9s 4d to John MacLey of Edinburgh for legal expenses, covering the years 1636 and 1637, but he was only able to pay £3,361 14s. This left £373 17s 8d, which was added to his existing debt of £3,333 6s 8d. It meant that around a third of the rent from his estates was effectively mortgaged to his Edinburgh lawyer. Twenty years later, Sir James MacDonald of Sleat owed £2,974 19s 8d to Mr John Bayne, mostly for legal expenses for the year 1656. Several Highland landlords and clan chiefs even took to retaining the services of an Edinburgh lawyer on a permanent footing, thus incurring yet more expense.

Temptations of Conspicuous Consumption

Highland landlords and clan chiefs were also tempted into conspicuous consumption by trying to rival the sophisticated lifestyles of Lowland magnates, so emphasising their own status. The household accounts of the MacLeods of Dunvegan for the 1650s are especially revealing. A bill was presented in 1653 for £404 13s 8d by a Glasgow merchant, which included London cloth at £15 an ell, and twenty-four gold buttons, while another such account for 1656 came to £439 5s 8d, owed to a tailor in Edinburgh. The MacLeods were spending even greater sums in the 1690s, and they were not alone.

An account to Sir James Mor MacDonald of Sleat in 1674 came to more than £900, including £102 12s for taffeta. It is hardly surprising that he owed debts of more than £66,666 13s 8d at his death four years later in 1678. It took the united actions of fourteen of his kinsmen as the leading gentry of the clan, and themselves his principal creditors, who determined under the 'Oath of the Friends', to 'free this family of debt'. By excluding Sir James and his heir from administering their estates, they saved the family from almost certain bankruptcy.

The gaming tables of Edinburgh or London were another temptation. As Iain Lom chided Aeneas, Lord MacDonnell and Aros: 'You seem to me to be a long time in England, being ruined by gaming. I would prefer you in a coat and plaid, rather than a cloak that fastens; and that you should walk in a sprightly manner in trews made of tartan, and visit for a spell in grassy Glenquoich.' Indeed, Angus MacDonald of Glengarry lived the typical life of an absentee landlord after 1660, when he was granted an annual pension of £3,600 Scots for life, as well as his peerage. By then, he had accumulated debts of £148,000 Scots from his support of the Royalist cause, and now he adopted the habits and fashions of a courtier. His example was followed by several other Highland chiefs. Not content with life in Edinburgh, they often insisted on making their mark at the court in London.

Accumulation of Debts

But it was not just the adoption of Lowland ways that threatened bankruptcy. Admittedly, Donald MacKay, first Lord Reay and Chief of MacKay, had incurred great expenses at the court in London before 1638. However, by undertaking to recruit a regiment for service in the Thirty Years' War at his own expense, expecting to be reimbursed, he had greatly increased his financial difficulties. By 1637, his debts came to £102,912 Scots, which was more than three times the annual rental from his estates in Strathnaver. Moreover, as an avowed Royalist after 1638, many of his creditors were staunch Covenanters. Among them was John Gordon, thirteenth Earl of Sutherland, who provoked a rent strike by MacKay clansmen in Strathnaver, which lasted from 1642 until the death of Lord Reay seven years later.

Then MacKay's son John, second Lord Reay, accumulated further debts through his own support of the Royalist cause, adding another £80,000 Scots to his debts by the time Charles II was restored to his throne in 1660. More than £30,000 Scots was awarded against him in reparation for damage caused to lands belonging to the Earl of Sutherland. His debts took another twenty years to clear, and then only with the help of his leading clan-gentry, not just from the MacKays of Strathnaver but also from the Munros of Fowlis.

Equally, other Highland chiefs blamed their indebtedness on their support for the Royalist cause. John MacDonald of Clan Ranald had already found security for his debts of £22,000 Scots, by mortgaging his estates in Moidart and Arisaig in 1633, when he was first forced to admit the feudal superiority of the Campbells, earls of Argyll, under Lord Lorne. Then he became deeply involved with his son Donald MacDonald in campaigning with Alasdair MacDonald after 1644, retiring to the safety of their own estates after his son had finally returned from Ireland in 1649. Their estates were forfeited, and they took little part in the Highland resistance to the Cromwellian occupation of Scotland. Even so, they still had debts in excess of £73,000 Scots by

1660, secured by mortgaging their estates on South Uist, Eigg and Canna. Their debts 'left them always in distress, and their posterity'. Yet in 1669, despite being encumbered with such debts, Donald MacDonald of Clan Ranald was presented with a bill for more than £700 for expensive cloths, lace, French ribbon and silver buttons. By 1674, Archibald Campbell, ninth Earl of Argyll, had gained feudal superiority over all the estates of Clan Ranald by buying up such debts.

The MacLeods of Dunvegan likewise accumulated debts after John MacLeod had inherited debts of £12,172 Scots on his father's death in 1626. Despite increasing the rents on his estates, he left debts of £66,700 at his death in 1649 through his commitment to the Royalist cause. Afterwards, his son Rory the elder not only incurred fines of £30,000 Scots by opposing the Cromwellian regime, but he was also a 'prodigal, vitious [corrupt] spend-thrift'. Even increasing the rents upon his estates did not prevent his debts from mounting to £129,000 Scots when he died in 1663.

Such debts were only reduced by good management to £41,360 Scots by the time his brother John MacLeod had died in 1693. He had to underwrite loans in excess of £29,000 Scots during his lifetime, and to accept the superiority of Archibald Campbell, ninth Earl of Argyll, over his lands of Glenelg. But he was succeeded by his son Rory MacLeod the younger, who was another wastrel and a habitual absentee from his estates. His spendthrift ways ran up debts of more than £45,000 Scots during the later 1690s.

Argyll's Financial Difficulties

The problem of servicing debts was particularly acute with the Campbells, earls of Argyll. As the foremost supporter of the National Covenant, Archibald Campbell, eighth Earl and Marquis of Argyll, was promised more than £333,024 Scots by the Parliaments of Scotland and England. The sum was intended to pay for his services against Charles I, and for all the losses he had suffered since 1638, but the money was never paid. However, he was granted the estates belonging to George Gordon, Marquis of Huntly, when they were forfeited by the Covenanting regime at the time of Huntly's execu-tion in 1649. After Argyll was executed in 1661, his estates were forfeited, and George Gordon, ninth Earl and fourth Marquis of Huntly received back his lands, as already mentioned in connection with the Keppoch murders. But when Argyll's son Archibald, now recognised as the ninth Earl of Argyll, was restored to his father's estates in 1663, he not only lost Huntly's lands but he was still held responsible for the debts contracted by his father against these lands. Without the revenue from Huntly's lands, Argyll was quite unable to pay off his debts. Indeed, he inherited debts in excess of

£360,000 Scots, owed to his father's creditors, along with another £232,101 Scots of debts which he had contracted jointly with his father. All told, his debts were nearly £600,000 Scots, equivalent to more than eighteen years' rents from his estates.

Faced with such a burden of debt, and pressed by his creditors, who wanted him to sell off his estates, Argyll increased his rents fourfold over the twenty years from 1665, when his estates were fully restored to him. They eventually brought him in £61,327 Scots at the time of his execution in 1685. Moreover, acting under the patronage of John Maitland, second Earl of Lauderdale, he embarked on legal action in 1669 to restore his own finances, exploiting his hereditary position as Justice-General of Argyll and the Isles. Since his own courts at Inveraray heard all criminal and civil cases, apart from treason, Argyll could act quite unscrupulously to protect himself from his creditors while using all his judicial powers to squeeze money from his debtors. Moreover, despite the burden of his own debts, Argyll bought up the debts of others, hoping to profit by a ruling by the Privy Council that all debts had to be secured against the possession of land. It was the ruthless pursuit of his legal rights, 'forced upon him by dire necessity', that so alienated the other Highland clans, and especially the MacLeans of Duart.

Action against the MacLeans of Duart

Although they held their lands in Mull, Ardgour, Morvern and Jura from the Crown, the MacLeans of Duart were foremost among the Highland clans owing substantial amounts of money to the earls of Argyll. Already seriously indebted in 1637, it was the arrears in taxes owed by Sir Lachlan MacLean of Duart to the Covenanting regime that eventually precipitated their downfall. Their debts were first purchased by Archibald Campbell, eighth Earl and Marquis of Argyll. He held Sir Lachlan MacLean a prisoner until he acknowledged that he owed Argyll a grossly inflated sum, said to be £60,000 Scots. Matters were made worse by Lachlan's son Sir Hector MacLean. He made an agreement with the Marquis of Argyll, hoping to protect his lands in Mull from Campbell attack before the battle of Inverkeithing, where he was killed fighting for the Royalist cause. Even after Charles II was restored in 1660, this debt was not written off. It now amounted to £121,000 Scots, or so Argyll claimed. Foolishly, the MacLeans rejected Argyll's offer to assign these debts directly to his creditors, so that they might collect the money themselves. Pressed by his own creditors, Argyll was left with no choice but to enforce the payment of all the debts owing to him.

By 1669, the ninth Earl of Argyll was pursuing Hector's son and heir Sir Alan MacLean of Duart through the courts for repayment of this debt, which had almost doubled over the previous decade. Meanwhile, Argyll exerted his influence on the government under Lauderdale to grant him a charter to the MacLean estates, originally held from the Crown, while encouraging his followers to settle upon isolated MacLean outposts, such as the Garvellach Islands, virtually by right of conquest. Argyll himself undertook provocative expeditions to dive for treasure from the Spanish galleon sunk off Tobermory Bay. Keeping up the pressure, he then imposed an excessive land tax upon Mull, and quartered troops upon the MacLean lands when it was not paid.

Argyll's efforts were opposed not just by the MacLeans themselves, but by the MacDonalds of Keppoch and Glengarry, the MacDonalds of Glencoe, and the Camerons of Lochiel, who all sent men to Mull in the late 1660s to stiffen MacLean opposition to a Campbell takeover. Highland politics were once again becoming dangerously polarised, as the anti-Campbell clans built a confederacy to oppose Campbell hegemony. Then, early in 1674, Argyll had a stroke of good fortune, when Sir Alan MacLean of Duart died, leaving only his four-year-old son John as his heir.

Attempts to Invade Mull

Archibald Campbell, ninth Earl of Argyll, now planned an armed expedition against Mull, buying ammunition and provisions and summoning his leading gentry to meet him at Inveraray. In response, Lachlan MacLean of Brolas seized and fortified Duart Castle with his own clansmen, while provisioning it with cattle lifted from the surrounding countryside. Summoned before the justice-court at Inveraray, held under the jurisdiction of Argyll himself, it is hardly surprisingly that he declined to appear. The Privy Council responded by issuing letters of fire and sword to Argyll, since the armed resistance of the MacLeans was effectively an act of rebellion against the Crown. The government thus gave its official sanction for Argyll to embark on his first expedition against the MacLeans of Mull in pursuit of his private interests.

Argyll was accompanied on his expedition to Mull by the Campbell chiefs of Glenorchy, Cawdor, and Lochnell, while the government provided 500 troops to augment 1,800 of Argyll's own clansmen. They included contingents from the Stewarts of Appin, the MacDonalds of Clan Ranald, and the Camerons of Lochiel, whose chiefs all held their lands under the feudal superiority of Argyll. The expeditionary force landed in three places on Mull and Iona. Lachlan MacLean of Brolas drove his own stock into the hills for safety, after cattle were ruthlessly hamstrung by the Campbell forces to deny food supplies to the MacLeans. Duart Castle was retaken, and an agreement reached after Glenorchy and Lochnell had persuaded Argyll to negotiate with the rebels.

But over the following winter the MacLeans came to suspect Argyll's real intentions, after he had obtained letters of eviction against Hector MacLean of Torloisk, joint tutor to the young John MacLean of Duart, and several hundred lesser tenants on the island of Mull. Torloisk himself remained watching events on the sidelines, like the MacLean chiefs of Lochbuie and Coll. However, their sons joined Brolas in his rebellion against Argyll, and he was also supported by the MacLean chiefs of Kinlochaline and Ardgour on the mainland. Together, they swore a league with other MacLean gentry to resist Argyll, garrisoning the formidable fortress of Cairnburgh in the Treshnish Islands, and occupying the island of Tiree. When Argyll went to Mull in April 1675 to claim what was due to him, he was repulsed by a large party of MacLean clansmen in an armed standoff.

Argyll now obtained another commission of fire and sword from the Privy Council, while Lachlan MacLean of Brolas sought the assistance of Aeneas, Lord MacDonnell and Aros, chief of Glengarry. By September 1675, Argyll had assembled an expeditionary force of 1,500 men at Dunstaffnage, which now included regular troops supplied by the government. He then started to ship them to Mull across the Firth of Lorne in order to reinforce the Campbell garrison in Duart Castle. They still included the MacDonalds of Clan Ranald, and the Campbell forces were now also joined by the MacLeods of Dunvegan.

Alliance of Lochiel with Lord MacDonnell

The Camerons of Lochiel were also expected, but Ewan Cameron suddenly wrote to Argyll, saying that his clansmen would not serve under him to suppress the rebels. Instead, they appeared with their chief in the ranks of Aeneas, Lord MacDonnell and Aros, swelling his numbers to 1,100 men in support of the MacLeans. Together, they crossed the Sound of Mull from Morvern, hoping to 'mediate' in the quarrel. Then a storm arose, scattering the boats Argyll had sent to land reinforcements elsewhere on Mull. Forced to admit defeat for the time being, Argyll withdrew to the mainland, where he stationed 900 men at various points along the coast to protect Argyllshire and its off-shore islands from any raids.

Even so, the Camerons spent the next winter in plundering Ardnamurchan, Lorne, and Lismore, until Ewan Cameron of Lochiel called a halt. Other attacks were launched by the MacLeans against the Garvellachs, where fifty-two cows, twelve stirks, 120 sheep, several clothes chests, thirty stones of butter and forty bolls of victuals were carried off, together with brass and ironwork to the value of £436. This included one great cauldron worth £40, four pans worth £12, iron pots worth £40, ironwork worth £12, twelve silver spoons worth £80, and four silver dishes worth £100. The raid left destitute the thirty-two inhabitants on the islands. Another raid on the lands of Migharie and Carwallan carried off 1,300 sheep, one hundred and sixty-one horses, five hundred goats, two hundred bolls of corn and twenty-four bolls of bere (barley).

Stalemate ensued over the next two years, when Aeneas, Lord MacDonnell and Aros, sent a large force of MacDonalds and Camerons each year to Mull, so forestalling any action by Argyll against the MacLeans. He evidently hoped by this means to be recognised as the head of Clan Donald in a confederacy against Argyll, but Sir James MacDonald of Sleat remained neutral, while Donald MacDonald of Clan Ranald still honoured his obligations to the Earl of Argyll. However, the other great magnates in the Highlands became so alarmed by the 'ambitious grasping' of Argyll that Lord MacDonnell and Aros was joined by Kenneth MacKenzie, third Earl of Seaforth, John Murray, second Earl and Marquis of Atholl, and John MacLeod of Dunvegan in 'a combination to bear him down', or so it was reported in 1676.

The armed standoff between Argyll and Lord MacDonnell now encouraged widespread disorder, which threatened to get out of control. Early in 1676, Lochaber men were raiding Badenoch, Strathspey and Glen Urquhart, while the MacDonalds of Clan Ranald attacked the upland districts of Moray during July. Later that year, Camerons raided Argyll's estates in Lorne, while other bands of Camerons and MacDonalds, joined by the 'Halket Stirk', struck south into Perthshire, where the MacNabs joined them in raiding as far afield as Fife. Sir James Campbell of Lawers was even kidnapped for a ransom, and only obtained his release, and the subsequent execution of his captors, by forging a letter of remission.

Actions of the Privy Council

The government reacted early in 1677 by renewing its commission of justiciary to Sir James Campbell of Lawers, so replacing Major George Grant in this office. He was given full powers to apprehend

> all thieves, sorners, and broken men, committers of theft, robbery, murder, depredations, fire-raisings and other such crimes tending to the disturbance of our peace, where any of the said persons may be found in the country or in any burgh within the shires of Inverness, on the south side of Ness, Nairn, Moray, Banff, Aberdeen, Mearns, Angus, Perth, Argyll, Clackmannan, Menteith, Stirling and Dumbarton.

Inverlochy Castle was to be repaired, and a garrison installed. Argyll and

Glenorchy were appointed to a justiciary court, along with the Earl of Moray and Lord Aboyne. Later that year, Sir James Campbell of Lawers was joined in his office by Aeneas, Lord MacDonnell and Aros, as already mentioned, perhaps in an attempt to counterbalance the Campbell interest.

Argyll's campaign against the MacLeans was disrupted early in 1678 by the dispatch of the 'Highland Host' to contain religious dissent in the Lowlands, as recounted in the next chapter. But later in 1678, more than 100 landlords, clan chiefs and heads of families were summoned to Inverlochy to give yearly bonds for their good behaviour. The move was evidently intended to paralyse Argyll's opponents by breaking the confederacy against him, since among their number were MacDonald of Keppoch, MacIain of Glencoe, Stewart of Appin, and MacPherson of Cluny. Meanwhile, Archibald Campbell, ninth Earl of Argyll, and John Campbell of Glenorchy were given commissions to raise two regiments of foot as two more Independent Companies, each consisting of 150 men. They were placed under the command of Colonel James Menzies of Culdares and Sir James Campbell of Lawers.

However, it was only late in 1678 that Argyll finally took the initiative against the MacLeans, reinforced with troops and ammunition from the government. Already, Ewan Cameron of Lochiel had changed sides again, bought off by the Earl of Argyll, who cancelled a debt of 40,000 merks against him. As the MacLeans wryly commented: 'Ewan has lost his God, but the Earl his money.' Argyll landed on Mull with 1,500 men in mid-December 1678. Meeting no resistance, he soon held the whole island, after capturing MacLean of Lochbuie. He agreed to pardon the lesser tenants on generous terms, but not the tacksmen, who held their lands directly from the MacLean chiefs. Meanwhile, Argyll's brother Neil Campbell invaded the mainland opposite Mull, where Lochiel joined him with 400 Camerons, forcing MacLean of Ardgour to take refuge in Kinlochaline Castle. But the MacLeans and their allies were not cowed, since Lachlan MacLean of Brolas launched cattle-raids against Mull from his refuge on the island-fortress of Cairnburgh, while MacDonalds, Stewarts, Camerons and MacCouls raided Mull from the mainland.

Lord MacDonnell in Rebellion

Argyll now made a political blunder in the aftermath of the 'Popish Plot' in England. The work of Titus Oates, it revealed what was supposedly a conspiracy to murder Charles II in order to place his Catholic brother James, Duke of York, upon the throne. By reviving fears of 'popery', it precipitated the Exclusion Crisis of 1679–81, when Parliament at Westminister attempted to exclude James from the throne on the grounds of his religion. Calling upon all Catholics in Scotland to disarm, the Privy Council incurred the wrath of Aeneas, Lord MacDonnell and Aros, who defied its orders. Argyll was thus able to obtain a commission in April 1679 to disarm Lord MacDonnell and his fellow Catholics, among whom were MacDonald of Keppoch, and the still-defiant MacLean rebels, apparently never thinking that it would revive the anti-Campbell confederacy of Highland clans, who feared that they would be 'forever ruined and enslaved by him'.

Soon afterwards, the MacLeans recaptured Mull, where the regular forces under Argyll were now reduced to starvation, such were the difficulties of supplying them with meal from the mainland. Then the rebels crossed to Lochaber on the mainland to reinforce the forces of Aeneas, Lord MacDonnell and Aros. By now, they were around 2,000 strong, including the MacDonalds of Glencoe and the men of Rannoch. Advancing south of Loch Leven to the Braes of Glencoe, they threatened Argyll, now occupying Kilchurn Castle at the head of Loch Awe.

An armed conflict looked almost inevitable, since as Campbell of Lawers commented in a letter to Glenorchy: 'In all appearance the E. A. [Earl of Argyll] will not cease till the Highlands be in a combustion.' Indeed, Argyll withdrew to Inveraray, intent on raising more forces to confront Lord MacDonnell and the MacLeans. But the rebels only advanced to Beinn Buidhe near the head of Loch Fyne, before they fell back north after raiding Glen Shira and Glen Aray. Indeed, not long afterwards, the MacLeans returned to Mull, leaving the MacDonalds to fight a rearguard action as Argyll advanced into Lochaber.

Surprisingly, Argyll now had the advantage, which he seized in sailing to Mull with the bulk of his forces, leaving the rest to hold Lochaber under the command of Ewan Cameron of Lochiel. He encountered little resistance on reaching Mull, where only Cairnburgh in the Treshnish islands remained in MacLean hands. Again, he offered generous terms to the lesser tenants, while dividing up Mull among his own Campbell tacksmen. However, the King's brother James, Duke of York, had by now arrived in Scotland, intent on preserving 'that ancient and Loyal Clan of the MacLanes'. On the King's urging, he forced Argyll to provide the young John MacLean of Duart with an income of £300 a year by granting him the island of Tiree, but all the other lands once held by his family were lost. Meanwhile, five new garrisons were established to reinforce the one already at Inverlochy. Two garrisons at Duart and Lochaline ensured the permanent dispossession of the MacLeans, while three other garrisons were placed on the mainland at Mingary, Dunollie and Barcaldine to protect the Campbell estates of Ardnamurchan and Lorne from any attack.

Chapter Ten

END OF THE RESTORATION
REGIME

While these events unfolded to his private advantage, Archibald Campbell, ninth Earl of Argyll, remained blind to a serious crisis in the nation's affairs. The 1670s had seen the penal laws against religious dissent flouted throughout much of the Lowlands of Scotland, despite the issuing of Indulgences to ministers prepared to compromise their Presbyterian principles. The government under John Maitland, now Duke of Lauderdale, eventually responded by passing repressive measures, which merely inflamed the situation by making martyrs of the Covenanters. They still refused to acknowledge the supreme authority of the King under the 1669 Act of Supremacy. Preaching at an armed conventicle in the field was now made an offence punishable by death. However, the clumsy attempt by Lauderdale to enforce religious conformity upon the landed gentry and their tenants precipitated a crisis in 1678.

The policy adopted by Lauderdale involved the taking of a bond from landowners, requiring them to prevent their families, domestic servants and tenants from attending conventicles. To enforce this policy, Lauderdale intended to quarter troops on landowners who proved recalcitrant, especially in the west. Seemingly, he even feared another Presbyterian uprising, since he called upon reinforcements from Ireland and the north of England. However, they were not deployed in the event, since he called upon what became known as the 'Highland Host', which mustered at Stirling on 24 January 1678.

The Highland Host

Since the irregular troops making up the 'Highland Host' were mostly drawn from the south-eastern fringes of the Highlands, the name itself is rather a misnomer. John Murray, second Earl and now Marquis of Atholl, raised more than 2,000 foot from 'his own lands, property and superiority', among whom were presumably the Robertsons of Struan and the Stewarts of Atholl. John Campbell of Glenorchy, recently created Earl of Caithness, raised nearly 1,600 foot. Among their ranks were the MacDonalds of Glencoe, whom he feared to leave behind where they might attack his lands. Smaller forces were raised by the Earl of Perth with more than 500 foot from Strathearn, and by the Earl of Mar with 700 foot from the Braes of Mar. The Earl of Moray raised 200 foot, which mostly came from his lands in Menteith.

All told, the Highlanders numbered around 5,000 men. They were augmented by another 1,000 foot from the Angus militia, and nearly 600 horse from other Lowland militias, mostly belonging to Atholl, Perth and Angus. Regular forces including a foot regiment and a cavalry troop brought the strength of the 'Highland Host' to slightly under 8,000 men. They first marched west to Glasgow, and then occupied the shires of Renfrew, Lanark and Ayr. Although well-armed, albeit with old-fashioned matchlocks, many of the Highlanders evidently lacked adequate footwear. The shoemakers' guild in Edinburgh was ordered to provide 2,000 pairs of double-soled shoes, and another 1,000 pairs were to be made in Glasgow. Several hundred more pairs would be needed in the weeks ahead.

Yet while the Privy Council authorised payment for the shoes, it was said that when the Highlanders began to return home early in March 1678:

> You would have thought by their baggage that they had been at the sack of a besieged city, and therefore when they passed Stirling Bridge every man drew his sword to show the world they had returned conquerors from their enemies' land, but they might as well have shown the pots, pans, girdles, shoes taken off countrymen's feet, and other bodily and household furniture with which they were loaded, and among them all none purchased so well as the Earls, Airlie and Strathmore, chiefly the last, who sent home money not in purses, but in bags and great quantities [as well as] bed clothes, wearing clothes, rug-coats, grey coats and the like.

All these goods were plundered indiscriminately from the Covenanting households on which they had lived at free quarter. The losses from Ayrshire alone were estimated at £200,000 Scots. Although they were meant to enforce the signing of the bond, and to disarm the western shires, leaving only gentlemen of quality in possession of their swords, they greatly exceeded their commission from the Privy Council. Indeed, their lack of military discipline, their poor command of the Scots language, and their religious convictions as staunch Episcopalians, if not Catholics, made the Gaelic-speaking Highlanders in particular quite unsuited to enforcing religious conformity, whatever the merits of such a policy.

Apart from the burgesses of Glasgow, most landowners resolutely refused to sign the bond, and the only practical result achieved was the demolishing of Presbyterian meeting-houses, and the burning of their timbers in sight of the populace. The Privy Council virtually admitted defeat when it sanctioned the withdrawal of the 'Highland Host' in March 1678. Little bloodshed was recorded apart from the single death of a Highlander in a brawl. Nevertheless, the behaviour of such a 'barbarous, savage people, accustomed to rapine and spoil', who were 'more terrible than Turks or Tartars', left a lasting impression upon Lowland Scotland. It reinforced the bitter memories of Highland savagery during Montrose's campaigns forty years earlier.

George Sinclair, Earl of Caithness

After the 'Highland Host' had returned home, John Campbell of Glenorchy went back to resume the struggle against the MacLeans on behalf of his kinsman, the Earl of Argyll. But first, in April 1678, he married Mary Campbell, sister of the ninth Earl of Argyll, and widow of George Sinclair, sixth Earl of Caithness. Ever since the 1660s, Glenorchy had been buying up the debts of her first husband, who had succeeded while still a child to the earldom of Caithness after the death of his great-grandfather in 1643. Encumbered by vast debts, the power and influence of the Sinclairs, earls of Caithness, was already broken. They were overshadowed in the north by the supremacy of the Gordons, earls of Sutherland, who had remained in the ascendant as fervent supporters of the National Covenant after 1638.

Thereafter, George Sinclair, sixth Earl of Caithness, had reaped the consequences of his marriage when his father-in-law Archibald Campbell, eighth Earl and Marquis of Argyll, was executed in 1661. Out of favour with the Restoration regime, George Sinclair had failed even to become sheriff of Caithness. He first quarrelled with William Sinclair of Dunbeath, now acting in his place as the sheriff-depute of Caithness, and then joined him in a commission of fire and sword against the MacKays of Strathnaver. Over the last two decades, the MacKays had taken advantage of the disturbed state of the country in raiding Caithness, after a MacKay from Strathnaver had been killed in 1649 in a fracas at Thurso.

But while the Privy Council authorised action against the MacKays of Strathnaver early in 1667, it was more than a year later that William Sinclair of Dunbeath put it into effect. Only then did he lead a raiding party, 1,200 strong, against the lands of Strathnaver, accompanied by George Sinclair, sixth Earl of Caithness. However, they greatly exceeded the terms of their commission when they kidnapped several gentlemen. Among them was William MacKay of Scourie, who died of ill-treatment at their hands.

George Sinclair, sixth Earl of Caithness, was summoned to Edinburgh, and briefly imprisoned in Edinburgh Castle. However, he soon obtained a remission, along with many others, pardoning him for 'making war on his Majesty's lieges, manslaughter, robbery, fireraising, and general oppression'. Meanwhile, William Sinclair of Dunbeath had escaped north from custody in Edinburgh, attacking a party sent to recapture him, and killing William MacKay's brother Hector. His murder left Hugh MacKay of Scourie as the sole survivor of his family. The Privy Council reacted by granting a commission of fire and sword against the Sinclairs, but realising that it might just make matters worse, it soon afterwards substituted a fine of 50,204 merks, equivalent to £33,469 6s 8d Scots.

Then in July 1669, John Campbell of Glenorchy was given a commission by the Privy Council to bring William Sinclair of Dunbeath to justice. Marching north with 300 men, including some regular troops, Glenorchy garrisoned Dunbeath Castle. But his expedition achieved very little, apart from holding a dozen Sinclair gentry captive for three months after they had refused to sign a bond swearing that they and their tenants would not shelter Dunbeath. Eventually, Glenorchy admitted defeat, and returned south, but his ill-treatment of the Sinclair gentry would be remembered in Caithness.

Dispute over Caithness's Inheritance

Soon afterwards, George Sinclair, sixth Earl of Caithness, ever credulous, was tricked by his distant kinsman Sir Robert Sinclair of Longformacus. He offered his services as an Edinburgh lawyer to buy up Caithness's debts at a discount from his many creditors. His true motives were only revealed when he proposed that he should receive all of Caithness's estates in return for paying him a small annuity. But John Campbell of Glenorchy had also been pursuing the same strategy, acting apparently on behalf of Argyll as well as himself. Then in 1672, Sir Robert Sinclair of Longformacus tried again to gain control of the Caithness estates. In response to this new threat, George Sinclair, sixth Earl of Caithness, who had no children, conveyed all his dignities, landed estates and hereditable jurisdictions at his death into the hands of John Campbell of Glenorchy, whom he now owed £3,800 sterling as his principal creditor, in return for an annuity of 12,000 merks, or £8,000 Scots.

When George Sinclair, sixth Earl of Caithness, died in March 1676, his title was claimed by George Sinclair of Keiss. He was a grandson of the fifth Earl of Caithness, but still a minor. However, John Campbell of Glenorchy had a legitimate claim upon his estates. Then in June 1677, favoured by the Duchess of Lauderdale, Glenorchy was created Earl of Caithness, and directed to assume the name of Sinclair, and to bear the arms of Caithness. A year later, in April 1678, he married the widowed Countess of Caithness to strengthen his position in the north. But already in September 1677, after coming of age, George Sinclair of Keiss had landed in Caithness, where he seized his family estates.

Crisis in National Affairs

John Campbell of Glenorchy, and now the erstwhile Earl of Caithness, could not retaliate immediately. He was first involved in the dispatch of the 'Highland Host' to quell religious dissent in the west of Scotland, and he was then involved in the aftermath of these measures. Indeed, the repressive steps taken against the Covenanters had merely made matters worse. Another brief rebellion by the Covenanters broke out hardly a year later, after Archbishop James Sharp of St Andrews was brutally murdered in full view of his daughter while crossing Magus Muir, just two miles east of the town. Hated by the more extreme Covenanters, his death at their hands on 3 May 1679 triggered an armed uprising in the west. The Covenanters first inflicted a minor defeat on government forces under John Graham of Claverhouse at Drumclog near the head of Strathaven, only to be defeated three weeks later on 22 June 1679 at Bothwell Bridge by an army of 10,000 men under Charles II's natural son James, Duke of Monmouth.

Threatened by Lord MacDonnell's forces in May and June 1679, Archibald Campbell, ninth Earl of Argyll, had ignored this crisis in the nation's affairs. Imperilled as he was in his own territories by a crisis largely of his own making, he pursued instead his own selfish interests, despite the Privy Council urging him to 'disentangle yourself from the expedition . . . against the rebellious people in the Highlands'. He paid no attention until he had finally crushed all resistance in Mull, and occupied the island. Only John Campbell of Glenorchy responded to the repeated appeals of the Privy Council to march against the rebels. He dispatched a force of 600 men which reached Stirling on the same day as Monmouth defeated the Covenanters at Bothwell Bridge.

Expeditions against Caithness

Meanwhile, after John Campbell of Glenorchy had failed in a legal action to regain control of Caithness over the summer of 1679, he ordered a small party of fifty men north in the guise of the Perthshire militia. En route, they plundered Sutherland indiscriminately before occupying Castle Sinclair in Caithness. But they were starved out within a fortnight by George Sinclair of

Keiss, who then seized full possession of the earldom, collecting the rents and exporting its produce. The erstwhile Earl of Caithness reacted by obtaining permission from the Privy Council in November 1679 to raise a force of 1,200 men to march north. But it was not until June 1680 that Glenorchy finally mustered his select force of Campbells, MacGregors, and MacIntyres, amounting to only five or seven hundred men, and captained by several of his Campbell kinsmen. Many were his own clansmen, but others were local militiamen as well as regular troops from the Independent Companies. Marching north, they were opposed by 300 men from Caithness and Sutherland, together with 100 townsmen of Thurso, reluctantly pressed into the service of George Sinclair of Keiss.

Glenorchy's intention was to avoid an armed confrontation at all costs. On reaching Caithness, he first marched towards Thurso. He then doubled back towards Wick, only to come under heavy cannon and musket fire near Spital. But he restrained his own forces, arguing that the rebels 'are all my own tenants and vassals'. After occupying Wick for the next four days, he was forced by lack of provisions to march out of the town on 13 July 1680. Still wishing to avoid an encounter with the rebel forces, who were poised on the high road to Thurso, he took a minor road further north, which crossed the Allt nam Mearlach, north of the Wick River. But his ruse was discovered by the rebel forces, who followed him as he marched north out of Wick.

Battle of Allt nam Mearlach

Threatened in his rear by the rebels who had loaded their cannon, John Campbell of Glenorchy had little option but to turn and fight. The first volley was fired against the Campbells, killing one man and wounding several others. After returning fire, the Campbell forces then charged the rebels, who almost immediately broke ranks and started to flee. Even though Glenorchy tried to restrain his troops, calling upon them to give quarter, the losses suffered by the Sinclairs over the next few minutes were 107 dead, if not more. They included a fifth of the Thurso contingent and a child, while another 100 men were captured. The pipe tune 'The Campbells are Coming' was composed in memory of this expedition.

As Paul Hopkins comments in his monumental study *Glencoe and the End of the Highland War*, bloodshed on this scale had been avoided in the Highlands ever since the restoration of Charles II. It was an extreme irony that the ever-conciliatory Glenorchy was its agent, rather than the ninth Earl of Argyll, always impetuous and aggressive. Even though John Campbell of Glenorchy now succeeded in occupying Thurso, where he started to collect his rents, he soon afterwards fell from favour, when Lauderdale was removed from office, after failing to contain the Covenanting threat in the Lowlands, or to curb the excesses of Argyll in the Highlands.

George Sinclair of Keiss successfully petitioned the Privy Council in 1681 to recognise his right to the earldom of Caithness as the grandson of George Sinclair, fifth Earl of Caithness. Sir John Campbell of Glenorchy had to relinquish his title, but he was created instead the first Earl of Breadalbane, while George Sinclair of Keiss became the seventh Earl of Caithness. After his death in 1698, the title reverted to other branches of the Sinclair family, who still hold the earldom at the present day.

James, Duke of York

Scottish politics was now briefly dominated by James, Duke of York, who was Charles II's brother and the future James VII of Scotland. He had come north during the course of the Exclusion Crisis in 1679, when he took the place of Lauderdale as the King's Commissioner in Scotland. He arrived to find the security of the country still seriously threatened by religious dissent after the Covenanters were defeated at the battle of Bothwell Bridge on 22 June 1679, while equally the climax of Argyll's campaign against the MacLeans of Duart had spread fear and tension throughout the Highlands. As substantial numbers of regular troops could not be spared from maintaining law and order in the Lowlands, the Privy Council in September 1679 ordered 400 men north to guard the passes leading from the Highlands. They were to prevent 'broken men' from taking advantage of the unsettled state of the country by raiding the Lowlands.

The policies pursued in Scotland by James, Duke of York, were evidently intended to ease his accession to the throne by favouring those who would support him. As far as the Highlands were concerned, Argyll was still suspect as the staunchly Protestant son and heir of the Marquis of Argyll, who had betrayed Charles I and caused his death. Moreover, by asserting his legal rights in such a relentless and vindictive manner, Argyll had alienated many of the Highland clans who had earlier supported the Royalist campaign to restore Charles II to the throne. Indeed, even though Argyll was now the chief agent of government policy in the Highlands, he had persistently abused his judicial powers and feudal superiorities in pursuing his own private interests. The 'loyal clans' were briefly to come into their own. Indeed, Ewan Cameron of Lochiel was knighted in 1681 by James, Duke of York, in recognition of his service to the Royalist cause in the 1650s.

Soon after arriving in Scotland, James, Duke of York, had written to Charles II in February 1680, explaining that the 'extraordinary favours and partialities formerly shown to the Lord Argyll, could neither be answered nor without much difficulty amended, since that family had been so much advanced and so much power put imprudently into their hands'. Evidently, James hoped to curb Argyll's powers, while rewarding those 'loyal clans' favourable to his own interests in the Highlands. Chief among them were 'the ancient and loyal clan of the MacLeans'. The Crown would earn their gratitude by paying off their debts to Argyll, whereas if 'the Earl of Argyll has the MacLeans' estate, he would be greater than it were fit for a subject to be'.

Yet James had good relations with Argyll, and he evidently intended at first that Argyll should share his powers on an equal footing with Huntly, Atholl and Seaforth. The Privy Council agreed in February 1680 to make these four great magnates responsible for maintaining the peace of the Highlands. They would each be paid £500 sterling a year to raise Independent Companies to control their own four quarters of the Highlands.

Nevertheless, pressure grew on Argyll to reach an agreement with his creditors, while surrendering some of his feudal superiorities and judicial offices. As the Duchess of Lauderdale wrote early in 1681: 'I wish the Earl of Argyll would sell his estates, so as his family may not be a prey to his enemies, who are too many, and may be too powerful, if he not take good and speedy heed.' Moves were made by Parliament to open an inquiry into Argyll's exercise of his judicial powers. James first agreed to such an investigation, and then withdrew his approval. He gave as his reason that it was no concern of Parliament to ask how Argyll had used the powers given to him by the Crown under the royal prerogative. Yet it perhaps suggested to Argyll that James was fearful of taking any action against him, since he now displayed 'the foolhardy and provocative arrogance of a man who believed himself invulnerable', to quote David Stevenson.

Argyll's downfall was quite possibly engineered by James, Duke of York, hoping to deprive him of all his hereditary jurisdictions and other offices, which he thought 'too much for any one Subject'. Recalled in July 1681, Parliament first passed the Act of Succession, which confirmed the hereditary right of succession to James, Duke of York, despite his religion, which was now avowedly Catholic. It then passed the Test Act, which required all members of Parliament and their electors, as well as every other holder of public office in Church and State, to take an oath of loyalty. It acknowledged the supremacy of the Crown in all matters temporal and spiritual, while upholding the 1560 Confession of Faith. Argyll had the temerity to propose during the debate that all the members of the royal family should also be required to take the oath, apart from James. This may well have given James good cause to fear that Argyll would follow the traditions of his family in championing an extreme Protestantism by opposing his own accession to rule as the Catholic king over a Protestant country.

Designed as a 'Test' to uphold the Protestant Church as established in Scotland under the Stuart monarchy, the oath of loyalty 'could hardly be taken without qualification by any conscientious man', since the 1560 Confession of Faith conflicted with the assertion of royal supremacy. Argyll took the oath of loyalty in November 1681, but 'only so far as it was consistent with itself, and that he meant not to preclude himself, in a lawful way, from endeavouring to make such alterations to Church and State as he might judge beneficial'. His words made a mockery of the oath, which was now a central tenet of royal policy in Scotland, as it had earlier been in England. By uttering these reckless words of outright defiance, however justified, Argyll laid himself open to his enemies. They insisted in Parliament that he should be arrested for so flagrant an act of open contempt, directed against the Crown. Brought to trial under the jurisdiction of his arch-enemy James Graham, third Marquis of Montrose, he was found guilty of treason, and condemned to death.

Yet even now it seems that James, Duke of York, did not contemplate Argyll's utter destruction. Instead, he intended that Argyll should be taught not to act with utter impunity against the interests of the Crown. Even though his life and lands were to be spared, however, James wrote to his brother in London, proposing 'to make use of this occasion to get him [Argyll] more into their power, and forfeit certain jurisdictions and superiorities which he and his predecessors had surreptitiously acquired, and most tyrannically exercised'. Charles II agreed, since he thought Argyll's powers were 'too much for any one subject, and was glad (he said) he had got them out of so ill hands'.

Argyll's conviction for uttering a single remark, however ill-judged in the circumstances, seemed a flagrant miscarriage of justice to many Scots, so making him a martyr to the Presbyterian cause. Indeed, the Test Act itself was a mistake, since it simply served to emphasise how widely the country opposed the succession of James, Duke of York. Several of the clergy resigned after refusing to take the oath, and Sir James Dalrymple of Stair, President of the Court of Session, and Alexander Fletcher of Saltoun, went abroad to exile in Holland. They were joined there by Argyll, who had escaped from captivity in Edinburgh Castle, disguised as a page to his step-daughter Lady Sophia Lindsay. Denounced as a traitor, he had first sought sanctuary in London beyond the jurisdiction of the Scottish courts, and then fled to Holland. He remained in exile at the court of William of Orange until his abortive rebellion against James VII in 1685.

Faced with his defection, Charles II had no alternative but to forfeit all of Argyll's lands and titles, just as he had done twenty years previously after the executuion of Argyll's own father in 1661. Yet although the feudal superiorities held by Argyll were forfeited along with all his other property, they were not annexed by the Crown. Argyll's vassals thus did not become directly dependent on the Crown as their feudal superior. As David Stevenson has emphasised, only after losing his throne in 1689 did James VII promise the Highland chiefs to 'free them from all mannar of vassalage and dependence on the great men their neighbours' so that they could be 'freed from the tyranny and oppression of these superiors' and 'have their sole dependence on the Crown'. Instead, Argyll's feudal superiorities were transferred to other Highland magnates, among whom was George Gordon, ninth Earl and Marquis of Huntly, and soon to become the first Duke of Gordon. He received Argyll's feudal superiority over Sir Ewan Cameron's lands in Lochaber.

Argyll's son Archibald, Lord Lorne, and afterwards the tenth Earl of Argyll, was not forfeited along with his father, but he received only an allowance of £15,000 Scots a year, and indeed his own title of Lord Lorne was forfeited. Otherwise, the revenues from the family estates were intended to pay off the debts of his father and grandfather, and to compensate those families who had suffered ruin for their support of Charles I in the 1640s.

Pacifying the Highlands

Even before Argyll's downfall, the earlier plans of the Privy Council for keeping the peace in the Highlands were abandoned. Instead of assigning the task to Argyll, Atholl, Huntly and Seaforth, James now proposed to disband the existing companies, replacing them with two new Independent Companies. He argued they should be composed solely of Lowlanders, recruited from the regular army. Being 'neutral and disinterested persons', they would, or so he argued, 'receive more universal obedience from and be more terrible to all of them [the clans] than any natives can be'. It was agreed in March 1681 that such standing forces should be stationed in different parts of the Highlands, wherever they could maintain themselves by living off the lands forfeited from the rebels, and especially their cattle and corn.

Evidently, this proposal was put into effect, since two companies of regular troops were ordered north by the Privy Council in September 1681. They were to quarter themselves on the country around Inverlochy and the head of Loch Ness, so that they could keep the peace and collect the taxes owed to the government. But only six months later, Sir Ewan Cameron of Lochiel had attacked the garrison at Inverlochy in February 1682 with four or five hundred of his clansmen. They stripped the regular troops of their clothes and weapons, leaving them to make their own way south to safety.

The Privy Council responded by establishing the Commission for Securing the Peace of the Highlands in August 1682. It consisted not of such great magnates as Argyll, Atholl, Huntly and Seaforth, but of seventy-five other gentry and lesser chiefs acting as Commissioners. Surprisingly, Sir Ewan Cameron of Lochiel was among their number, despite organising the attack on the government forces at Inverlochy by his clansmen, only six months earlier. He was joined by Alasdair MacDonald, now chief of Glengarry after the death in 1680 of his uncle Aeneas, Lord MacDonnell and Aros, and later by John Campbell of Glenorchy, first Earl of Breadalbane. By making such clan chiefs responsible for keeping the peace of the Highlands, James, Duke of York, laid the foundations for the overwhelming support that they would later give to the Jacobite cause.

In fact, four separate commissions were appointed for different parts of the country. Justiciary courts were to be held at Lochnaver for the counties of Caithness and Sutherland; at Kilcumein at the head of Loch Ness for the counties of Inverness, Nairn, Elgin and Cromarty; at Kincardine O'Neil for the counties of Banff, Aberdeen, Kincardine, and Forfar; and at Balquhidder for the counties of Perth, Stirling, Dumbarton, and Argyll. The Independent Companies were placed at the disposal of the Commissioners, and twenty-four men were assigned to escort them as they made their judicial circuits around their respective quarters.

Although the record is incomplete, only the body covering the southern Highlands from Perthshire to Argyllshire was apparently at all active, holding courts at Crieff, Balquhidder, Killin and Finlarig. Yet the Commission for Securing the Peace of the Highlands marked a significant change in policy by the government. It seemed the regime now wanted the active co-operation of the clan chiefs and their leading gentry, acting in a genuine spirit of conciliation in pursuing its policies towards the Highlands.

This was further emphasised by the decision to take bonds of surety from all the heritors in the Highlands, who held their estates by hereditary title, and not just from the more important chiefs and larger landowners. More than 500 such bonds were taken during 1683–4 in the southern district alone. Moreover, as these bonds were taken parish by parish, the clan chiefs no longer needed to appear each year before the Privy Council in Edinburgh with all the expense that entailed, and which they found especially onerous.

The taking of such bonds also gave official recognition to the landed status now enjoyed by the clan gentry. They had often gained their estates by advancing loans to their clan chief in the form of the redeemable mortgage known in Scots law as a wadset. This gave them a title to the land in question, but only until the loan itself was paid off from the rents charged on the land by the clan chiefs. However, as they became ever more saddled with debt, this often proved to be impossible. It forced the clan chiefs to transfer portions of their estates to the clan gentry as their creditors. They thus became landed proprietors in their own right, holding their estates under feudal charter from their former debtors and clan chiefs. It gave them a vested interest in maintaining law and order, as they were now responsible for the good conduct of their own tenants and dependants as landowners in their own right.

Even though the Commissioners gave the Privy Council glowing reports in 1684 of their apparent success in quelling disorder, Argyllshire was still suspected as a breeding ground for Campbell plots against the Government. After James Graham, third Marquis of Montrose, died in the same year, John Murray, second Earl and Marquis of Atholl, was appointed as Lord Lieutenant of Argyll in his place. Instructed by the Privy Council to arrest several leading Campbells, he raised a force of 1,000 of his own men in August 1684, and marched without any opposition into Argyllshire. After arresting Colin Campbell of Ardkinglas, who was suspected of supplying money to the exiled Earl of Argyll, he took bonds from the other gentry to appear before the Privy Council in Edinburgh. He then departed, leaving Inveraray garrisoned with a small force under his bailie, Patrick Steuart of Ballechin.

'The Killing Time'

Six months later, in February 1685, Charles II died and his younger brother James, Duke of York, was proclaimed James VII of Scotland. His brief reign ended with his flight in 1688 after his Protestant son-in-law, William of Orange, had invaded England. James VII did not take the Coronation Oath to defend the Protestant religion, and the indemnity he proclaimed on his accession did not extend to the Covenanters. Indeed, after two gentlemen of the King's bodyguard were murdered, Parliament declared the taking of the Covenants to be treason, while the mere presence of Presbyterians at conventicles in the field was also made punishable by death. The religious persecution of extreme Presbyterians, which had started even before James came north in 1679 as the Duke of York, now reached its horrendous climax, known as the 'Killing Time'. Among its victims were the members of the extreme sect known as the Cameronians, or the 'Hill Society'.

The sect itself was named after Richard Cameron, who had returned as an ordained minister from Holland in 1679, soon after the rout at Bothwell Bridge. He joined forces with Donald Cargill, and together they rode into Sanquhar on the first anniversary of the battle of Bothwell Bridge in 1680 at the head of twenty armed men. Nailing their Declaration of Sanquhar to the Mercat Cross, they had publicly excommunicated Charles II for his immorality, tyranny, and breach of the National Covenant, declaring war against him 'under the standard of Our Lord Jesus Christ, Captain of Salvation'. Richard Cameron was himself killed a month later in a skirmish with government dragoons at Airds Moss, north of Cumnock in Ayrshire, but his followers continued his godly crusade.

Among the Covenanters taken prisoner at Airds Moss was David Hackston of Rathillet in Fife, who had witnessed the murder of Archbishop Sharp of St Andrews in 1679. Hackston suffered execution in a most gruesome fashion, his hands first being cut off before he was hanged and disembowelled. His body was then dismembered, and his limbs displayed publicly at St Andrews, Glasgow, Leith and Burntisland. Donald Cargill remained at liberty until 1681, preaching fiery sermons against the King and his ministers, but eventually he too was captured and beheaded at the Mercat Cross in Edinburgh.

Revival of the Cameronians

Yet despite such executions, and the persecution of its followers, religious extremism still remained endemic in the south-west of Scotland. Indeed, the Cameronian sect was revived under the leadership of James Renwick, whose tract of October 1684 incited his followers to murder. Government officials, Episcopalian ministers, and anyone giving evidence against the Cameronians, all deserved punishment as the enemies of God. Thus justified, several murders took place among other attacks, and the government reacted with even more savage persecution, especially after the accession of James VII in 1685. Indeed, the decade as a whole witnessed perhaps 100 executions, often summary in nature, while perhaps the same number of people were hunted down and killed by government forces while worshipping in the field at the illegal conventicles.

Argyll's Expedition to Scotland

Such was the atmosphere of religious bigotry and intolerance when James VII succeeded to the throne in February 1685. Almost immediately, his rule was challenged in England by the armed rebellion of James, Duke of Monmouth, eldest son of Charles II by his liaison with Lucy Walters. Already exiled by his father, Monmouth joined forces with Archibald Campbell, ninth Earl of Argyll, and other Scottish exiles in Holland, all of whom were staunch Protestants. The two-pronged attack involved Monmouth landing in Dorset, while Argyll planned to invade his own territories in the west of Scotland to rally support against James VII from among his own followers.

Setting sail from Amsterdam on 2 May 1685, Argyll first reached the Orkney Isles with his flotilla of three small vessels, laden with arms, ammunition and provisions. But foolishly he allowed his physician and secretary to go ashore, where they were taken prisoner by the Bishop of Orkney, who alerted the government in Edinburgh to Argyll's presence. He then sailed for the Campbell stronghold of Dunstaffnage, arriving there on 13 May 1685. His younger son Colonel Charles Campbell landed to sound out his friends and vassals, only to bring back discouraging news. Even though Duncan MacDougall of Dunollie had just died, leaving no leader to oppose the insurgents locally, few leading Campbells were prepared to join their chief in his rebellion. More than a dozen of the Campbell gentry had already been ordered to Edinburgh, where they were detained, while others even refused to meet Argyll. Among the leading families, only Sir Duncan Campbell of Auchinbreck, Donald Campbell of Barbreck, who was Breadalbane's brother-in-law, Dugald Campbell of Kilberry, and the Campbells of Ellangreg joined Colonel Charles Campbell in raising perhaps 1,200 men from their own territories.

Argyll now sailed for Islay, where Patrick Steuart of Ballechin had already gone on government orders to disarm the tenants of Sir Hugh Campbell of Cawdor. Argyll then embarked for Campbeltown in the south of Kintyre. But he succeeded in raising very few men from among his own clansmen and tenants, apart from on Gigha, largely because his own financial difficulties had made him a harsh landlord. When he marched north from Campeltown to a rendezvous at Tarbert on 28 May with his son Charles Campbell, his forces consisted mostly of Lowland settlers from Kintyre, who shared his staunchly Presbyterian religion. Together, they could only muster 1,800 men.

Reaction of the Government

By this time, the government had mobilised its own forces. Leaving Edinburgh on 18 May, John Murray, Marquis of Atholl, raised 2,000 men, receiving some officers from the Earl of Mar's Regiment, among whom was Captain Kenneth MacKenzie of Suddie. Among the Campbells loyal to James VII was John Campbell, first Earl of Breadalbane, who reached Balloch on 20 May, declaring his intention of occupying his stronghold of Kilchurn Castle with his own men. Once there, he sent word to Patrick Steuart of Ballechin, who had returned to Inveraray after garrisoning several castles in Kintyre against the Campbell forces. Farther north, the northern clans were ordered to rendezvous on 9 June under the command of George Gordon, fourth Marquis of Huntly, who was now the Duke of Gordon, and Lord Lieutenant of the North.

By 30 May 1685, Atholl had marched to Inveraray at the head of 3,000 men, after meeting up with the Earl of Breadalbane. They were soon afterwards reinforced by more than 1,500 men from the Highland clans. Among them were the Robertsons of Struan, the Stewarts of Appin, the MacDonalds of Glencoe, the MacDonalds of Glengarry, Keppoch and Clan Ranald, the MacDougalls of Lorne, the Camerons of Lochiel, the MacIntoshes of Clan Chattan, and the MacLeans of Duart. Nearly all these clans had joined Montrose and Alasdair MacDonald in laying waste to the lands of Argyll in the 1640s. The Privy Council issued Atholl in secret with the brutal order: 'All men who joined [Argyll's rebellion], and are not come off . . . are to be killed, or disabled ever from fighting again, and burn all houses except honest men's, and destroy Inveraray and all the Castles . . . Let the Women and Children be transported to remote Isles.' Even if such a draconian order was subsequently rendered redundant by events, the government clearly viewed Argyll's rebellion as a serious challenge against the Crown, especially as he might well be joined in arms by radical Presbyterians from the Lowlands.

Argyll's Movements

Meanwhile, Argyll had shipped his own men to Bute, after Captain Kenneth MacKenzie of Suddie had repulsed an attempt by Colonel Charles Campbell to land in Cowal. Atholl now ordered Patrick Steuart of Ballechin to advance with 500 men to cut off Argyll's rear at Tarbert, while the rest of Atholl's forces stayed at Inveraray to prevent Argyll from escaping north. By now, Argyll had moved his camp with all his stores to Ellangreg Castle, situated on an island in Loch Riddon, just north of Bute. A few days later, English warships entered the Kyles of Bute, and Argyll was cut off from the sea.

Atholl only left Inveraray on 13 June to march around the head of Loch Fyne towards Glendaruel after he had learnt of this blockade by the English navy. His caution had allowed Argyll to escape east towards Loch Long, which he crossed late on the evening of 15 June to reach Rosneath and Garelochhead. By then, the Duke of Gordon was advancing with his own forces from the north towards Stirling, while other columns of government troops were massing in the Lowlands. Against the advice of his commanders, Argyll now insisted on marching into the Lowlands, hoping to reach Glasgow, where Presbyterian sympathies were strong.

Execution of Argyll

Argyll's rebellion against James VII came to an abrupt end at Kilpatrick on the banks of the River Clyde, where his forces, now numbering less than 500 men, broke up and dispersed on 18 June 1685. Argyll himself was captured near Paisley, and brought to Edinburgh. As he had already been convicted of treason in 1681, and condemned to death, the Privy Council abandoned any pretext of a new trial, resolving on the orders of James VII to put the existing sentence into effect. Argyll was beheaded at the Mercat Cross in Edinburgh on 30 June 1685, meeting his fate with great courage and dignity. Indeed, he was seen sleeping calmly two hours before the time set for his execution, and even on the scaffold, noticing that the block did not lie evenly, he pointed out the defect to a carpenter, so that it could be remedied.

Atholl was ordered to execute all the heritors among the rebel forces, who held their lands by inheritance, together with 100 of the principal men from among the tenants and commons. In the event, however, Argyll's death was followed by only another seventeen executions, which took place at Inveraray. Otherwise, the rebels did not suffer the savage persecution suffered by the English Puritans after the defeat of Monmouth's rebellion at the battle of Sedgemoor on 6 July 1685. Sir Duncan Campbell of Auchinbreck was forfeited along with thirty-five others, and perhaps 150 lesser men were transported, mostly to Jamaica, along with the survivors of 187 Covenanters, held in the notorious 'Whigs Vault' of Dunnottar Castle.

Last Battle of the Clans

The success of the government in suppressing Argyll's rebellion did not quell disorder in the Highlands. Indeed, the government forces indulged in widespread looting as they dispersed, and it was not just confined to the Highland clansmen. Even the Marquis of Atholl returned to Perthshire with trees uprooted from Argyll's plantations at Inveraray. Campbell territories were plundered indiscriminately throughout mid-Argyll, Cowal and Kintyre, especially where the Earls of Argyll had already planted Lowland settlers with their Presbyterian sympathies. It was not until 20 July 1686 that the Commission for Securing the Peace of the Highlands was restored, but it had little effect in reducing the widespread disorders that followed in the wake of Argyll's rebellion. The policy of co-operating with the clan elite was virtually abandoned as detachments of regular troops from Lowland regiments were dispatched north under the command of Lieutenant-General William Drummond, Lord Strathallan, to bolster the Independent Companies. Their presence merely made the disorder worse. Indeed, when the Commissioners ventured to hold a court at Inverlochy, Lochiel provoked a riot against them, making it an excuse to escort them from Lochaber for their own safety.

Then, the Privy Council in February 1688 renewed the commission of fire and sword given in 1681 to Lachlan MacIntosh of Torcastle against the MacDonalds of Keppoch, who still refused to accept him as their feudal superior. MacIntosh had already invaded their lands in 1682 with a force of 1,100 men, building a small fort at Keppoch, which was later captured and demolished by 'Coll of the Cows', who succeeded his father Archibald MacDonald of Keppoch in the same year.

Lachlan MacIntosh of Torcastle now obtained the support of government troops in his feud with Keppoch. Stationed at Inverness under the command of Captain Kenneth MacKenzie of Suddie, they brought his strength up to perhaps 1,000 men. However, the swollen waters of the River Spean prevented them from taking any action during July. Only on 4 August 1688 were they able to cross the river, and advance up Glen Roy. The forces under Coll MacDonald of Keppoch were rather fewer in number, perhaps amounting to 700 men, including the MacMartins of Letterfinlay, and a large contingent from the Camerons of Lochiel. But they had the advantage of height, drawn up on the shoulder of Maol Ruadh, which gave the name of Mulroy to the battle that followed.

As the invading forces under MacKenzie of Suddie advanced up the hill, the MacDonalds of Keppoch launched a classic Highland charge, firing a single volley before attacking their enemy in hand-to-hand fighting with swords and Lochaber axes. Heavy casualties were inflicted on both sides during the battle, which reportedly lasted an hour. Among the dead and wounded was Captain MacKenzie of Suddie, killed along with several leading members of Clan Chattan. Although government troops were involved, it proved to be the last private battle between the Highland clans.

The Privy Council in Edinburgh reacted by ordering north a company of 150 foot and sixty dragoons. Their orders were to lay waste to Keppoch, sparing neither man, woman nor child, or so it was later recorded. However, such reprisals were mostly avoided as the MacDonalds of Keppoch withdrew into the mountains with their womenfolk and children, although their stocks of corn were burnt and their houses destroyed. Then, a month later, the government troops were suddenly recalled to meet the threat of an impending invasion by William of Orange, which brought the reign of James VII to an end. Whig propaganda would later hail his overthrow as the 'Glorious Revolution'.

Background to the 'Glorious Revolution'

Despite the undoubted success in suppressing Argyll's rebellion, and indeed the more serious challenge of the Duke of Monmouth, James VII after his accession in 1685 adopted religious policies that were to destroy the Stuart monarchy. As an observer at the French Court later commented: 'Our good King James was a brave and honest man, but the silliest I have ever seen in my life.' Indeed, he seemed quite unable to appreciate the likely consequences of his actions, lacking any sense of the religious susceptibilities of his subjects, especially in England.

He was equally a poor judge of people. Thomas Bruce, Earl of Ailesbury, noted with irony: 'Those the King loved had no faults.' Given his own profession of faith, it is hardly surprising that he wished to grant religious and civil equality to his fellow-Catholics. But so blindly did he pursue this aim, however laudable to the modern mind, and with such disastrous results, that he destroyed the very alliance between the Tory Party and the Anglican Church which had kept his elder brother Charles II secure upon the throne against the plotting of the Whigs.

Birth of the Old Pretender

The final crisis only broke on 10 June 1688, when James VII's second marriage was blessed with a male heir. He was christened James Francis Edward Stuart, Prince of Wales. History would come to know him as the Chevalier St George, or the Old Pretender. His birth effectively disinherited James VII's eldest daughter Mary as the heir-presumptive. Born in 1662 of James's first marriage, and herself a Protestant, she was now married to William, Prince of Orange. He was not only James's son-in-law by this marriage, but also his nephew, since his mother was Mary Stuart, daughter of Charles I. Although his ancestral title came from Orange in the south of France, he now ruled over Holland as its *stadtholder* or governor.

Moreover, as an ardent Protestant ruling over a Calvinist country, William of Orange had spent the years since 1672 in a bitter struggle against Louis XIV of France and his expansionist policies in the Low Countries. Indeed, his marriage in 1677 to James's daughter Mary was an attempt to bring England into a wider alliance against France, which sought to unite the Catholic countries of Austria, Spain and even Rome itself with the Protestant countries of Holland and Germany. William's aim would be achieved by the 'Glorious Revolution' of 1688.

Invitation to William of Orange

It was James VII's blatant attempt to offer religious indulgence to dissenting Protestants as well as Catholics, suspending the penal laws against them, and admitting them to public life, including service as officers in the army, that proved the final straw. Matters came to a head on 30 June 1688 when seven bishops of the Anglican Church in England, among whom was the Archbishop of Canterbury, were acquitted of a charge of seditious libel against the Crown, after they had refused the King's command for their clergy to read a second Declaration of Indulgence from their pulpits. It provoked an alliance of seven Tory and Whig leaders, who wrote to William of Orange, urging him to intervene in the affairs of the kingdom.

They seemingly hoped that James VII could be persuaded of the error of his ways, and indeed William of Orange agreed after some delay to their invitation. He would come to England to ensure that all the pressing concerns of Church and State were settled by a free Parliament. But his terms were humiliating to James VII, involving as they did not only the calling of a 'free' Parliament, but also a declaration of war against France, and even a commission to investigate whether or not the infant Prince of Wales was legitimate.

William of Orange was only invited to England to remonstrate with James VII, but he perhaps came determined to depose his own father-in-law as King. Yet he evidently wished to be thought a liberator, not a conqueror. His own struggles with Louis XIV of France had reached crisis point, and soon afterwards culminated in the outbreak of the Nine Years' War (1689–97). He desperately needed the military and financial resources of England, and especially her navy, to defeat France. William of Orange embarked with an army of 14,000 men in a fleet of fifty vessels from Holland, carrying contingents from all over Protestant Europe. The fiction would later arise that his forces were simply intended as a personal bodyguard. But it was James VII who eased his passage down the English Channel under a 'fair Protestant wind' by spurning the protection of Louis XIV of France. Among the exiles accompanying him was Archibald Campbell, Lord Lorne, who would soon be restored to his title as the tenth Earl of Argyll.

Flight of James VII

When he landed at Torbay in Devon on 5 November 1688, William of Orange attracted little support at first, and it is not even clear how he expected to gain the throne. But James VII played into his hands, since he had what can only be described as a failure of nerve, variously described as the onset of syphilis or a stroke. His ever more bizarre and erratic behaviour was aggravated by almost incessant nosebleeds. Even though he had gathered together a large army, 40,000 strong, it had only marched as far west as Salisbury before its officers started to desert. Among them was John Churchill, afterwards Duke of Marlborough, and the Major-General of his army.

James VII himself fled back to London, where he ordered his forces to disband on 10 December 1688. By then, he had already sent his Queen and their infant son to safety in France, and he now resolved to escape the country. But while waiting for the tide after taking ship at Sheerness, he was detained by some fishermen. They suspected him of being a 'hatchet-faced Jesuit' before recognising him as the King. Sent back to London under a military escort by the Lord-Lieutenant of the county, much to the annoyance of William of Orange, he received an ecstatic welcome from the people.

Yet once again he resolved to flee the country, after failing to reach any accommodation with William of Orange, who remained cold and distant. James perhaps feared that 'there is but a little distance between the prisons and graves of Kings', seeing no reason to suffer the same fate as his father Charles I on the block. He received permission from William of Orange to go to Rochester, where he embarked for France on 23 December, arriving on Christmas Day 1688. He had effectively thrown away his Crown in an act of utter folly, along with the Great Seal, which he dropped into the waters of the Thames as he fled downriver.

The 'Glorious Revolution'

Meanwhile, William of Orange had entered London to take up residence at St James's Palace. The English Parliament was now recalled after new elections to sit as a Convention in the absence of the King. It declared that James VII had effectively abdicated by fleeing the country. Its first act was to draw up the Declaration of Rights, which did away with the Divine Right of Kings, as practised by the Stuart monarchy, by placing Parliament – however corrupt – above the Crown. Once they had given their assent to its provisions, the Parliamentary Convention then offered the throne on 13 February 1689 to William of Orange and his wife Mary, to rule as joint sovereigns, since William would not agree to act as Regent or Prince Consort. They were crowned on 11 April 1689. England would spend almost the next twenty-five years at war with France, apart from 1697–1702.

Once William of Orange had arrived in London, he was urged to accept responsibility for the administration of Scotland, where public affairs had lapsed into a state of near-anarchy. Indeed, most men of substance had hurried south to London on hearing that James VII had fled the country. Almost immediately, the Cameronians started to evict Episcopalian ministers forcibly from their parishes in the south-west of the country. Tradition has it that 200 were expelled with their families on Christmas Day 1688 in what became known as the 'rabbling of the curates', just as extreme Presbyterians had been expelled from their parishes in 1663. William of Orange responded by authorising a Parliamentary Convention to meet in Edinburgh, which it did after elections were held in mid-March 1689. But, intimidated by the presence in Edinburgh of well over 1,000 armed Cameronians from Glasgow and the West of Scotland, reinforced by Argyll's Highlanders, only nominally under the command of David Melville, third Earl of Leven, the new Convention's counsels were divided. Indeed, the loyalists who still supported James VII proposed to hold a rival Convention at Stirling.

The Parliamentary Convention

Almost as soon as it met in March 1689, the resolve of the King's supporters in the Parliamentary Convention was fatally weakened by a letter sent by James VII from Brest, where he was about to embark for Ireland. Lacking any sense of diplomacy, he condemned his opponents for abandoning their natural allegiance to the Crown. He even threatened them with 'infamy and disgrace . . . in this world and the Condemnation due to the Rebellious in the next'. He would only concede that a Parliament should be called to fulfil his 'existing promises' to his loyal subjects. By alienating nearly all his natural supporters in the Parliamentary Convention, he acted with 'almost unbeliev-able arrogance and ineptitude', to quote Bruce Lenman in his account, *The Jacobite Risings in Britain*. Only John Graham of Claverhouse, newly enno-bled as Viscount Dundee in the final weeks of the old regime, stood firm in still professing loyalty to James VII. But threatened by a plot against his life by the more extreme Cameronians, whom he had persecuted in the past, he fled from Edinburgh on 18 March 1689.

Claim of Right

A month later, now under the domination of the extreme Presbyterians, the Convention in Edinburgh adopted the Claim of Right, which was far more radical than its English equivalent. It declared that James VII had forfeited the throne of Scotland by refusing to take the Coronation Oath with its pledge to defend the Protestant religion. Along with his avowal of the Catholic religion, and his exercise of 'arbitrary despotic power', he was further charged with subverting the 'fundamental constitution of this Kingdom' and violating the laws and liberties of the nation. It resolved to offer the throne of Scotland instead to William and Mary, and three representatives were sent south to London to administer the Oath to the new King and Queen. Archibald Campbell, newly restored to his title as the tenth Earl of Argyll, represented the peers, while Sir Robert Montgomerie of Skelmorlie and Sir John Dalrymple, Master of Stair, acted for the other two Estates of the Scottish Parliament.

Divisions within the Country

Meanwhile, the Parliamentary Convention in Edinburgh instructed the clergy throughout the country to offer prayers for King William and Queen Mary. Many refused, especially in the north of the country beyond the Firth of Tay. They still felt bound in their consciences to the oath of allegiance they had given to James VII. By November 1689, the Privy Council acting under William Lindsay, Earl of Crawford, had expelled 182 clergy from their livings in what was an illegal purge, lacking any official sanction. Such loyalty to the Stuart dynasty formed the bedrock on which the Jacobite rebellions were founded, not just among many of the Highland clans, but throughout much of the country north of the River Tay. Only in the far north of Scotland did such clans as the MacKays, the Gunns, the Rosses and the Munros accept the new dispensation, influenced no doubt by the Presbyterian sympathies of the Earls of Sutherland. South of the Tay, Presbyterian strongholds were found, not just in Glasgow and far south-west, but elsewhere in the Lothians and the Borders, as well as in parts of Fife, Stirlingshire and Argyll.

Chapter Eleven

OUTBREAK OF
THE HIGHLAND WAR

When John Graham of Claverhouse, Viscount Dundee, took flight from Edinburgh, he spent the night of 18 March at Linlithgow. Then, on the next day, he rode past Stirling to reach Dunblane, where he conferred with Alexander Drummond of Balhaldie, son-in-law to Sir Ewan Cameron of Lochiel. Balhaldie was in fact a MacGregor forced to take another name. Later, he would be accepted as chief of the clan. He reported that Lochiel was even then mobilising a 'confederacy of the clans' in support of the exiled King, who had knighted him in 1681. Despite the appalling weather, Lochiel had already consulted Alasdair MacDonald of Glengarry, Donald MacDonald of Benbecula, tutor of Clan Ranald, and the leading MacLean gentry in Mull in the absence abroad of the young Sir John MacLean of Duart. Together, they had agreed to a rendezvous in Lochaber on 18 May 1689.

What prompted Sir Ewan Cameron of Lochiel to play the role of Alasdair macColla to Dundee's Montrose in support of James VII remains a matter for debate. There can be hardly any doubt that the chieftains of the western Highland clans were deeply alarmed by the prospect of Argyll's restoration, which threatened them all to varying degrees. Indeed, nearly all the clans who had joined the Marquis of Atholl in putting down the 1685 rebellion of Argyll's father eventually rallied to Dundee's standard. Only the MacIntoshes of Clan Chattan were absent, but they were hardly likely to join the MacDonalds of Keppoch in supporting James VII, given their recent defeat at Mulroy by their hereditary enemies.

Even so, Sir Ewan Cameron of Lochiel had perhaps the most to gain among all the west Highland chieftains. James VII had just erected Lochaber into a separate jurisdiction 'for he would have Lochiel master of his own Clan, and only accountable to him or his Council for them'. Pursuing this policy, he had persuaded George Gordon, ninth Earl and fourth Marquis of Huntly, now the Duke of Gordon, to give up his feudal superiority over

Lochiel's lands in Lochaber, which he had received after the ninth Earl of Argyll was executed in 1685. Moreover, Lochiel's ancestral lands of Sunart and Ardnamurchan had recently been restored to him as a gift from James VII after Alexander Campbell of Lochnell had forfeited them as a vassal of the ninth Earl of Argyll.

In fact, Sir Ewan Cameron of Lochiel was the King's favourite among all the Highland chiefs, despite his lawless actions in the 1680s, when he quite blatantly violated the King's peace in Lochaber by attacking the garrisons at Inverlochy. Yet James VII seems drawn to Lochiel, fascinated by his vivid personality, while viewing him at the same time with deep suspicion and mistrust. Indeed, when Lochiel was knighted in 1681, James had wished to use Lochiel's own sword in the ceremony. But it stuck as he attempted to draw it from its scabbard, and Lochiel had to free it for him. As James remarked, Lochiel's sword would clearly obey no hand but his own. Then in 1685, he introduced his protégé to the Court as the 'King of the Thieves', joking light-heartedly about the safety of the horses in the royal stable. Sir Ewan Cameron of Lochiel for his part evidently saw himself in the same heroic mould as Montrose, whose name was 'always in his mouth'.

Indeed, Lochiel was among the few Royalists still alive who had fought for Charles II at the battle of Worcester in 1651, and afterwards during Glencairn's Rising. James VII was nothing if not loyal to the Highland clans which had supported his family in the Civil Wars, forty years earlier, and such loyalty was returned. Indeed, as Paul Hopkins has emphasised, disingenuous and often lacking any clear rationale for his policies, James VII regarded several of the Highland clans, and especially the Campbells, as incorrigibly disloyal, and prone to 'atavistic acquisitiveness', perhaps even afflicted by some hereditary disorder, whilst favouring the 'loyal clans' who were their ancient enemies.

Raising the Jacobite Standard

Only after the Parliamentary Convention in Edinburgh had declared Dundee a fugitive and a rebel did he raise the Jacobite standard at the summit of Dundee Law on 16 April 1689. He then rode north with a small party of followers. Already, James VII had landed on 12 March 1689 at Kinsale in the south of Ireland with 7,000 Frenchmen. They reinforced what was now a largely Catholic army in Ireland, commanded by the Lord Deputy Richard Talbot, whom James VII had earlier created Earl of Tyrconnel. Only the Protestants in Ulster, mostly lowland Scots in origin, declared their allegiance to William and Mary. They were forced after the 'Break of Dromore' to take refuge behind the city walls of Londonderry and Enniskillen. If they could be overcome, James VII would himself cross to Scotland with a force of 5,000 men, after securing the whole of Ireland.

Riding out from Dundee with no more than sixty troopers, John Graham of Claverhouse, Viscount Dundee, first crossed the Cairn O'Mount into Deeside from Angus. Passing north through Kincardine O'Neil, Huntly and Keith, he first reached Gordon Castle near Fochabers, before making for Inverness. But then, at Forres, he doubled back to the Cairn O'Mount, hoping to recruit the dragoons now quartered at Dundee to the Jacobite cause. However, on learning that Sir Hugh MacKay of Scourie was advancing in strength against him, Dundee was forced to return north to Gordon Castle. MacKay had landed a month earlier at Leith on 25 March 1689 with 1,000 men of the Dutch Brigade, armed with a commission from King William to act as Major-General of the regime's forces in Scotland. His own regiment was accompanied by two others, commanded by Colonel George Ramsey and Brigadier-General Barthold Balfour.

MacKay was now head of his family, after his two elder brothers had lost their lives at the hands of William Sinclair of Dunbeath, as already recounted. A staunch Presbyterian, and a Gaelic speaker, he had gone abroad at the restoration of Charles II in 1660 to become a professional soldier. After serving Louis XIV under James, Duke of Monmouth, he later transferred his allegiance to William of Orange, when Charles II repudiated his alliance with France in 1674. Afterwards, he was briefly recalled to England, where he fought against Monmouth's rebellion, before returning to serve William of Orange.

Reverse in the North

Meanwhile, Dundee's hopes of raising the Gordon country in the north-east of Scotland came to nothing. Only James Seton, fourth Earl of Dunfermline, and brother-in-law to George, Duke of Gordon, rallied to the Jacobite standard, together with 100 gentlemen. Then, riding towards Inverness on 1 May 1689, Dundee found Coll MacDonald of Keppoch already encamped outside the town with a mixed force of Camerons, Stewarts and MacGregors, as well as his own clansmen. Ever since the reprisals after the battle of Mulroy, he had lived off the land with his followers. Indeed, it was not for nothing he was called 'Coll of the Cows'. Later, he was described in disparaging terms as 'little more than a highway robber, and his policy was always to be the enemy of the existing English government . . . For the rest, he was a tough little man, intelligent and enterprising, but he had no regard for his word or for the law.'

By mid-March 1689 at the latest, Keppoch had raised his clan in arms, and, advancing through Stratherrick and Strathnairn, ravaged the MacIntosh lands, before reaching Inverness on 28 April with perhaps as many as 900 men. There, he demanded a payment of 4,000 merks from the town council in compensation for his being imprisoned by the magistrates in 1683, which had occurred at the urging of Lachlan MacIntosh of Torcastle. It was paid by Dundee, who however sharply rebuked Keppoch for his behaviour. It had alienated Hugh Rose of Kilravock, who otherwise might have rallied to Dundee's standard. Instead, he raised 300 men to defend Elgin, where Dundee had hoped to quarter Keppoch's men.

Dundee and his forces were now threatened by the advance of Sir Hugh MacKay and his forces, who had reached Elgin after responding to an appeal for its defence. But the Camerons would not fight, excusing themselves by saying they had to ask permission from Sir Ewan Cameron of Lochiel, while the MacDonalds of Keppoch merely wanted to return home with their plunder. Dundee was thus forced to abandon Inverness on 8 May 1689, allowing the town to be occupied by the government troops under Sir Hugh MacKay of Scourie. They were soon reinforced by 500 men under David Ross of Balnagown, while John Gordon, Lord Strathnaver, and afterwards the sixteenth Earl of Sutherland, went north to raise his own men in Sutherland. Sir Hugh MacKay also ordered another 600 men from the Dutch Brigade to advance north by way of Atholl and Badenoch under the command of Colonel George Ramsey.

Dundee's First Raid

Meanwhile, Dundee rode south-west along the Great Glen with what remained of his forces. After a brief visit to Invergarry, where he consulted Alasdair MacDonald of Glengarry, he doubled back with perhaps 200 men to spend the night of 8 May at Kilcumein (now Fort Augustus). Next day, he crossed the Corrieyairack Pass with his followers to reach Cluny Castle in Badenoch, stronghold of the MacPhersons, who were sympathetic to the Jacobite cause. Then, he rode south to gain Glen Truim by nightfall, where 'he issued the Royal letter to all the faithful clans, bidding them to be ready with their men by the Kalends of May [18 May], to follow the orders and the camp of the Graham Viscount Dundee'.

Next morning, Dundee rode south across the Drumochter Pass to reach Blair Castle, where he was welcomed by Patrick Steuart of Ballechin. Then, scarcely pausing in the saddle, Dundee rode south with his men through the Pass of Killiecrankie and past Pitlochry to reach Dunkeld. Entering the town, he captured a captain of horse, relieving him of what government revenues he had been collecting. At nightfall on the same day, 10 May 1689,

Dundee continued south in a bold move against the city of Perth, garrisoned by government troops against just such an incursion.

By 2 o'clock on the morning of 11 May, he had entered Perth, gaining control of the streets. He then arrested two officers in charge of the garrison, and William Blair, Laird of Blair, who was recruiting a troop of horse. Next morning, Dundee rode out of Perth with his prisoners to Scone Palace, where he forced Lord Stormont to give him dinner. He spent the next night at Stobhall Castle, a few miles to the north, and the seat of James Drummond, fourth Earl of Perth. After a day spent collecting taxes on behalf of King James from the surrounding countryside, Dundee left Stobhall as darkness fell on 12 May, riding past Coupar Angus and Meigle to arrive next morning at Glamis Castle. After resting only briefly, he set out across the Sidlaw Hills for Dundee, arriving before the town walls in the late afternoon of 13 May.

But the town gates were firmly closed against him, and the town walls guarded, so that any Jacobite sympathisers among the town's garrison were unable to join him. Dundee now turned north and west, leading his weary troop back past Dunkeld and then along the River Tay to Weem, where he crossed the hills to Loch Rannoch. Then skirting the Moor of Rannoch to the east, he rode along Loch Treig into Glen Spean, arriving in Lochaber on 16 May, two days before the date of the rendezvous arranged by Sir Ewan Cameron of Lochiel.

Rallying the Clans

Such a lightning raid against the Lowlands of Perthshire and Angus was a deed worthy of Montrose, and a superb piece of propaganda. Its very daring encouraged the Highland clans to rally to Dundee's standard, while giving heart to lowland Jacobites. But it also greatly alarmed the government in Edinburgh, which sent reinforcements north to guard the country from any more raids. Meanwhile on 18 May, the Highland chiefs loyal to King James started to rally at Mucomir at the southern end of Loch Lochy.

Among the first to arrive was the young Alasdair Dubh MacDonald of Glengarry with 300 clansmen, followed by Donald MacDonald of Benbecula, tutor of Clan Ranald, with 200 clansmen, Alasdair MacIain with 100 MacDonalds from Glencoe, and Coll MacDonald of Keppoch with 200 of his clansmen. Their ranks were further swelled by 200 Stewarts of Appin, 120 Frasers under William Fraser of Foyers, and sixty Grants of Glenmoriston. Already present were the 400 clansmen raised by Sir Ewan Cameron of Lochiel, along with their chief. Still absent were any MacLeans from Mull, or any MacDonalds of Sleat. Dundee spent the next week waiting vainly for their arrival.

Incursion against Kintyre

Despite his earlier promise of military aid, James VII could only spare Dundee a few hundred men from his forces in Ireland. He was still laying siege to Londonderry, which the Ulster Protestants held by sheer strength of arms. But among the Jacobite commanders was Sir Donald MacDonald, third Baronet of Sleat, who landed on the small island of Cara at the southern end of Gigha on 2 May. He was followed a few days later by Sir John MacLean of Duart, and his kinsman Sir Alexander MacLean of Otter. Rallying the Kintyre clans, Sir Donald MacDonald, third Baronet of Sleat, laid siege to Skipness Castle, aided by Donald MacNeil of Gigha, Alexander MacAlister of Loup, and Archibald MacDonald of Largie, along with a few surviving MacDonalds from Islay and Jura.

The government in Edinburgh responded to this threat by ordering 500 men to cross by sea to Kintyre under the command of Captain William Young. Sir Duncan Campbell of Auchinbreck was also instructed to march south into Kintyre with what men were available at Inveraray. By 15 May, Captain Young had landed his men at Tarbert, and next day they scattered the Jacobite forces just south of Loup. Nearly all of them escaped by boat to Gigha, while Captain Young remained on the mainland with his government forces, now 1,200 strong.

Meanwhile, the Irishmen under Sir Alexander MacLean of Otter, accompanied by Sir John MacLean of Duart, had sailed north to Mull. Then, in mid-May, some MacLean clansmen seized a French merchantman, after it had been captured earlier by Angus Campbell of Kilberry. Sailing to Mull, they armed the boat with cannon so that it could act as the flagship to a flotilla of the MacLean birlinns. Sir Alexander MacLean of Otter now sailed back to Gigha with reinforcements. Before a squadron of English frigates could arrive under the command of Captain George Rooke, he managed on 26 May to evacuate the MacDonalds of Largie from the island of Arran, where they had taken refuge after the skirmish at Loup.

Only a few hours later, the English squadron appeared off Gigha, and started to bombard the island with its cannon. However, small-arms fire from the Jacobite forces on the island prevented any landing, and Rooke retired to transport an invasion force that Captain Young had assembled on the mainland of Kintyre. Taking advantage of the lull in the fighting, Sir Alexander MacLean of Otter embarked all his men, now 400 strong, at the north end of Gigha. Sailing north in the darkness, they were pursued by the English frigates, but after landing first in Argyll, they eventually reached Mull with hardly any losses on 31 May 1689. It was therefore only in early June that the MacLeans eventually joined Dundee, bringing in much-needed reinforcements.

Dundee's Strathspey Campaign

Meanwhile, Dundee had left Lochaber on 25 May at the head of a small army, perhaps 2,000 strong. Marching up Glen Roy, he first crossed the higher ground to reach the headwaters of the River Spey at Garvamore. He then descended its wide valley to enter the lands in Badenoch held by Duncan MacPherson of Cluny. His animosity to Lachlan MacIntosh of Clan Chattan, who had refused to recognise his family's claims to independence, made him sympathetic to the Jacobite cause. Indeed, Lachlan MacIntosh had himself sided with the government in Edinburgh, which looked likely to offer him its support in his bitter and long-lasting feud with Coll MacDonald of Keppoch following the battle of Mulroy in 1688. Although reluctant to declare himself personally for King James, Duncan MacPherson of Cluny was prepared to allow 200 of his clansmen surreptitiously to join the Jacobite cause. Another fifty men under John Farquharson of Inverey, the 'Black Colonel', would join Dundee's ranks as he marched down Strathspey.

Dundee's strategy in marching into Badenoch was evidently to march down Strathspey to reach the Gordon lands of north-eastern Scotland. But already he knew from Patrick Steuart of Ballechin that Colonel George Ramsey was marching north into Atholl from the Lowlands, as ordered by Sir Hugh MacKay of Scourie, who was still at Inverness with his own forces. They had planned a rendezvous between their two armies at Ruthven Castle in Badenoch. It was already garrisoned by a company of Grant's regiment, raised by Ludovick Grant, chief of Clan Grant. But when Ramsey reached Blair Castle on 24 May, he found the men of Atholl in arms under Patrick Steuart of Ballechin. He thought it best to retreat back to Perth the very next day.

Meanwhile, Sir Hugh MacKay of Scourie, with 450 regular soldiers, strengthened by another 400 Rosses and MacKays from the north, had marched across country towards Strathspey from Inverness, intending to block Dundee's advance north-east. The two armies came into sight of one another on 28 May, but in the confusion it seems Sir Ewan Cameron of Lochiel mistook Dundee's orders. Instead of attacking the enemy, he withdrew the Highland clans for several miles, allowing MacKay to escape down Strathspey to Culnakyle, which lies just beyond the point where the Nethy enters the Spey.

Dundee now laid siege to Ruthven Castle, and its garrison surrendered before it was put to the flames by Coll MacDonald of Keppoch. Dunachton House, chief residence of Lachlan MacIntosh of Clan Chattan, was also burnt in passing by Keppoch, provoking a furious and very public rebuke from Dundee. Keppoch apologised, saying somewhat disingenuously that he thought MacIntosh was an enemy of the King, even though he was pursuing his own vendetta against him. In fact, Dundee relied on 'Coll of the Cows' to feed his army, since Keppoch had an uncanny ability to find cattle secreted among the hills.

Dundee now advanced down Strathspey, forcing MacKay to abandon his defensive position at Culnakyle on 2 June. Leaving only a garrison at Ballachastell (now Castle Grant) to guard the Grant country, he fled overnight with his own hungry forces down the valley of the River Spey to Craigellachie, where he turned east to halt at Balvenie Castle. But still pursued by Dundee, who had advanced down Glenlivet, he resumed his flight eastwards on the evening of 3 June, reaching the headwaters of the River Deveron only as darkness fell. Dundee's forces just failed to intercept the fleeing army. Only a rearguard action by MacKay's dragoons allowed MacKay to stagger south across Suie Hill to the south of Huntly with his now-exhausted army. Dundee had called off the pursuit on reaching Edinglassie Castle, fearful of encountering the enemy cavalry on the flat-lying ground of Strathbogie.

Dundee in Retreat

Dundee spent the next day at Edinglassie Castle, only to fall ill with dysentery. Then, he learnt that MacKay's forces had been reinforced by Sir James Leslie's regiment of foot, 700 strong, and Colonel Berkeley's dragoons, 300 strong, which were now advancing against him. Realising the tide had turned, he decided on retreat. By the evening of 5 June, he had reached Cromdale, before he withdrew more slowly along the Spey towards Boat of Garten. He was joined there around 7 June by an advance guard of MacLeans under Hector MacLean of Lochbuie. However, out foraging for food, they were caught by surprise by Sir Thomas Livingston, who attacked them at the head of more than 200 dragoons.

While some fled, and others were taken prisoner, a remnant of the MacLean forces, around 100 strong, managed to regroup at the foot of Knockbrecht Hill. They slowly retreated up its steep slopes to safety, holding off their attackers with musket-fire, and keeping the enemy at bay until the morning of 8 June by rolling boulders down upon the dragoons. Then, they mounted a Highland charge, breaking through the enemy ranks, and killing a captain, before they regained Dundee's camp. The dragoons retaliated in anger by killing around forty of their MacLean prisoners, even if Lochbuie's brother was spared.

Encouraged by this engagement, Dundee resumed the march back to Badenoch. Even before he reached Ruthven, his forces were further strengthened by another 200 MacLeans under Sir Alexander MacLean of Otter. However, as they reached striking distance of their own country, the Highland clans under Dundee started to disperse, driving home the cattle they had looted and carrying off their other booty. Dundee now withdrew west into Lochaber, where he formally dismissed his forces 'upon their giving assurance that they would be ready to join him upon twenty-four-hours advertisement', in the words of his son-in-law Balhaldie. MacKay advanced as far as Ruthven to confirm that Dundee's forces were no longer a threat. Colonel George Ramsey joined him there, having advanced slowly through Atholl after his earlier foray north, and together they withdrew to Inverness with their own exhausted forces.

Attempts to Rally Support

Recovering from his illness, Dundee remained in Lochaber for the next few weeks until he marched south to fight the battle of Killiecrankie on 27 July 1689. His standing was strengthened on 22 June, when messengers finally brought him a commission as Lieutenant-General from James VII in Ireland, giving him plenipotentiary powers over all of Scotland. By then, the reinforcements he expected from Ireland had finally arrived. But their numbers were a grave disappointment, amounting to only 400 ill-trained men, augmented by a few dragoons. It was now more important than ever to rally more support to the Jacobite cause from among the Highland clans.

Among the many Highland clans who had still not declared for King James were the MacLeods of Dunvegan. They had suffered disastrously in the Civil Wars, especially at the battle of Worcester in 1651, without receiving any reward at the restoration of Charles II. Now their chief Iain Breac MacLeod remained aloof from the struggle, secure in Dunvegan Castle. Sir Donald MacDonald, third Baronet of Sleat, spent much of July in Skye with his own clansmen, trying to force the MacLeods, and more particularly the MacKinnons of Strathordle, to join Dundee. But only the MacLeods of Raasay, descended from the now-extinct MacLeods of Lewis, served with distinction for King James.

Further north, Kenneth MacKenzie, fourth Earl of Seaforth, was sympathetic to the Jacobite cause as a recent convert to Catholicism. Indeed, he had followed James VII into exile, accompanying him on his expedition to Ireland. But his influence was countered by his kinsman Sir George MacKenzie of Tarbat, afterwards first Earl of Cromartie. Now nearly sixty years of age, he had served the Royalist cause as a young man in Glencairn's rebellion against Cromwell, and although excluded from high office for many years by the Earl of Lauderdale, he was made Lord Justice-General of Scotland in 1678.

Even though he had Jacobite sympathies, which threatened his position with the new regime, Tarbat soon ingratiated himself with the government in Edinburgh by advising them on the threat posed by the Highland clans. He would later put forward a scheme for their pacification, which was eventually taken up by Sir John Campbell of Glenorchy, first Earl of Breadalbane. Meanwhile, the Munros of Fowlis, and the Rosses of Balnagown, who lived in the shadow of the MacKenzies, had rallied to the cause of King William, whom they served under the command of Sir Hugh MacKay of Scourie.

Beyond the Dornoch Firth, the country was dominated by the Gordons, Earls of Sutherland. They adhered to the Protestant religion, unlike the Gordons, Earls of Huntly, who were the senior branch of the family. Indeed, it seems that George, fourteenth Earl of Sutherland, left Scotland to live in Holland in the 1680s, only returning to the country in 1688 with William of Orange. He left his affairs in the hands of his elder son John, Lord Strathnaver, afterwards the fifteenth Earl. Although Lord Strathnaver had supported James VII against the 1685 rebellion of Archibald Campbell, ninth Earl of Argyll, he now rallied to the Protestant cause, raising a regiment of 600 foot.

Closely allied to the Earls of Sutherland were the MacKays of Strathnaver. They could hardly be expected to support the Jacobite cause. George, third Lord Reay, and Chief of MacKay, was still a minor, completing his Protestant education in Holland. Moreover, he was a grand-nephew of Sir Hugh MacKay of Scourie, and he would remain stalwart in opposing the Jacobite rebellions of 1715 and 1745. Only William Sinclair of Dunbeath offered Dundee 200 horse and 800 foot, but this inveterate troublemaker, isolated in the far north of Scotland, never made good his offer.

Other erstwhile supporters of the Jacobite cause were equally lukewarm in their actions. Even though George, first Duke of Gordon, ninth Earl and fourth Marquis of Huntly, held Edinburgh Castle for King James while the Parliamentary Convention was meeting under its walls, he did little to rally the north-east to the Jacobite cause. Dundee had visited him after climbing the Castle Rock, just before he rode out of Edinburgh. But it was said devastatingly of Huntly that he 'has sense, and some very good links in him, but 'tis impossible to make a chain of them'. Even so, forced to surrender on 13 June 1689 for lack of food, Gordon remained a prisoner of the Convention until he eventually left Scotland under parole for France.

Elsewhere, Dundee had hopes of calling out the smaller clans of Argyllshire, but again with very little success. Only Iain MacNauchtan of Dundarave was prepared to join him, but hardly any of his tenants would follow. Even though Archibald Campbell, tenth Earl of Argyll, was not yet restored to his estates, he was engaged in raising a regiment of foot for the government in Edinburgh. Indeed, as already recounted, one company under Sir Duncan Campbell of Auchinbreck had repulsed the MacLeans when they attempted to land in Kintyre. Evidently, the likely resurgence of Argyll's power under King William was enough to inhibit all but the boldest.

Correspondence with Breadalbane

Yet the most surprising of all the Highland magnates in close correspondence with Dundee was John Campbell of Glenorchy, first Earl of Breadalbane, as Paul Hopkins has emphasised in his study *Glencoe and the End of the Highland War*. According to a contemporary, he was 'grave as a Spaniard, cunning as a fox, wise as a serpent, but slippery as an eel, whom no government can trust but where his own private interest is [clearly] in view'. He had taken little part in the Parliamentary Convention in Edinburgh before he retired to Kilchurn Castle, pleading gout as an excuse. Doubtless, Dundee would not have concentrated his early campaigning in the north-east had he then expected Breadalbane to join the Jacobite cause. But a few weeks later, after he received his commission from James VII on 22 June, allowing him to 'act with the power of our whole council', Dundee evidently made an agreement on King James's authority with Breadalbane.

Indeed, Dundee even hoped that Breadalbane would himself persuade Argyll to change sides. The suggestion was met with self-righteous indignation, but only a year later Argyll would be embroiled in a Jacobite plot against the government. Even so, Dundee tempted Breadalbane by observing: 'There are few considerable cadets so just to their chief – if Argyll were out of the way Breadalbane would be all in these countries and have the whole name to follow him.' They agreed that Breadalbane should raise an army of 1,600 men from his territories in support of King James. But this prospect was shattered by the death of 'Bonnie Dundee' at the battle of Killiecrankie.

MacKay's Plan to Garrison Inverlochy

While Dundee thus attempted to build a coalition for King James, Sir Hugh MacKay of Scourie remained in Inverness until the end of June, ignoring calls from Edinburgh that he should withdraw all his troops to the Lowlands. Indeed, when he finally marched south, he left a strong garrison behind to guard Inverness in case Dundee should move north to raise the MacKenzies and the Frasers. Then, on 2 July, he ordered a detachment of foot and horse under William, Master of Forbes, to advance up the Dee to seize Braemar Castle and its unruly occupant, John Farquharson of Inverey. A dawn attack was planned, but the 'Black Colonel' managed to escape with his men 'in their shirts'. Later they returned to burn the castle in a surprise attack, forcing the government forces to flee. MacKay then advanced in strength to establish a garrison in Abergeldie Castle, only a few miles down the Dee from Braemar, but this diversion delayed his arrival in Edinburgh until 12 July.

MacKay now proposed to emulate General Monck in establishing a garrison at Inverlochy to cow the Lochaber clans. But unlike Monck, who had planted and supplied the Commonwealth garrison at Inverlochy by sea, MacKay intended to advance overland through Atholl. It seems he was now dangerously complacent about the fighting qualities of the Highland clans under Dundee. Indeed, apart from minor battles like Mulroy, government forces had not experienced a full-blooded Highland Charge for well over a generation. Their commanders had forgotten what devastation it could cause among their ranks. As Paul Hopkins has commented, this pattern was repeated for more than a century, until the use of cannon at Culloden ushered in its death-knell.

Jacobite Sympathies in Atholl

Atholl was also divided in its loyalty to the government in Edinburgh. No longer a young man, John Murray, first Marquis of Atholl, had first embraced the cause of King James, after he suffered a rebuff in seeking office under King William. But he had lost his nerve, eventually retiring in late May to take the waters at Bath. He left his affairs in the hands of his eldest son, Lord John Murray, afterwards second Marquis and first Duke of Atholl. He had orders to resist Dundee if he were to advance again through Atholl. But his attempts to resist any such advance were thwarted by the evident reluctance of the men of Atholl to fight for King William.

Indeed, the Murrays of Atholl were themselves a family divided, since three of Lord John Murray's younger brothers were Jacobite sympathisers. Moreover, occupying powerful positions as their bailie and chamberlain were Patrick Steuart of Ballechin, and his brother Alexander. They were even more ardent supporters of King James, along with their sons, including the Reverend Robert Steuart. Indeed, as already recounted, Colonel George Ramsey's first foray north in May 1689 had foundered when he encountered the men of Atholl in arms under Patrick Steuart of Ballechin.

When Ramsey had arrived back in Perth after this abortive expedition, Lord John Murray had ridden north to find out what had happened, arriving in Dunkeld on 28 May. But Patrick Steuart of Ballechin misled him, saying the men of Atholl had only been protecting their cattle from plunder by Ramsey's forces. Lord Murray returned south to reassure the government in Edinburgh that all was well, leaving only a small garrison in Blair Castle. Dundee, however, was only biding his time. On 9 July he sent orders by David Halyburton of Pitcur, instructing Patrick Steuart of Ballechin to occupy Blair Castle, which he did under the guise of sending in 'reinforcements'.

Then, on 13 July, Sir Alexander MacLean of Otter arrived in Atholl with his own regiment, 300 strong, forcing the local gentry to retire from a blockade of Blair Castle. He then marched for Braemar, meeting up with John Farquharson of Inverey, and together they attacked the lands of John Gordon of Brackley, evading the garrison in Abergeldie Castle. Lord John Murray hurried back to raise his tenants, but even with a force of 1,000 men, he lacked the means to seize Blair Castle, now occupied by the Jacobite forces under Patrick Steuart of Ballechin.

Advance to Killiecrankie

Events now began to move very fast. The reinforcements that Dundee expected from Ireland eventually arrived in three French frigates towards the middle of July, as already recounted. But apart from Brigadier-General Alexander Cannon, and several others with commissions from James VII to raise regiments on his behalf, there were only around seventy-five junior officers, and 300 raw troops under Colonel James Purcell. Soon afterwards, Sir Donald MacDonald, third Baronet of Sleat, arrived in Lochaber with his own clansmen. Dundee now judged that time was running short, since Argyll threatened him from the south-west, while MacKay was collecting his own forces to march north through Atholl to establish the garrison at Inverlochy. He therefore declared a general rendezvous for the end of July, but it was intended only to mislead the enemy. On the morning of 23 July, he abruptly marched his own forces out of camp, leaving so suddenly that a government spy in his camp did not even know of his orders.

Even though Dundee marched through Glen Roy, he was not joined by the MacDonalds of Keppoch, who were always more concerned with plundering. Nor did the MacPhersons of Cluny rally to his standard as he entered Badenoch, although Duncan MacPherson provided provisions for his small army. Then, guided by Alexander Steuart of Ballechin, Dundee marched over Drumochter Pass to camp three miles north of Blair Castle on the evening of 26 July. Meanwhile, learning of Dundee's approach, Lord John Murray had fallen back through the Pass of Killiecrankie with three or four hundred of his own men, leaving a small guard at its head, while the rest melted away, driving their cattle into the hills for safety.

MacKay's March into Atholl

Unaware that Dundee was even then marching south towards Atholl, Sir Hugh MacKay of Scourie had reached Perth on 25 July. He intended to continue overland by way of Atholl to Inverlochy, where he planned to establish a garrison. He left Perth the very next day, despite being warned of Dundee's approach by Robert Menzies of Weem, whom he ignored. His forces were nearly 4,000 strong, consisting of three battalions of infantry from the regiments of the Dutch brigade, reinforced by two troops of horse, and three more companies of foot. Accompanied by a baggage train of 1,200 horses, carrying provisions for a fortnight and other supplies, MacKay reached Dunkeld by the evening of 26 July. Only then did he learn from Lord John Murray of Dundee's movements. 200 fusiliers under Lieutenant-Colonel George Lauder were sent forward to guard the northern entrance to the Pass of Killiecrankie, where they found that Murray's guard had vanished.

Next morning, the government forces marched north towards Killiecrankie. They were joined at Ballinluig by an Independent Company under Robert Menzies of Weem. When he reached Moulin, just above Pitlochry, MacKay was joined by Lord John Murray, who however could not persuade what remained of his own men to join MacKay's army. Fearing that his baggage train might be plundered, MacKay ordered Hasting's regiment and Annandale's horse to guard the rear of his column. Then, advancing towards the Pass of Killiecrankie, he took the precaution of sending forward another 200 men from Leven's regiment, even though he heard from Lauder that the way north into Atholl was clear.

MacKay could not have entered the Pass of Killiecrankie with all his forces without a sense of trepidation, even if he merely described it in his memoirs as 'a strait and difficult pass'. According to Mowbray Morris, writing in 1888,

> it forms the highest and narrowest part of a magnificent wooded defile in which the waters of the Tummel flowing eastward from Loch Rannoch meet the waters of the Garry as it plunges down from the Grampians . . . The only road that then led through this Valley of the Shadow of Death was a rugged path, so narrow that no more than three men could walk abreast, winding along the edge of a precipitous cliff at the foot of which thundered the black waters of the Garry.

Yet by the early afternoon of 27 July, MacKay's force had passed unscathed through the pass, apart from the attentions of a single sniper. Slowly, they emerged in a long straggle over the next two hours to gain the flatter ground forming the valley below Blair Castle.

Dundee's Tactics before Killiecrankie

Even as MacKay advanced north from Dunkeld on the morning of 27 July 1689, Dundee had entered Blair Castle to hold a council of war with his commanders. His regular officers advised him to rest his forces, while engaging in guerilla warfare against the enemy as it advanced. But his Highland commanders urged him to strike immediately against the enemy, as their clansmen no doubt expected. Indeed, as Sir Ewan Cameron of Lochiel later recounted in his memoirs, he was unable to promise Dundee a victory

> if we are not the aggressors. But be assured, my Lord, that if we are once fairly engaged, we will either lose our army, or carry a complete victory. Our men love always to be in action . . . Employ them in hasty and desperate enterprises, and you will oblige them; and I have still observed, that when I fought under the greatest disadvantage of numbers, I still had the greatest victories.

Dundee agreed whole-heartedly, but he could not be persuaded against risking his own life, arguing that he must lead his forces at their head if he were to command their respect.

By now, it was mid-afternoon, and MacKay's forces had emerged from the Pass of Killiecrankie in their march towards Blair Castle. Dundee ordered forward a small troop of horse to advance down Strathgarry from Blair Castle as a diversion. They were spotted at a distance by MacKay as he reached a small hamlet on the banks of the Allt Chluain, where it enters the Garry from the north. He promptly drew up his army to face an attack from the direction of Blair Castle, and issued ammunition to his infantry. But then, MacKay suddenly became aware that Dundee had gained the high ground overlooking his army to the east.

Dundee had executed what can only be described as a brilliant *tour-de-force*, taking advantage of the topography to gain the tactical advantage. It would prove crucial to the outcome of the battle, given that his forces were outnumbered. While he launched the diversionary feint down Strathgarry, he had crossed the Bridge of Tilt with the rest of his army. He then marched his men almost at a run up Glen Fender, and around the back of the Hill of Lude, where Montrose had raised the Royalist standard for Charles I nearly half a century earlier. Gaining the headwaters of Allt Chluain, he then descended its valley towards the south, before skirting around the southern flanks of Creag Eallaich. Only now were his forces, deployed above its lower slopes, high above the valley of the River Garry, in sight of MacKay and his men. By securing the high ground, they now looked out from a position of strength over the right wing of MacKay's army, lying some 200 to 300 feet below them at a distance of several hundred yards.

As soon as he realised the danger, MacKay wheeled his forces to the right, so that his regiments now faced the enemy in their order of march. He then advanced uphill to reach a terrace of flatter ground, just above Urrard House. It is now crossed by the A9 road with scant regard for history. But in MacKay's own words, it was ground 'fair enough to receive the enemy, but not to attack them', since a cavalry charge could not be mounted uphill with any chance of success. Indeed, Dundee 'had his back to a very high hill, which is the ordinary maxim of the Highlanders, who never fight against regular forces upon anything of equal terms, without a sure retreat at their back, particularly if their enemy be provided of horse'.

Prelude to the Battle

Dundee now had the initiative, but he rested his men until the early evening. Tradition has it that he exhorted his men with an eloquent speech, speaking of King, religion and country. Reminding them that King William was an usurper, he promised them 'the reward of a gracious King' if they were successful in fighting for 'King James and the Church of Scotland'. The reference was of course to the Episcopalian Church, as established at the Restoration.

MacKay also addressed his forces in rather more prosaic terms, calling upon his men not to betray the cause of King William and the Protestant religion by 'criminal faint-heartedness'. If they did, they would surely be cut down by naked Highlanders, who could easily outrun them, and even if they escaped, there remained the men of Atholl, who 'were in arms ready to strip and knock in the head all runaways'. His words can hardly have reassured his troops. Indeed, their morale was now flagging as the Highlanders above them took up an eerie howling, following the example of the Camerons of Lochiel, which sounded like the wailing of banshees. The government forces only answered with what Lochiel later described as 'a dead, hollow and feeble noise'. He was certain that the enemy 'were all doomed to die by our hands this very night'.

It was seven o'clock in the evening, when the sun was already low in the west, that Dundee finally gave the order to attack. He had already instructed his own forces to form up 'deep in file'. This meant that his men were packed tightly together in solid phalanxes, each composed of a major clan and its septs, and able to pierce the enemy line at its weakest point. They were spaced out at intervals on the slopes above their enemy. MacKay now risked being outflanked on his right wing, which would cut off his only means of retreat down the Pass of Killiecrankie. But he made a serious error when he lengthened his line by reducing it only three ranks deep – apart from Kenmuir's regiment at its centre, made up of inexperienced men – while allowing gaps to open up between his other regiments. It was far too fragile a line to receive the full force of a Highland charge.

Highland Charge at Killiecrankie

As the Highlanders started to advance, they threw off 'their plaids, haver-sacks and all other utensils, and marched resolutely and deliberately in their shirts and doublets, with their fusils [muskets], swords, targes, and pistols ready'. They were met by several volleys of musket fire, and Lochiel later observed that it was 'incredible with what intrepidity the Highlanders endured the enemy's fire'. Despite the appalling casualties, numbering around several hundred men at the very least, the concentrated fire of 4,000 footsoldiers was not enough to check the ferocity of the Highland assault over the last 100 yards. Only at the very last moment did the Highlanders let loose a single volley against the enemy, 'pouring fire . . . in upon them all at once, like one great clap of thunder'. Then throwing away their muskets, they charged the enemy over the last few yards to break through the enemy lines in hand-to-hand fighting.

MacKay's forces were at a disadvantage. Indeed, they had hardly time to ram their old-fashioned bayonets into the muzzles of their muskets before they were cut down by the broadswords and claymores of the Highlanders. As Lochiel wrote afterwards, soon after the Highlanders 'fell pell-mell among the thickest of them with their broadswords . . . the noise seemed hushed; and the fire ceasing on both sides, nothing was heard . . . but the sullen and hollow clashes of broadswords, with the dismal groans and cries of dying and wounded men'. The actual fighting lasted perhaps ten minutes.

Course of the Battle

Dundee's far right wing was composed of 200 MacLeans under Sir John MacLean of Duart. Early in the battle they were joined by sixty Camerons, who had withdrawn under fire after sniping against the enemy from a forward position. They faced 200 fusiliers under Lieutenant-Colonel George Lauder, occupying a wooded hill, perhaps 500 yards away, together with Balfour's regiment of foot to their right. Brigadier-General Barthold Balfour had him-self been given command of MacKay's left wing, separated as it was from his centre by marshy ground, making communication difficult.

MacKay's left wing broke almost at once under the onslaught, as Balfour's infantry fled downhill towards the river, and then tried to escape down the valley towards the Pass of Killiecrankie. Pursued by the MacLeans, many men were cut down before they even reached its mouth, while the survivors were killed as they became jammed together on the narrow path through the gorge. One fortunate soldier managed to leap to safety across the Garry at the Soldier's Leap. Among the dead was Balfour himself, supposedly slain by the Reverend Robert Steuart of Ballechin after he had contemptuously refused an offer of quarter.

Lauder's fusiliers broke at the same time, although their commander managed to escape with his life through the pass. Next in line to Balfour's regiment on MacKay's left wing was Ramsey's regiment. It took the brunt of the Irish regiment, commanded by Colonel James Purcell, even though his men charged downhill like a 'stampede of cattle', flanked by the MacDonalds of Clan Ranald and Glengarry. Ramsey's regiment stood its ground at first, but it was not long before it broke as well, fleeing after Balfour's regiment towards the Pass of Killiecrankie. Colonel George Ramsey later managed to gather together some 200 survivors of the battle, and joining up with MacKay, crossed the hills to the safety of Weem.

MacKay's left wing had thus collapsed disastrously, leaving Kenmuir's raw regiment dangerously exposed on what was now his left flank. More than three deep, they initially held their ground, firing vigorously as the MacDonalds of Clan Ranald and Glengarry charged against them, supported to their left by the MacDonalds of Glencoe, and the Grants of Glenmoriston. But their ranks were broken by their own cavalry, which MacKay had ordered forward from his position at the centre of his line. Wheeling suddenly left, perhaps to press home their attack, or more likely, panic-stricken at the sight of Dundee as he charged downhill at the head of his own cavalry, Belhaven's troop of horse careered back through their own ranks without their commander, causing utter confusion in Kenmuir's regiment.

Leven's regiment lay immediately to MacKay's right, facing the Camerons under Lochiel. They escaped the full force of the Highland charge. The Camerons were apparently intent on attacking MacKay's own regiment on his right wing, rather than Leven's regiment, closer to the centre. Indeed, Leven's regiment loosed off a devastating volley of musket fire into their flanks, as the Camerons of Lochiel crossed in front of them. But immediately afterwards, half of Leven's regiment turned and fled as Annandale's troop of horse, which MacKay had ordered forward to attack the Camerons, veered right to avoid Dundee's charge, and galloped back through their own ranks. Yet the remnant of Leven's regiment stood its ground, its members keeping to their ranks.

MacKay's regiment on his right wing received the full brunt of the

Highland charge mounted by the Camerons of Lochiel, together with the clans on Dundee's left wing, among whom were the MacLeans of Otter, the MacDonalds of Kintyre, and the MacNeills of Barra. Even though they managed to loose off two volleys of musket fire, MacKay's regiment broke and fled almost before the Highlanders were upon them, leaving their officers to be killed or wounded. Among them was MacKay's own brother Lieutenant-Colonel James MacKay, who had command of the regiment.

Apart from the remnant of Leven's regiment, the only fighting force left to MacKay was Hastings' regiment on his far right wing. Charged by the MacDonalds of Sleat at the very end of Dundee's left wing, it only slowly gave ground to the Highlanders in hand-to-hand fighting. But then Colonel Fernando Hastings ordered his regiment to wheel to their left, so allowing the MacDonalds to pass in front of his lines. They continued on downhill, pursuing the scattered remnants of MacKay's army as it fled from the field.

MacKay now rallied around 400 footsoldiers who had survived from the remnants of Leven's and Hastings' regiments, and took flight from the scene of his defeat. After meeting up with Colonel George Ramsey with another 200 men, he crossed the Garry upstream of the battlefield. Then, taking to the hills to avoid being pursued by Dundee's cavalry, he crossed Strathtummel, and eventually reached the safety of Weem, where he arrived in the early hours of 28 July 1689. Later the same day, he took horse to Drummond Castle, and finally arrived in Stirling with most of his senior officers, and a few hundred survivors from his army.

Casualties at Killiecrankie

Collapsing under the ferocity of the Highland charge at Killiecrankie, MacKay's forces suffered dreadful casualties. Eyewitnesses later recorded that

> officers and soldiers were cut down through the skull and neck, to the very breast; others had skulls cut off above the ears . . . Some had both their bodies and cross belts cut through at one blow; pikes and small swords were cut like willows; and whomever doubts of this, may consult the eyewitnesses of the tragedy.

Another account by Balhaldie described how

> The enemy lay in heaps almost in the order they were posted; but so disfigured with wounds, and so hashed and mangled, that even the victors could not look upon the amazing proofs of their own agility and strength without surprise and horror.

Nearly a third of MacKay's army lost their lives upon the field of battle, and perhaps the same number were killed as they attempted to escape. The Highland clans suffered similarly heavy losses, especially in the first volleys of musket fire, amounting to around a third of Dundee's own forces. Even so, given their numerical inferiority, they had inflicted three times as many casualties upon the enemy. But among the Jacobite dead was Dundee himself, mortally wounded by a musket ball to his left side. It had pierced his body just below his breast-plate. Another shot had perhaps hit him 'betwixt the eyebrows', causing him to fall from his horse.

Death of 'Bonnie Dundee'

Dundee had charged towards the enemy lines, making for their very centre, 'intent on the action, and carried on by the impetuosity of his courage', in Balhaldie's words. Galloping behind him were James Seton, fourth Earl of Dunfermline, David Halyburton of Pitcur, and a handful of other horsemen. They were followed by a larger troop of horse with Sir William Wallace at its head. But reaching the flatter ground, he suddenly veered to his left, apparently intent on attacking MacKay's regiment. Wallace's action left Dundee dangerously exposed, especially to musket-fire from the remnants of Leven's regiment on his left. Dunfermline saw Dundee's horse swerve to the right, as its rider rose in the saddle, as if waving forward Wallace's horse. Dundee then disappeared from his view amid the smoke discharged from the enemy's muskets.

After silencing the enemy cannon and driving off MacKay's cavalry from the field, Dunfermline and Pitcur returned to the battlefield with their small troop of cavalry. Now intending to join in the attack on Hastings' regiment, they rallied the few Highlanders who had not pursued the enemy from the field. But moving off, they suddenly found themselves under attack by the remnants of Leven's regiment, still standing in their line of battle. Only then as they were forced to retreat did Dunfermline see John Graham, Viscount Dundee, lying on the ground. He was at the point of death.

Just as they came to his aid, Leven's men opened fire, fatally wounding Pitcur, and felling Dunfermline's horse. Dundee's body was left where it lay, only to be stripped during the night by some Camerons, who took his armour and most of his clothes. His near-naked body, 'white and shameless, and all unclothed' to quote Iain Lom, was only found next morning. He was buried in the churchyard at Blair. The significance of his death for the Jacobite cause is best expressed by a translation of a Latin elegy written only a few weeks later in Edinburgh by Dr Archibald Pitcairn:

Oh last and best of Scots, who didst maintain
Thy Country's freedom from a foreign reign,
New people fill the land now thou art gone,
New Gods the temples, and new Kings the throne.
Farewell, who dying didst support the State
And could not fall but with thy Country's fate.

Chapter Twelve

END OF THE HIGHLAND WAR

Even though Jacobite forces kept to the field for another ten months until after their defeat at Cromdale on 1 May 1690, Dundee's victory at Killiecrankie was rendered empty by his death. His command passed to Major-General Alexander Cannon, who lacked Dundee's qualities of leadership, and his charismatic appeal in the eyes of the Highland clans. Indeed, Dundee's death proved a disaster for the Jacobite cause, as the government in Edinburgh realised with relief as soon as it learnt only a few days later that Cannon had been appointed in his place. As King William himself said somewhat prematurely: 'Armies are needless: the war is over with Dundee's life.'

Indeed, had Dundee lived, there can be little doubt that the 1689 rising would have taken on a momentum of its own. Already, the Highland clans left behind on the precipitate march south to Killiecrankie had arrived in the Jacobite camp. Among them were 500 Camerons under Lochiel's son John, 250 MacPhersons, 150 MacDonalds of Keppoch, and 300 other clansmen, mostly Stewarts of Appin and MacDonalds of Glencoe, with a few MacGregors.

The men of Atholl also came out for King James, ignoring the appeals of Lord John Murray. On hearing of MacKay's defeat, he had withdrawn what men he still commanded to Tulliemet, just south of Pitlochry. Disbanding them, he left hurriedly for Edinburgh, while they promptly declared for King James under the leadership of his younger brother Lord James Murray. Meanwhile, news arrived in the Jacobite camp that William Drummond, second Lord Strathallan, had raised Strathearn and Balquhidder, acting for his father John Drummond, first Earl of Melfort, who was among the closest of King James' advisers in Ireland.

Dundee's death ended any likelihood that John Campbell of Glenorchy, first Earl of Breadalbane, would declare for King James, bringing in much needed reinforcements. Despite the urging of Dundee's successors, who reputedly offered to make him General of what was now known as the

Highland Army, he remained at Kilchurn Castle, 'sitting by the fireside with sore foot'. Later he would need an indemnity from the government, pardoning him for advising Cannon on Jacobite tactics and even communicating with King James in Ireland. Dubious of success, he was evidently determined to see which way the dice would fall before he committed himself. No doubt, there were many others like him among the aristocracy who would have rallied to the Jacobite cause after Killiecrankie, had Dundee survived the battle to lead it.

But even had he lived, Dundee would have faced the same strategic difficulties as Montrose had done before him. Cannon made no attempt to seize Perth in the immediate aftermath of Killiecrankie, simply sending a party 300 strong under Alexander Robertson of Struan to raid its stores of meal after its garrison had fled. They were surprised there early on 1 August 1689 by Hugh MacKay of Scourie at the head of a cavalry force, 400 strong. He was determined to regain the initiative after reaching Stirling early on the morning of 29 July, thirty-six hours after his defeat.

Dundee would surely have foreseen the danger, advancing in strength upon Perth before it was seized by MacKay. Admittedly, Argyll's three regiments at Inveraray might have threatened his rear, and indeed Cannon allowed the Stewarts of Appin and the MacDonalds of Glencoe to return home from Atholl to defend their own lands from just such a danger. But believing the early reports that MacKay was dead, the government in Edinburgh had ordered the immediate withdrawal of Argyll's regiments to Glasgow. They arrived there so exhausted after a forced march through atrocious weather that they were quite unfit for service.

Reinforced by Jacobite sympathisers like Breadalbane, Dundee might then have succeeded in taking Edinburgh at the head of a sizeable army. Indeed, the political situation in the Scottish capital had still not resolved itself. Many of the nobility had pursued a vacillating and opportunist course in the last few months, switching allegiance according to the dictates of their own self-interest. Now it appeared that they were prepared to turn their coats again, but not when they learnt that Dundee was dead. However, even if he had managed to overthrow the existing regime with its Presbyterian sympathies, forces would surely have massed elsewhere against him, just as they did against Montrose.

Already, the Presbyterians in the west had assembled in arms at the news of MacKay's defeat at Killiecrankie, and their strength is demonstrated by the 14,000 men that later rallied at a lesser emergency in 1690. But such numbers were dwarfed by Schomberg's army, which was even now being assembled by King William for an invasion of Ireland. Diverted to Scotland, and reinforced by English forces from south of the border, Schomberg would surely have defeated Dundee, just as General David Leslie had defeated Montrose at Philiphaugh. The history of Ireland might well have taken a different course if Londonderry had not been relieved only a few days after Killiecrankie, and the battle of the Boyne fought just a year later. Yet it is difficult to believe that it was only Dundee's death at Killiecrankie that prevented James VII from regaining the throne of Great Britain.

Yet Dundee had perhaps acted too precipitately in 1689. His early thrust down Strathspey showed that he hoped for support from the north-east, with its strong Episcopalian traditions. It was not forthcoming at the time, since the growth of Jacobite sentiment in the north-east was restrained in 1689 until it became clear that bigotry and prejudice would lie at the very heart of the Glorious Revolution's settlement of the Church, as it affected the Episcopalian clergy and their patrons. In reaction to such bigotry, the north-east had become far more receptive to the Jacobite cause by 1690, as Sir Hugh MacKay of Scourie later admitted. By then, many of the Episcopalian clergy, fearful of losing their livelihoods, were actively encouraging rebellion on behalf of King James. Certainly, the support of the north-east with its Episcopalian sympathies and conservative traditions was crucial to any success that the 1715 rebellion might have achieved, had it not been led by John Erskine, sixth Earl of Mar. Had Dundee waited, he could well have found a groundswell of Jacobite support in the north-east that was denied to his lacklustre successors. Dundee's death at Killiecrankie has thus tended to obscure the political and military support that the Jacobite movement attracted over the next two years.

'Extraordinary Long March'

Now with Major-General Alexander Cannon in command, the Highland Army started to march north-east from Atholl on 4 August 1689, eight days after its victory at Killiecrankie. The Highland chiefs had wanted to move south-west along the edge of the Highlands, where recruits to the Jacobite cause from Strathearn and Balquhidder would reinforce their ranks. Instead, Cannon was intent on moving north, hoping to gather recruits from the north-east with its strong Episcopalian sympathies. While marching north towards Strathbogie, he sent Alasdair MacDonald of Glengarry to blockade Abergeldie Castle, while further north, the garrison of Balvenie Castle fled on the approach of a Jacobite raiding party.

MacKay trailed behind the Highland Army as it advanced north-east from Perth with his own cavalry, moving along Strathmore to reach Forfar, and then Aberdeen. By then, Argyll had been ordered north to garrison Perth, but a quarrel with Sir Duncan Campbell of Auchinbreck meant that he remained in Glasgow, while the remnants of MacKay's own army to survive Killiecrankie still occupied Stirling. Colonel George Ramsey took command of the Perth garrison. It consisted of several regiments of infantry, mostly on the verge of mutiny. Then, after summoning Livingston's dragoons from Inverness, MacKay left Aberdeen for a rendezvous in Strathbogie, accompanied by his own cavalry and Heyford's dragoons from Angus. He intended to use his cavalry forces, now 1,200 strong, to drive Cannon's forces, estimated at 4,000 foot and 150 horse, back into the Highlands.

Meanwhile, Cannon had not succeeded in raising the north-east for the Jacobite cause. Apart from the Farquharsons of Inverey, his forces were only swelled by local gentry, who perhaps doubled his cavalry to 300 horse. The Highland chiefs, disillusioned by the lack of any obvious strategy, held a council of war at Auchindoun Castle. When Cannon and his regular commanders refused to mount an offensive, Sir Ewan Cameron of Lochiel, and Sir Donald MacDonald, eldest son of the third Baronet of Sleat, returned home. They did however leave behind their own men in the Jacobite camp, unlike Coll MacDonald of Keppoch, who left with all his followers. Within a fortnight, he would contact Sir Hugh Campbell of Cawdor, offering to submit to the government in Edinburgh.

Perhaps hoping to regain the initiative, Cannon now embarked on another of those 'extraordinary long marches' for which the Highlanders are justly renowned. Moving south from Strathbogie on 17 August, he had crossed the Dee by the morning of 18 August, ignoring a challenge from MacKay to stay and give battle. It seems he intended to cross the hills into Angus by the Cairn O'Mount, but an advance party was repulsed at Fettercairn by government forces under Sir John Lanier. Cannon therefore turned southwest after learning that an infantry regiment had occupied Dunkeld only a few days previously. It had been raised by James Douglas, Earl of Angus, and in fact consisted largely of fanatical Cameronians, drawn from his father's estates in the Lowlands. 'Mad men not to be Governed even by master Shields their oracle', they were commanded by Lieutenant-Colonel William Cleland.

On reaching Dunkeld on 17 August, the Cameronians of Angus's regiment had almost mutinied, fearing that they were surrounded by their enemies. But reassured by Cleland, they started erecting defences within the town. Early on 19 August, they were reinforced by five troops of horse and dragoons under Henry Erskine, third Lord Cardross. Alexander Steuart of Ballechin, whom Cannon had left behind in Atholl, now raised Atholl and Strathtay against this threat. By the morning of 20 August, he appeared with perhaps 1,000 men on the hills above Dunkeld. Cardross sallied out of Dunkeld to meet the Jacobite forces, and skirmishing occurred all day, until the vanguard of Cannon's Highland Army suddenly arrived in the evening. The rest of his forces had surrounded Dunkeld by dawn on the following morning.

Battle of Dunkeld

The battle of Dunkeld might never have been fought but for the incompetence of Colonel George Ramsey in Perth. On learning from Sir John Lanier that Cannon's Highland Army was marching towards Dunkeld, he was sufficiently alarmed to order Cardross's regiment of horse to withdraw at once to Perth. His instructions were however ignored for a whole day as Cardross and his dragoons engaged the enemy on 20 August, only to retire south in the evening. But Ramsey failed to realise that he also had command of Angus's regiment of Cameronians. He therefore neglected to order it to withdraw from Dunkeld at the same time, waiting instead for instructions from Sir John Lanier. The Cameronians threatened to mutiny again, and they were only persuaded then to stay in Dunkeld by Cleland and his officers, who offered to shoot their own horses so they could not abandon their men. It was a badly demoralised force of less than 700 men that now faced the Highland Army, four or five thousand strong according to official estimates.

Dunkeld itself was then only a cluster of houses built in three rows around the ruined cathedral and its graveyard. Dunkeld House, built only a few years previously, dominated the town just north of the cathedral, towering over the surrounding buildings. The town itself was built upon the low ground forming the northern bank of the River Tay, but it was overlooked by the steep slopes of Shiochies Hill flanking the town to the north-east, while Bishop's Hill lay just west of the cathedral. It would not be easy to defend.

The battle started at 7 o'clock on the morning of 21 August 1689. The Jacobite forces first attacked from the north-east, where Sir Alexander MacLean of Otter seized Shiochies Hill with 100 of his men, supported by two cavalry troops on their left flank, advancing over flatter ground to the south to prevent any escape. A second attack was launched on the eastern entrance to the town, forcing back a Cameronian outpost to defend a barricade at the Cross, just east of the cathedral. Another outpost was attacked from the west, and the defenders retreated to take refuge in the ruined cathedral. Meanwhile, two other troops of Jacobite cavalry had circled around Bishop's Hill to prevent the garrison escaping over the ford that crossed the River Tay to the south.

Although the Cameronians were now trapped within the town, only ferocious hand-to-hand fighting slowly pushed them back to take up defensive positions in Dunkeld House, the cathedral, and the few Canons' houses. The Highlanders everywhere deployed their classic tactic of firing a single volley at close quarters from their muskets, and then charging the enemy with sword and targe. But the momentum of such a charge was broken by the low walls separating the back yards of the houses, while they came under sustained fire from the defenders. Even so, Cleland and his second-in-command were killed an hour after the fighting had begun, leaving Captain George Munro in charge.

Yet the Jacobite attack slowly lost its momentum, and eventually petered out. By 11 o'clock, just as the defenders were preparing for a last desperate stand in Dunkeld House with hardly any ammunition, the Highlanders drew off. Castigated by the clans as 'a devil of a commander who was out of sight of his enemies', Cannon was blamed for leading from the rear. But equally the Highlanders were 'not accustomed to stand against a wall for protection, as was done at Dunkeld. The stalwart young men . . . [were] felled by bullets fired by cowherds'. A prisoner afterwards admitted that the clans had baulked at returning to attack 'mad and desperate Men', despite the urging of their officers. Cannon later claimed that his forces had exhausted their ammunition. Late in the afternoon, the Cameronian garrison was relieved by Cardross's dragoons advancing from Perth, while the Highland Army withdrew north along the River Tay to Blair Atholl. Little more than a week later, the Jacobite forces would disperse beyond Loch Rannoch, as the clansmen returned home in time for the harvest, only agreeing to muster again in September.

Containing the Jacobite Threat

Dunkeld ended any likelihood that the Highland Army would break out south into the Lowlands of Scotland. MacKay arrived four days later in Perth on 25 August, where he mustered a large army, consisting of seven battalions of infantry, four regiments of horse and dragoons, and three Independent Companies of horse. Leaving Perth well-guarded, he marched north into Atholl with his forces, arriving there on 28 August to garrison Blair Castle with 500 men. Already, Lord James Murray had submitted, and now MacKay allowed the men of Atholl to take the indemnity already offered by the government in Edinburgh, providing they laid down their arms by 10 September. But despite their submission, their lands were laid waste by Argyll's regiment in revenge for the devastation they had caused four years earlier in Argyllshire.

MacKay did not venture any farther into the Highlands, returning instead to the Lowlands after establishing a garrison at Weem. His English regiments were then ordered to Ireland for active service, or marched south to gain more recruits, leaving him depleted of men. Indeed, the Convention, now sitting as the Scots Parliament, continued to refuse to vote money for the regiments' upkeep, determined to keep up the pressure on King William to meet all their demands concerning the settlement of the Church. It meant that MacKay's remaining forces started to disintegrate in October, when the Treasury ran out of funds. MacKay now hoped to contain the Jacobite threat within the western Highlands by establishing a series of garrisons as a 'cordon sanitaire' around their 250-mile perimeter.

The urgent need for such garrisons was revealed soon after MacKay's return to Edinburgh. Early in September, a raiding party 140 strong under Donald MacGregor of Glengyle, accompanied by his young son Rob Roy MacGregor, seized cattle from the lands of Lord Cardross under the express orders of Major-General Cannon. Such raids for provisions would be needed over the coming winter, if the Jacobite forces were not to succumb to starvation. Indeed, the tactic had some success, since it was reported in November that there was 'plenty of French Wine, and good store of Beef, but great scarcity of Bread'. Even so, several Jacobite officers, and a number of their prisoners, died from a lack of food, especially on Mull.

Lord Cardross reacted to the raid upon his lands by planting a government garrison at Finlarig to guard the western end of Loch Tay. By occupying a stronghold of John Campbell of Glenorchy, first Earl of Breadalbane, the garrison was intended to prevent the MacGregors from breaking out of their fastness around Loch Rannoch and the head of Glen Lyon. Breadalbane had already submitted to the government, so it appeared to Cannon that he had perhaps agreed to the garrison itself, despite his Jacobite sympathies. Cannon therefore decided to forestall any further garrisons by ordering the burning of Breadalbane's tower-house at Achallader, which guarded the southern edge of the Moor of Rannoch. Breadalbane was outraged. However, as Paul Hopkins has argued, his anger was directed more at his own tenants who had colluded in its destruction, rather than blaming the MacDonalds of Glencoe, who were among the raiding party. Indeed, when he learnt that Cannon had himself given the order for its burning, he became preoccupied by how his own intentions could be so misunderstood. Thereafter, he would adopt a neutral stance, standing aloof from both parties to the conflict.

A month later, another notorious raid took place against the lands of Robert Campbell of Glenlyon. Sixteen months later, he would play a leading role in the Glencoe Massacre. Beset with financial difficulties, he had already taken a commission with Argyll's regiment before Killiecrankie. After the battle of Dunkeld, he had acted as a guide to a detachment of government forces that MacKay sent out from Blair Castle to capture Alexander Robertson of Struan and several other Jacobites. Then on 7 October, MacKay ordered

Robert Menzies of Weem to establish a garrison at Meggernie Castle in Glenlyon, thereby making it a legitimate target for raiding by the Highland Army. Indeed, although no written orders have survived, there can be little doubt that the raid was sanctioned by Cannon, as Paul Hopkins has argued. The plundering was thorough, since Glenlyon lost more than £7,500 Scots in cattle and goods. Legend has it that a baby was even stripped of its blankets.

Even so, Glenlyon's later petition to Parliament, asking that he should be compensated for his losses, fails even to mention the role played by the MacDonalds of Glencoe, although they undoubtedly took part. Instead, he blamed the MacDonalds of Keppoch, along with the Robertsons, the MacGregors, and the tenants of Atholl and Weem, from among his neighbours. Moreover, he was threatened with the loss of his estates to John Murray, Marquis of Atholl, whom he needed to pay £39,000 Scots by Whitsun 1690 to redeem his debts. Unable to do so, he alleged that Atholl had somehow connived with Robert Menzies of Weem to secure his destruction by providing the Jacobite forces with a pretext for raiding his lands.

The MacDonalds of Glencoe under their chief Alasdair MacIain were party to yet another raid, 500 strong, which occurred in November, and which was again authorised by Cannon. It plundered the lands of William Cochrane of Kilmaronock, south-east of Loch Lomond. He was an officer in MacKay's army, despite being Dundee's brother-in-law, and thus his lands were a legitimate target. Other raids occurred farther north, where Cannon issued a warrant to lay waste to the lands of Duncan Forbes of Culloden at Ferintosh in the Black Isle. The attack was carried out in mid-October by a force of Jacobites, among whom were the Grants of Glenmoriston and the Chisholms of Knockfin. They had suffered in the immediate aftermath of Killiecrankie, when John Gordon, Lord Strathnaver, had ravaged Glenmoriston with 500 troops and some dragoons, burning down John Grant's house at Invermoriston.

Winter Campaign by Glengarry

Now in the aftermath of the October raid on the Black Isle, Sir James Leslie as the Governor of Inverness feared a full-scale Jacobite attack. He had his own infantry regiment, as well as two other regiments and seven troops of horse and dragoons, to defend the lowlands of Ross and Moray. Indeed, on 3 December 1689, Alasdair MacDonald of Glengarry advanced along the Great Glen with Lewis Crichton, fourth Viscount Frendraught, and upwards of 100 men. They were joined by 400 men from Glenmoriston and Strathglass in laying siege to Castle Urquhart. Further reinforcements were expected from Kintail in Wester Ross, raised by the Earl of Seaforth's uncle, Colin MacKenzie.

Their plans, however, were frustrated. Sir Ewan Cameron of Lochiel had stood aloof from the Jacobite cause ever since Killiecrankie, while hundreds of his clansmen had, since early November, laid waste to the Airds, just west of Inverness. Now, they plundered indiscriminately the lands of Glenmoriston and Strathglass, left vacant by the attack with Glengarry on Castle Urquhart. Glengarry was forced to retire before Colin MacKenzie could even join him. Then in late December, Sir Thomas Livingston arrived in Inverness with his regiment to take command of the garrison. He would play a crucial role in the final defeat of the Jacobite forces at Cromdale in May 1690.

Jacobite Resurgence in the North-East

By then, the Highland Army was commanded by Major-General Thomas Buchan of Auchmacoy. He had sailed from Dublin on 24 January 1690, accompanied by several professional officers. But he was not James FitzJames, first Duke of Berwick, King James' natural son, and nor was he accompanied by 8,000 men, as King James had promised. Only a spirited speech by Sir Ewan Cameron of Lochiel at a council of war at Inverlochy in mid-February prevented the Highland chiefs from seeking terms from Edinburgh. Yet Lochiel had his own reasons, since Buchan then supported him in his petition to King James, requesting a grant to the lands of Sunart and Ardnamurchan. Among the other chiefs only Sir John MacLean of Duart remained fanatical in his attachment to King James, since he had most to lose by defeat. However, still hoping for reinforcements from Ireland, the Jacobites agreed a rendezvous for 15 March, when each chieftain promised to raise 100 men.

Owing to the lateness of the season, it was only in mid-April that Buchan was able to resume active campaigning. He first marched to the head of Loch Ness, while Coll MacDonald of Keppoch harried all of Stratherrick and Strathnairn with his clansmen, returning with sufficient meal to feed Buchan's forces for the time being. Buchan then crossed into Badenoch, most likely by the Corrieyairack Pass, where he stayed for ten days, before moving down Strathspey in a north-easterly direction. By then, his force of MacLeans, MacDonalds, Camerons, MacNachtans, Grants of Glenmoriston, and the Irish troops had been reinforced by the MacPhersons, 200 strong. Indeed, as he marched from Lochaber, his army 'increased like a snowball daily', until it perhaps numbered 1,500 men, all on foot.

By 29 April, the Highland Army under Buchan had reached Culnakyle.

There, Buchan held a council of war and, overruling his commanders, determined to continue his advance along the valley of the River Spey. Next evening, his troops were encamped below the Haughs of Cromdale, occupying the low ground on the east bank of the Spey at Dalchapple, while another contingent bivouacked on the low hills around Lethendry Castle, a mile to the south. Only the MacDonalds of Keppoch took up a more defensive position beyond Dalchapple at the foot of Tom an Uird. The Grant stronghold at Ballachastell was little more than a mile away on the opposite bank of the Spey, where it was garrisoned by a company of Grant's regiment under Captain John Grant of Easter Elchies.

Misjudging the situation, Buchan had almost deliberately laid his troops open to a possible attack. It seems he knew of local Jacobite sympathisers, who would only join the Highland Army if it appeared that they were coerced into doing so. But it was a dangerous tactic, since Buchan knew already that Livingston had left Inverness, marching out to Brodie on 27 April with 800 foot and 400 horse. Yet to guard against any such attack across the River Spey from the direction of Ballachastell Castle, Buchan made another disastrous error, which compounded his earlier misjudgment. He had sounded out the depths of the River Spey with some of his officers, finding out that it could only be forded in three places. He then placed outposts, forty-five strong, to guard these crossings of the river, while another 240 men protected their rear, lying halfway between the outposts and the main encampments. What Buchan quite failed to realise was that there were no horsemen to raise the alarm, should the enemy cavalry overwhelm his forward outposts, and gallop directly against his own positions, as indeed happened.

Rout at Cromdale

Meanwhile, Livingston had left Brodie on 30 April, after learning of Buchan's whereabouts. Marching across the hills through rough country, he reached Ballachastell with his army in the early hours of 1 May 1690. By half past two in the morning, he was ready to attack, spurred on eagerly by his men. By following a small valley down to the River Spey, he managed to gain its banks without being detected. 200 men were then ordered to attack the main ford at Cromdale Church as a diversion, while he led the rest of his forces downstream to cross the river at the lower ford. He found it left unguarded. The forward detachment guarding the ford was either negligent, or it had gone to stem his diversionary attack at the church. Two troops of dragoons, and MacKay's Highland Company, crossed the river before they were even observed, and the remainder soon followed.

As men ran back to raise the alarm, Livingston galloped forward with four troops of horse and dragoons. The remaining cavalry were left behind with all his infantry to guard his rear, apart from some Grants who rode forward, mounted as pillions behind the dragoons. Buchan's forces were taken utterly by surprise, and confusion reigned as Livingston's cavalry broke upon them. Some men were still asleep, while others ran up and down half-naked. Buchan ordered his nephew and some other officers to defend the ruins of Lethendry Castle, where they eventually surrendered. Apart from the MacPhersons from Badenoch, whom Buchan admitted fought well, only the MacLeans managed to keep together as a fighting force.

Retreating in a body towards the Haughs of Cromdale, the MacLeans suddenly turned, hoping to repulse the enemy. But their spirited defence was futile, and soon they too were forced to flee, along with the other survivors of the Highland Army. They left perhaps three or four hundred dead upon the field. Many more would have been killed if a sudden mist had not come down upon Livingston's cavalry as it pursued the fugitives uphill over the Haughs of Cromdale. According to Livingston, he had no dead, and only three or four wounded. Such was the rout of the Highland Army at Cromdale.

Among the Jacobite commanders, Major-General Alexander Cannon fled up Strathspey to take refuge with Duncan MacPherson of Cluny. Buchan fled over the hills to Glenlivet, before making his way back to the west. His official report castigated his army as 'the very worst men among the Clans, the Chiefs never venturing their best but where they go themselves'. The comment made him 'the most ungrateful man in the Highlands', to quote Sir John MacLean of Duart. The MacDonalds of Keppoch never even attempted to engage the government forces. Instead, they retreated to safety up the slopes of Tom an Uird with their chief Coll, who it was said 'was ever keen for plunder, but never once fought for his King'. Afterwards, he withdrew with his clansmen up the east bank of the Spey, and returned to Lochaber. Shortage of food eventually forced Livingston back to Inverness, but only after he had advanced into Badenoch to overawe Cluny, and then briefly returned down Strathspey to occupy Ballindalloch.

The rout at Cromdale is often depicted as the dying fall of the first Jacobite rebellion. Yet when MacKay marched north seven weeks later on 21 June 1690, he was afterwards bitterly reproached for risking losing Scotland to gain Inverlochy. Indeed, he had to appeal directly to King William for his marching orders, since the Council in Edinburgh would not agree to them. Later in June, as Cannon and Buchan joined forces to raid the Lowlands, the government called out the fencible men of the Presbyterian south-west to defend the country. Rallying to the call, and 14,000 strong, they flocked to

Glasgow in what was almost the exact opposite of the 'Highland Host' of 1678. Their numbers were such that all but 4,500 of the 'Lowland Host' had to be dismissed on 24 July, leaving the remnant to garrison Glasgow, Stirling and Falkirk.

Naval Expedition to the Western Isles

After its victory at Cromdale the government in Edinburgh first ordered a naval expedition against the Jacobite rebels in the Western Isles. Consisting of three English men-of-war, including the 32-gun frigate *Dartmouth* as its flagship, and four other ships, it sailed from Greenock on 14 May 1690. It carried six or eight hundred infantrymen under a Major Ferguson, mostly from the three regiments of the Dutch Brigade. Sailing round the Mull of Kintyre, they first laid waste to the islands of Gigha, Cara, and Colonsay, and also to parts of Jura, burning houses and destroying cattle and corn, before the squadron reached Mull. Although they burned the country around Lochbuie and Aros, they were not strong enough to attack Duart Castle, which was defended by 600 MacLeans. Ferguson requested reinforcements, which Argyll was ordered to raise, but they would only be ready in late June.

Meanwhile, the squadron separated to attack the small isles of Coll, Eigg, Rhum and Canna, and then sailed for Skye. Anchoring off Isle Ornsay, Ferguson landed with all his men, while fusillades of cannon-fire from the ships offshore prevented any active resistance from the MacDonalds of Sleat. Unwilling to risk further devastation to his lands, Sir Donald MacDonald, afterwards the fourth Baronet of Sleat, came aboard the *Dartmouth* off Armadale to give his word of honour not ever again to take up arms against the government. But the landing had not been accomplished without casualties, since three men had been killed, while a fourth man had been hanged after Sir Donald's clansmen had caught him hiding after the landing.

Massacre on Eigg

Determined to take revenge, but reluctant to offend the new-found loyalty of Sir Donald MacDonald, the squadron returned to Eigg in mid-June. The fighting men were absent, but Ferguson's soldiers proceeded to massacre all the other inhabitants who remained on the island, slaughtering women, children and old men, while his officers turned a blind eye. Only by heeding an old man's warning on his deathbed did a few manage to escape the slaughter. The ships' logs omitted to mention any such action, and it was only revealed later from the writings of the Reverend D. MacLeod on second sight, citing the warnings of the dying man. It seems quite likely that other atrocities had taken place, but equally they were not recorded.

Returning south from the massacre on Eigg, the squadron anchored off Dunstaffnage Castle, where the Campbell forces mustered by Argyll were now ready to embark. Other ships had already arrived with provisions destined for the garrison at Inverlochy. Together, they sailed up Loch Linnhe on 26 June to land their combined forces at Corpach, watched helplessly by Sir Ewan Cameron of Lochiel and Major-General Thomas Buchan. They had only 200 clansmen under their command, and urgent calls for reinforcements to Coll MacDonald of Keppoch and Alasdair MacDonald of Glengarry went unanswered. Indeed, they were both now threatened by the forces under Sir Hugh MacKay of Scourie. He was even then marching overland from Perth towards Inverlochy, which he would reach on 3 July. Major Ferguson took advantage of his enemies' weakness, seizing Lochiel's residence at Achnacarry, which he garrisoned with government forces. Once MacKay arrived at Inverlochy, the warships sailed for another brief cruise to the Inner Hebrides, leaving a garrison under Sir Duncan Campbell of Auchinbreck at Mingary Castle in Ardnamurchan, and bombarding Armadale House in Skye.

MacKay's Expedition to Inverlochy

Sir Hugh MacKay of Scourie had marched out of Perth on 21 June, accompanied by seven infantry battalions, his Dutch brigade, Menzies' Independent Company, and several troops of horse, amounting to more than 4,000 men. Now aware of the dangers of Highland campaigning after his defeat at Killiecrankie, his vanguard first made a feint towards Atholl. Meanwhile, his main forces marched up Strathardle to the east, before crossing the hills by Glenshee and perhaps the Cairnwell to reach Braemar. He then continued north to the head of Strathdon, before crossing the Ladder Hills into Strathavon, where he turned west to reach Culnakyle on the River Spey by 27 June. He was joined there by another two or three thousand men from Inverness under Sir Thomas Livingston.

In joining MacKay's army, Livingston had left only Strathnaver's regiment to guard Inverness and the surrounding districts, along with a few other detachments from among the northern clans. MacKay had taken another gamble. Kenneth MacKenzie, fourth Earl of Seaforth, had already landed from Ireland at his castle of Eilean Donnan on 20 May with a company of Irish grenadiers as a bodyguard, and a cargo of corn and ammunition. A Catholic convert, he had joined King James in France soon after fleeing the

country in December 1688. But although greeted with enthusiasm by large
numbers of his clansmen, they proved unwilling to rise again for the Jacobite
cause after the setbacks they had suffered earlier in the year.

MacKay now advanced up the Spey from Culnakyle. Badly short of
provisions, he had too few horses to carry enough meal for his army. As he
complained, he advanced 'somewhat contrary to the maxim of war', since he
did not know if his supply ships had arrived at Inverlochy. Reaching
Badenoch, he first sent a mounted detachment towards the head of the River
Spey on 1 July to deceive the enemy, who were waiting to ambush him in
Glen Roy with 800 men. He then marched across the hills to the south of
Loch Laggan with his main force. Under heavy sniper-fire, and despite a
frontal attack on his vanguard by 200 Highlanders, which was beaten back,
he marched down Glen Spean on 2 July. Next day, he reached Inverlochy.

The fort which MacKay now built on the shores of Loch Linnhe was
called Fort William in honour of King William. Constructed in just eleven
days, it consisted of an earthwork surmounted by a timber palisade, and
flanked by a ditch. It occupied the site of the old Cromwellian fortifications,
which had been razed to the ground in 1661. Lying just south of the mouth
of the River Nevis, a mile or so from Inverlochy Castle, the new fort followed
the pentagonal outlines of the older citadel. The waters of Loch Linnhe and
the River Nevis formed a natural defence to the north, so that the bulk of the
defences faced south and east, allowing a free field of fire across a glacis from
a covered way. The main entrance from the south was guarded by a detached
earthwork with three sides, known as a ravelin, which was overlooked by
the three-pointed bastion at the south-eastern corner of the fort. The other
corners consisted of two-pointed bastions, jutting out from the earthworks,
while a sallyport gave access to the banks of the River Nevis. After landing
twelve pieces of artillery from his supply ships, MacKay placed the heavier
pieces along the seaward side, facing out across Loch Linnhe to guard
against a possible attack by the French navy.

While his men laboured, MacKay was already under urgent orders to
return south. An invasion threatened England after the French navy had
decisively defeated the Anglo-Dutch fleet at Beachy Head on 30 June. But
only the next day, James VII was just as decisively defeated at the battle of the
Boyne on 1 July 1690. Although the war in Ireland would last another year,
he soon returned from Ireland to exile at the court of St Germain in France.
Meanwhile, MacKay had marched out of Fort William on 18 July, leaving
behind a garrison of 1,200 troops in charge of Colonel John Hill, who thus
returned to the post he had occupied more than thirty years previously at
the time of Cromwell. Leading his army up Glen Gloy to avoid the lower
stretches of Glen Roy, MacKay then crossed the hills into Badenoch. Leaving

a company of MacKays to garrison Ruthven Castle, he then crossed into Atholl, and finally reached Perth on 26 July 1690.

Jacobite Resurgence

MacKay had returned south to find yet another threat facing the government in Edinburgh. Quite unable to resist MacKay's advance towards Inverlochy on 3 July, Cannon and Buchan had gone their separate ways. Cannon rode south-east with thirty mounted men to Perthshire. He was joined there by several prominent gentry, among whom were Dundee's brother David Graham, now Viscount Dundee, as well as Iain MacNachtan of Dunderave, Alexander Robertson of Struan, and Patrick Steuart of Ballechin. Now sixty strong, Cannon rode unmolested into Balquhidder, where he raised 300 MacGregors for King James. They raided deep into the Lowlands south of the Forth, acting with impunity until the 'Lowland Host' was called out.

Meanwhile, Buchan had ridden east from Lochaber with seventy horse-men, hoping to raise the north-east of Scotland for the Jacobite cause. Routed at first by William, Master of Forbes, as he descended into Aberdeenshire, he was forced to rejoin Cannon in Perthshire. Together, they now moved north-east with their remaining cavalry to Braemar, where John Farquharson of Inverey, the 'Black Colonel', was still in arms for King James. Raising 800 men from Braemar and Cromar, and leaving a detachment to blockade Abergeldie Castle, they then marched across country to besiege Kildrummy Castle. They were met by eight troops of cavalry under the Master of Forbes. Buchan spread out his infantry, while placing baggage horses among his cavalry, to give the impression of strength. The ruse worked, as the Master of Forbes decided to fall back to Aberdeen, where he expected further reinforcements. But his tactical withdrawal turned into a panic-stricken flight, from which his reputation never recovered.

Kildrummy Castle was captured, and put to the flames. Then Buchan advanced on Aberdeen by way of the Garioch, gaining many more recruits from among the local gentry as he rode through the country. Their motives were mixed, since many were only persuaded to join Buchan by the obvious threat to their land and property. Others would have joined the Jacobite cause anyway, given their Episcopalian sympathies, once it looked like gaining momentum and impetus.

Now learning that Colonel Richard Cunningham was marching north with three infantry regiments to reinforce Aberdeen, Buchan turned south to enter the Mearns with a force reputed to be 1,800 strong. Cunningham himself halted at Montrose, waiting for Livingston's dragoons which were to reinforce his infantry. Although Livingston fell ill from dysentery, MacKay joined him instead, and together they advanced to Brechin on 17 August. Buchan did not dare oppose him directly with men whose loyalty he perhaps suspected. Retreating over the Cairn O'Mount, he rode hard towards Inverness with a rapidly dwindling force, now only 500 strong.

Buchan rode north in the hope that Kenneth MacKenzie, fourth Earl of Seaforth, might finally raise his clansmen for King James. But Seaforth prevaricated, just as he had done ever since landing in Kintail on 20 May. His indecision had already allowed MacKay to gamble on establishing the garrison at Fort William in the heart of Lochaber. He could hardly have risked such a campaign if Seaforth had threatened Inverness with perhaps 1,000 MacKenzie clansmen under arms. Now, almost as a half-hearted ges-ture, Seaforth belatedly started to raise the men of Kintail, Lochcarron and Lochalsh. He then advanced to Achilty near Contin with a force around 900 strong, which was 'fitter for a convoy. . . than an army'.

Meanwhile, MacKay had pursued Buchan and Cannon north with his horse and dragoons, leaving his infantry to follow. Surprised by MacKay's forces near Inverness, they fled west into the Aird, hoping desperately for support from the Frasers, and then retreated along Loch Ness to Glenmoriston. Seaforth could perhaps have joined them, although the Munros of Foulis might then have ravaged his lands. Instead, he opened negotiations through his mother with MacKay. He excused his conduct as being 'obliged in honour to make some appearance for King James', who had made him Marquis of Seaforth with a commission as Major-General.

But fearing for his health should he be imprisoned, Seaforth broke the agreement with MacKay, which was intended to save his face by having him 'captured' by government troops. MacKay reacted furiously by raising 900 MacKays, Rosses and Sutherland men, along with 200 men of Strathnaver's regiment. They were ordered to devastate the MacKenzie lands along the west coast, while his own mounted forces were to lay waste to the MacKenzie Lowlands in the east. Responding to this threat, Seaforth was urged by his followers to disband his forces, which he did on 2 September 1690. Guided by Colin MacKenzie, his officers made their way through the mountains into Lochaber, where they joined Buchan. Next day, Seaforth surrendered to Sir Hugh MacKay at Strathpeffer. Apart from a brief spell of freedom, he would spend the next seven years in prison, held captive in Edinburgh Castle, where his wife was eventually allowed to join him in 1692.

MacKay now settled a garrison in Inverness, and returned south through the north-east, where he quartered troops to prevent any repetition of Buchan's earlier campaign. Already, John Farquharson of Inverey was a spent force, having been defeated at the Pass of Ballater, and his lands destroyed. Yet Buchan and Cannon were still active for King James, advancing 300 strong to Glen Dochart, and raising another 200 foot in Balquhidder. Their forces briefly threatened Dunblane, and then advanced towards Perth with 400 horse and 100 foot, thought to be 'a very unusual proportion . . . in a Highland army'.

But suffering from shortages of food and forage, Buchan decided to withdraw north-west with his cavalry on 12 September, leaving his foot to fend for themselves. Later in September, he disbanded his remaining followers, as government forces advanced upon him from all sides, laying waste to the countryside. By late October, Buchan was settled for the coming winter with his Catholic officers at Invergarry, staying with Alasdair MacDonald of Glengarry, while Cannon had retired to Skye with his Protestant officers to stay with Sir Donald MacDonald, third Baronet of Sleat. It marked the start of a break between the two men which had serious consequences.

Argyll's Expedition to Mull

The government now had the advantage. As already recounted, the *Dartmouth* had already sailed once again for the Western Isles on 27 August, landing on Skye and Eigg to overawe the MacDonald clansmen, and perhaps even raiding Uist. Now, Archibald Campbell, tenth Earl of Argyll, was given authority to raise a force in Argyllshire to subdue Appin, Glencoe, Morvern, Ardnamurchan and Mull. Sailing first from Dunstaffnage, he returned from Fort William with four companies of his own regiment. Another 1,300 men joined his forces at Dunollie from the two Independent Companies under the Campbell lairds of Ardkinglas and Auchinbreck, together with another 100 gentry and their followers. Forty birlinns were pressed into the government service from all along the coast, along with 200 men to act as their rowers.

Meanwhile, the *Dartmouth* was ordered with two smaller ships to patrol the Sound of Mull, where it could threaten the MacLeans. However, before Argyll's expedition could even leave for Mull, a sudden storm on 9 October sank the ship, driving it against the rocks of Eilean Rubha an Rudire after its cables had parted off Scallastle Bay. It was lost with nearly all hands. Among the men who drowned was its captain, responsible for the massacre on Eigg. Local legend has it that a Mull witch put a spell on the ship, helped by covens from all over the Highlands, who made themselves manifest as crows and cats.

A week later, Argyll landed on Mull at Loch Spelve with 1,900 foot and sixty dragoons. While the MacLeans retreated to the mountains with their cattle, he advanced against Duart Castle, burning the country as he went. Another force camped at Aros Bay. Such a show of strength was enough to persuade some Highland chieftains to submit, at least for the time being.

Indeed, some of their tenants and lesser gentry had already submitted, especially among the Stewarts of Appin, and the MacDonalds of Glencoe, agreeing terms with Colonel John Hill, whom MacKay had left behind in Fort William as its Governor.

Even before reaching Fort William in July 1690, Hill had started negotiations with Sir Ewan Cameron of Lochiel and Alasdair MacDonald of Glengarry, together with Kenneth MacKenzie, fourth Earl of Seaforth. Lochiel and Glengarry were tempted with offers of money to buy off the superiorities which the Earl of Argyll, and the Duke of Gordon, held over them. But only Coll MacDonald of Keppoch, after visiting Lieutenant-Colonel Hill at Fort William, had offered his submission, provided that he could be given means to support himself, which was not forthcoming.

Now, however, Sir John MacLean of Duart gave his permission for his clan gentry and their tenants to submit, taking the oath of allegiance to King William, and surrendering their arms. He remained in the hills with 170 Irishmen, and some of his clansmen, while Duart Castle held out against Argyll's forces. After ten days, Argyll abandoned the siege of Duart Castle, and embarked on 8 November with the bulk of his own forces. He left a garrison in Lochbuie Castle, and another detachment of 250 men at Aros Bay. Other garrisons occupied Castle Stalker, after John Stewart of Ardsheal, tutor of Appin, had submitted earlier on 9 October, and Mingary Castle in Ardnamurchan. Faced with such odds, Sir John MacLean of Duart took refuge in the near-impregnable castle of Cairnaburgh in the Treshnish Islands.

Chapter Thirteen

'MURDER UNDER TRUST'

Argyll's campaign against Mull effectively ended the Highland War. Yet the government did not really have the resources to pacify the Highlands. The garrison at Fort William was close to mutiny, living only on meal, water and salt herring, and its pay hardly ever arrived. Death and desertion soon halved its numbers to only 600 men, many of them sick. Indeed, as many as seven troops of horse, and thirty-nine companies of foot, were needed to contain the Highland threat at an annual cost of £50,000 sterling, which the country could ill afford. Moreover, the threat to King William in Flanders, where Louis XIV of France captured the city of Mons after a three-week siege on 29 March 1691, meant that all his military resources and manpower were needed on the Continent. The time had evidently come to offer terms to the Jacobite clans.

In fact, Sir George MacKenzie, Viscount Tarbat, had advocated such a policy as early as April 1689, even before John Graham of Claverhouse, Viscount Dundee, had raised the Jacobite Standard on behalf of King James. Writing to his cousin George, Lord Melville, he had suggested that money might persuade the Highland clans to keep the peace. Soon afterwards, King William made Lord Melville his Secretary of State for Scotland, but it was not until March 1690 that Tarbat was given a warrant to negotiate with the clan chiefs. He argued that they mostly had their own reasons for rebelling against the government. By supporting the Jacobite cause, they most likely hoped to rid themselves of the feudal superiorities and other jurisdictions held over them by such magnates as Archibald Campbell, tenth Earl of Argyll, recently restored to the earldom forfeited by his father. Equally, they hoped to evade any payment of their debts, amassed over the years, which they mostly owed to the very same Earl of Argyll, after they were bought up by his predecessors.

Colonel John Hill was chosen by Tarbat to act as his agent in the negotiations, and it was presumably for this reason that he was made Deputy-Governor of Fort William in July 1690. However, Sir John Campbell of Glenorchy, Earl of Breadalbane, was also involved under the patronage of Sir John Dalrymple, Master of Stair, then acting as the Lord Advocate. Breadalbane had already fled to Kilchurn Castle in June 1690, after he was discovered plotting with the Jacobites. He spent the rest of the year in rebuilding the castle itself as virtually the last great essay in private fortification seen in the British Isles. Among his additions were two ranges of barracks, where he hoped to accommodate his own Independent Company, 200 strong. Commanded by himself, it would play a central role in the grandiose scheme he now entertained for pacifying the Highlands. But any attempt to negotiate with the Jacobite clans was suspect to the government. It might simply be a ploy to gain time until King James could send them help from Ireland, or an excuse to put off another Highland campaign to subdue them.

Negotiations with the Jacobite Chiefs

On the first day of 1691, Sir John Dalrymple, Master of Stair, was appointed as Secretary of State of Scotland under King William. Holding the post jointly with George, Lord Melville, newly created the Earl of Melville, he was soon to gain the upper hand over his political rival. Melville had failed to bring the Jacobite chieftains to declare themselves irrevocably for King William, despite the friendly relations they had established with Colonel John Hill at Fort William. Dalrymple now turned to Breadalbane to negotiate with the Jacobite clans, since the regime did not have the resources for another campaign against them. But first he needed the agreement of King William, which he finally obtained in May 1691, together with the promise of £12,000 sterling from the English Treasury, intended to pay off the Highland chiefs.

Breadalbane arrived at Kilchurn by 5 June 1691, where he opened negotiations with the chiefs, at first seeing them individually. Among his visitors were Sir Ewan Cameron of Lochiel, Sir John MacLean of Duart, and Alasdair MacDonald of Glengarry, as well as Major-General Thomas Buchan of Auchmacoy, commander-in-chief of what remained of the Jacobite forces. Then the scene shifted to the burnt-out ruins of Achallader Castle, where Breadalbane entertained the Highland chiefs and their retinues, some 500 strong, for a fortnight at his own expense. Telling the chiefs he was still a Jacobite at heart, he warned them that Sir Thomas Livingston, now commander-in-chief of King William's army in Scotland after Major-General Sir Hugh MacKay of Scourie had left for Ireland, was planning to attack them with fire and sword. He urged them to submit on the best possible terms which he promised to obtain for them. Alasdair MacDonald of Glengarry was violently opposed to any such negotiation, attempting to disrupt the proceeding by launching a raiding party, 500 strong, against the Rosses of Balnagown. It was repulsed by Sir James Leslie and his garrison in Inverness.

Agreement at Achallader

Sir Ewan Cameron of Lochiel spoke for the other Jacobite chiefs. He demanded that all their expenses incurred in the Highland War should be repaid, since otherwise they would have to live by raiding. He further argued that the feudal superiorities should be bought out with public money. Eventually it was agreed with Breadalbane how the sum of £12,000 sterling should be distributed: £3,000 to Coll MacDonald of Keppoch to buy out MacIntosh's superiority over him; £3,000 to Sir John MacLean of Duart to buy back estates from the Earl of Argyll worth £300 a year, as previously agreed in 1680; £2,800 to allow Sir Ewan Cameron of Lochiel to buy Sunart and Ardnamurchan from the Earl of Argyll, to be held under the Crown; £1,500 to allow Alasdair MacDonald of Glengarry, although still aggrieved, to buy Knoydart from the Earl of Argyll, and settle a debt on the estate; £600 to settle a debt of Alan MacDonald of Clan Ranald, owed to the Earl of Argyll; £300 to pay off the Earl of Argyll's claim upon the estate of Iain MacNachtan; £150 to settle the Earl of Argyll's claim upon the estate of Robert Stewart of Appin; £150 to compensate John Gordon of Brachley for his father's murder by John Farquharson of Inverey, the 'Black Colonel', who was to receive a pardon in return; £150 to Patrick Steuart of Ballechin, despite his refusal to attend; and £150 to Alasdair MacIain, chief of the MacDonalds of Glencoe, so that he could buy off Argyll's superiority over him. Given the circumstances, it was a generous settlement.

The sum of £150 to be paid to Alasdair MacIain is the most revealing in the light of subsequent events. It is notorious that Breadalbane quarrelled violently with the Glencoe chief at Achallader over the theft of some cattle by his MacDonald clansmen, and it is said that he threatened to do MacIain a mischief. Indeed, counting up the times his lawless activities had offended Breadalbane, the old chief became so alarmed that he withdrew with his two sons, telling them that he feared nobody as much as Breadalbane. Popular tradition later made this quarrel the pretext for the Glencoe Massacre, as Breadalbane reputedly plotted his revenge, even though it is mere supposition, lacking any evidence.

But just as Robert Campbell of Glenlyon never blamed Alasdair MacIain of Glencoe for the 1689 raid upon Glenlyon, denouncing it instead as an attempt by John Murray, Marquis of Atholl, to ruin him, neither does it seem that Breadalbane was especially hostile to the MacDonalds, or even Alasdair MacIain in particular. Indeed, he was playing for much higher stakes.

Significantly, as recorded by Paul Hopkins, he duly honoured his promise to obtain the sum of £150 for MacIain, even if it was never actually paid, and gained him a remission for murder. Moreover, MacIain had recently earned Breadalbane's gratitude, since only two months earlier his Glencoe clansmen had conveniently abducted a Presbyterian minister from Glenorchy, escorting him away from his parish one Sunday to the strains of the March of Death. The Episcopalian incumbent was restored, and administered to his parish undisturbed until his death in 1723.

Breadalbane's Movements after Achallader

Events now took on a momentum of their own, even though they were not preordained. Indeed, only the strictest and most literal of Calvinists, with their belief in Predestination, might argue the Glencoe Massacre was inevitable from the very start. The agreement made by Breadalbane with the Jacobite chiefs was signed on 30 June 1691. They were to submit to the government by 31 October, after getting King James to agree that they should lay down their arms on his behalf. Both sides were to observe a cessation of arms in the meantime. Well-satisfied, Breadalbane galloped south, reaching Finlarig on Loch Tay by nightfall, and then continued to Edinburgh. There he found to his dismay that Sir John Dalrymple was now abroad with King William in Flanders. It was not until the evening of 12 July that the King and his chief minister for Scotland heard of his successful negotiations at Achallader a fortnight previously.

As William's assent was needed in order to ratify the agreement, Dalrymple now expected Breadalbane to cross to Flanders. However, Breadalbane had already written on 28 June, suggesting instead that Dalrymple should come to London with the necessary instructions from King William. Breadalbane therefore remained in Edinburgh until 10 July, when he left for London. Arriving there a week later, he still had not heard from Flanders. He therefore decided to cross the Channel on 24 July to see William personally. His decision had disastrous consequences. Four days later, instructions arrived in London for Queen Mary to ratify the agreement, signed by the King on the very day before Breadalbane left the country. Had he delayed his departure, the Glencoe Massacre would never have occurred.

Worse followed. Breadalbane's return was delayed for more than two months by the difficulties of travelling back to London as rival armies faced one another on the continent. Already, his political rivals had seized on his absence abroad to undermine his grand scheme for pacifying the Highlands. Given his Jacobite past, they raised suspicions that he only intended to gain time until the campaigning season was over, or until fresh reinforcements could be sent from France to aid the Jacobites. Darlrymple himself became alarmed, only to have his fears allayed. Even so, he had King William write to Sir Thomas Livingston, trusting his regular troops were still guarding the fringes of the Highlands to prevent any further acts of rebellion. It was enough to make Queen Mary doubt what her husband intended, and she put off any decision until she heard directly.

Meanwhile, King William had made 'his company at table merry with his asking at my Lord Breadalbane, if there were any wolves in the Highlands, and upon his answering in the negative, with telling him that they had enough of two-footed wolves to need any four-footed ones'. Perhaps the King had in mind the MacGregors, who had spent the previous winter and spring raiding the Lowlands, and especially the country around Stirling. Indeed, another notorious raid, led by Rob Roy MacGregor, occurred later in the year, when villages around Kippen were burned, south of the River Forth.

Breadalbane only returned to London on 9 September, preceded by fresh instructions from King William, who now accepted that the Jacobite clans had shown their 'willingness to render themselves in subjection to our authority and laws, humbly asking our pardon for what is past', despite his joke about 'two-footed wolves'. The Privy Council was ordered to draw up a proclamation indemnifying and restoring all rebels who took an oath of allegiance to King William. It was issued on 27 August 1691. Owing to the delays, and the need for the Jacobite chiefs to get the agreement of King James to their submission, putting aside their oath of loyalty to him, the deadline set for their final submission was postponed to the fateful date of 1 January 1692.

Reactions of the Jacobite Chiefs

However, the Jacobite chiefs now began to doubt the good faith of the government in Edinburgh. Soon after the meeting at Achallader, Colonel John Hill had dispatched 400 men from Fort William to arrest Robert Stewart of Appin, after he had detained a soldier involved in a drunken brawl. Along with several other notables, Stewart was transferred to Glasgow on 29 July on the orders of the Privy Council. When they were not released for several weeks, Major Duncan Menzies of Fornooth came to Edinburgh, 'sent by the Generals and other gentlemen in the Highlands, to know whether my Lord Breadalbane had a power to treat with them, and, if he had, why the said treaty was not observed by the council of Scotland'. Indeed, their doubts were justified. The Privy Council had already instructed Archibald Campbell, tenth Earl of Argyll, to call for the immediate surrender of Duart and Cairnaburgh Castles, only four days after issuing the proclamation on 27 August with its deadline of 1 January 1692.

The 'Private Articles'

Moreover, Breadalbane found on his eventual return to the country in early September that a conspiracy was underway to sabotage the agreement he had made at Achallader. As Dalrymple's protégé, he was vulnerable to the machinations of George, fourth Earl of Melville, and more especially his allies. Already, 'Private Articles' were circulating, forged by Sir Aeneas MacPherson of Invereshie, as Paul Hopkins has shown, rather than by Alasdair MacDonald of Glengarry, the usual suspect. A self-confessed Jacobite, MacPherson would prove to be a double-agent. Implicated in plotting against the government, and burdened with debt, he had accepted £100 Scots and the promise of further reward to spy upon Breadalbane's dealings with the Highland chiefs at Achallader.

The agreement made at Achallader had placed Major-General Buchan in an awkward position as the commander-in-chief of the Jacobite forces in Scotland, since it proposed a cessation of arms until King James gave permission for the Highland chiefs to submit. Buchan therefore drew up a list of the terms that he had agreed verbally with Breadalbane, attempting by this means to justify his own actions in abandoning the Jacobite cause, so that he could not later be charged with disloyalty to King James. Seemingly, he then showed the list to his nephew, Lieutenant-Colonel Gordon, who then gave it to Sir Aeneas MacPherson.

The government would only pay MacPherson for his activities if he could obtain written evidence of Breadalbane's treason. He therefore used the document drawn up by Buchan as a basis for forging what became known as the 'Private Articles', passing it off as a formal agreement made in writing at Achallader with Breadalbane. The sting was in its tail. The fifth 'Article' stipulated that Breadalbane should join the Jacobite rebellion with 1,000 men if King William rejected the agreement with the Highland chiefs. Defending himself later from a charge of treason, Breadalbane emphasised it was an absurdly small number of men. If he had so intended to place his head on the block, he would surely have raised every man he had available.

Sir Aeneas MacPherson first showed the 'Private Articles' to Colonel John Hill at Fort William, who had his own reasons for opposing Breadalbane's scheme. Not only had Breadalbane overshadowed his own efforts to bring in the Jacobite clans, but his very position as Governor of the garrison at Fort William was threatened. Moreover, he was close to George MacKenzie, Viscount Tarbat, and through him to the Earl of Melville. Fearing for his position, on which he was utterly dependent, Hill promptly sent a copy of the 'Private Articles' to Sir Thomas Livingston, while another copy came into the hands of the Privy Council.

Meeting with Atholl

Yet it was the avarice and credulity of the Highland chieftains themselves that ultimately destroyed any hope of success. Resenting the favour shown to Breadalbane by King William, his arch-rival John Murray, second Earl and first Marquis of Atholl, invited several Highland chiefs to his house at Tulliemet in early September 1691. Alasdair MacDonald of Glengarry was the only one to appear, and even he at first refused Atholl's overtures. But eventually he gave way after Atholl had perjured himself by alleging that Breadalbane planned to embezzle a third of Glengarry's £1,500. However false, the accusation was enough to make Glengarry switch sides, allying himself with Atholl against Breadalbane in a bitter struggle for political power in the Highlands. Glengarry wrote immediately to Melville's son Raith, declaring that the 'Private Articles' were genuine. Meanwhile, his latent Jacobitism had broken out afresh, perhaps even encouraged by Atholl. An unholy alliance with Sir Aeneas MacPherson would bring the Highland chiefs to the brink of ruin by 1 January 1692, and destroy the MacDonalds of Glencoe.

Duplicity of the Jacobite Chiefs

Breadalbane himself was delayed for much of September in London, attending urgently to family business that otherwise threatened him with financial ruin. It was only on 25 September that he obtained the £12,000 from Treasury funds. Converting the money into bills of exchange, he left London three days later, arriving in Edinburgh on 2 October. Only a day later, the Treaty of Limerick was signed. It brought the war in Ireland to an end, more than a year after the defeat of King James at the battle of the Boyne. Henceforth, the government would harden its attitude to the Jacobite chiefs in the Highlands, secure in the knowledge that reinforcements could now only be sent from France. Yet that very prospect stiffened their resolve to obtain the very best terms for themselves. Apparently quite unaware of the impending danger, the Jacobite chiefs were even now prepared to repudiate the agreement they had made at Achallader, hoping to obtain better terms. Indeed, they had already sworn an oath that none should submit without the agreement of the majority.

Soon afterwards, the Jacobite sympathies of the Highland chiefs were further inflamed by Sir Aeneas MacPherson. He spent nearly a fortnight in mid-October travelling around the Highlands, encouraging them to resist the Achallader settlement. In return, the Highland chiefs, and Glengarry in particular, took to boasting that they had tricked the government into a cessation of arms. But they had only intended it as a ruse, which had prevented the army from attacking them over the summer. They now threatened to resume the Highland War. Glengarry even started to fortify Invergarry.

Yet they were playing a double game, since they were quite prepared to negotiate with Dalrymple's opponents, hoping to obtain even better terms by submitting to the government. Indeed, they seemingly delighted in their apparent cunning in playing off the opposite factions against one another. In particular, Sir John MacLean of Duart received an offer in November which he could not refuse. If he repudiated Breadalbane, he was promised back all his ancestral lands of Mull, Morvern and Coll, now in the hands of Archibald Campbell, tenth Earl of Argyll, who would only keep possession of Tiree. But Duart ignored the weakness of his position, since he had no guarantee that the government would keep its word, once he had submitted. Moreover, Argyll was bitterly opposed to the Achallader agreement, under which Sir John MacLean would gain far less at his own expense, so Argyll was hardly likely to favour an even more generous settlement.

Final Meeting with Breadalbane

In fact, the Highland chiefs were acting in such a reckless and foolhardy manner that it verged on sheer lunacy, even boycotting a meeting with Breadalbane until 10 November, when they finally agreed to meet him. As he wrote in despair: 'They are ruined and abused with lies that children of 10 years [of] age could not believe, and they talk as if they were to give terms & not to receive them, but they will find it a great mistake in [a] few weeks, notwithstanding all My Endeavours to the Contrary.' Indeed, preparations were already being made by Dalrymple for a winter campaign, directed especially against Glengarry.

As autumn turned to winter, Breadalbane eventually met all the chiefs apart from Glengarry for a week at Kilchurn Castle, starting on 10 November. He still had the active support of Sir Ewan Cameron of Lochiel, who 'would fain be at the sillr [silver]'. But even Lochiel was unwilling to act in his own interests against the majority. Others held back, fearing for their own reputations if they were seen to be the first to take the money. The oath of allegiance to King William also troubled them. Breadalbane vainly argued that the Protestant chiefs might accept the money without dishonour, while the Catholic chiefs might take the oath despite their religion. A final meeting on

23 November failed to end the deadlock. After all his efforts over the past six months, Breadalbane could only persuade John Farquharson of Inverey to submit, and the sum of £150 was paid to John Gordon of Brackley.

Role of King James

Underlying everything was the continued failure of King James to give the Jacobite chiefs permission to submit to King William. Only now did Breadalbane mention a fact that he had earlier kept hidden from Dalrymple for reasons of diplomacy: the agreement made at Achallader needed to be ratified by King James. But, afraid of compromising his own position, Breadalbane needed to be circumspect in dispatching messengers to the court of King James at St Germain. Lieutenant-Colonel William Rattray was the first to leave, sailing to France in mid-July in a French privateer. He found on his arrival a mood of resignation prevailing among the Jacobite court at St Germain. Indeed, letters to the Highland chiefs from King James had already been intercepted by the government, revealing 'how little they may expect from France and how easy therefore it will be to appease all disorders in Scotland'.

Yet in mid-September the mood suddenly changed when the French decided to send a fleet to relieve the siege of Limerick, even though it arrived too late to take any action. A letter addressed to Major-General Cannon from King James called upon him 'to endeavour . . . to break this negotiation betwixt the Highlanders and Breadalbane, till the latter end of January or the beginning of February [1692], against what time they should certainly be supplied' with men and arms. The letter came into Breadalbane's hands soon after his return to London, and he promptly suppressed it. Meanwhile, he sent Major Duncan Menzies of Fornooth with an urgent message to King James at St Germain, assuring him that his interests were best served by the Achallader agreement, and urging him to allow the Highland chiefs to submit.

Yet the truth was surely otherwise. Once the Jacobite forces had surrendered in Ireland, the Highlands remained the only centre of Jacobite resistance in the British Isles, apart from the Bass Rock, which held out until 1694. The Jacobites in England were strongly opposed to any further surrender, thinking that their cause would be irredeemably lost. Moreover, the treaty signed at Limerick allowed all the Jacobite forces fighting in Ireland for King James to return to France. As well as the French regiments, perhaps as many as 10,000 Irishmen embarked in what became known as the 'flight of the wild geese'. A plan was now hatched by King James to use these troops against Scotland, if Louis XIV would only agree. It was not until mid-November that the French king ruled against such an expedition, acting on the advice of his ministers. They evidently doubted if King James could succeed in Scotland where he had failed in Ireland.

Another fortnight elapsed before King James was finally persuaded to release the Highland chiefs from his service, and then it was only at the urging of John Drummond, first Earl of Melfort. A warrant to Major-General Buchan was signed on 2 December, allowing the clan chiefs to do whatever was necessary for their safety. Leaving St Germain on 5 December, Duncan Menzies of Fornooth sailed from Dunkirk with the warrant, bound for Scotland, and accompanied by another Jacobite officer, Sir George Barclay. But the warrant was discovered when they were captured by an English warship off Dover on 12 December, and brought to London. Menzies was eventually released on 17 December after taking an oath of allegiance to King William, which Barclay refused. By now, preparations were far advanced for a winter campaign against the Highland clans. Only now realising how implacable the government's attitude had become under Dalrymple, Menzies hurried north, desperately anxious for the Highland chiefs to meet the deadline of 1 January 1692.

Submission of the Jacobite Chiefs

Menzies reached Edinburgh on 21 December, and his home of Cardney House, just east of Dunkeld, on the following day. Utterly exhausted, he now sent off urgent letters with copies of King James's warrant to convince the chiefs that they should submit immediately without any further delay before the deadline finally expired. But he was widely distrusted in Edinburgh as Breadalbane's agent, and the original warrant from King James had been confiscated in London. He could only give his word that his copies were genuine. Indeed, contrary to a long-standing tradition, it seems almost certain that the Highland chiefs, for all their brave talk of resistance, had decided to submit even before they received Menzies's letters. Moreover, they did so individually, thus abandoning the united front they had earlier agreed amongst themselves. They thus threw away the chance of obtaining a remission that might pardon them all.

Sir Ewan Cameron of Lochiel submitted to Colonel John Hill at Fort William on 25 December, making it unlikely that he had received by then a letter dispatched to him by Menzies only three days earlier, given that the country was snow-bound. He then went to Inveraray along with several others to take the oath of allegiance, which was administered by Sir Colin Campbell of Ardkinglas as Sheriff-Depute of Argyll. Meanwhile, Coll MacDonald of Keppoch travelled the length of the Great Glen through the snow to Inverness, where he also took the oath of allegiance. Hill heard by 31 December that

Keppoch had submitted, making it likely that he had also set out before Menzies's letter had even reached him.

Alasdair MacDonald of Glengarry was among the last of the major chiefs to offer his submission, sending a messenger to Colonel John Hill at Fort William on 30 December. Significantly, he attempted to protect Coll MacDonald of Keppoch and Alasdair MacIain of Glencoe from the consequences of his own actions in fanning the flames of rebellion. They were both included under the terms of his submission, partly as he wished to be recognised as the head of Clan Donald. Disastrously as it turned out, their names were not even mentioned in the document signed on Glengarry's behalf, but only in a letter which Hill sent to George, fourth Earl of Melville. Before it arrived, Melville had lost his position as joint Secretary of State for Scotland. Although the document itself was passed to Sir John Dalrymple, he did not receive Hill's letter accompanying it, which would perhaps have lifted the threat to the MacDonalds of Glencoe.

Submission by Glencoe

As Paul Hopkins has argued, Alasdair MacIain of Glencoe played no part in the autumn's intrigues. He certainly did not lead the resistance to Achallader agreement, as historians such as MacAulay have suggested, even though one of his sons did attend the meeting on 23 November which finally rejected Breadalbane's terms. He evidently felt uneasy about his quarrel with Breadalbane at Achallader, while a clansman armed with second sight warned him that he would be murdered by night in his own house, or so tradition has it. He most likely heard rumours of the impending campaign against Glengarry as the deadline of 1 January approached, since Argyll's regiment was even then mustering at Dunstaffnage, after marching out of Stirling on 25 December.

It was only late on 31 December 1691 that MacIain appeared at Fort William to take the oath of allegiance, quite unaware that Colonel John Hill lacked the authority to administer it. Instead, he had to go to Inveraray. Hill gave him a letter for Sir Colin Campbell of Ardkinglas, arguing on his behalf that 'it was good to bring in a lost sheep at any time'. Hurrying south through a snowstorm, he did not even turn aside to visit his own house in Glencoe, so worried was he by the danger he now faced. He only reached Inveraray on 3 January. En route, a detachment of Argyll's regiment under Captain Thomas Drummond had detained him for twenty-four hours, despite the letter he carried from Hill. But when he reached Inveraray, he found that Ardkinglas had gone home. The storm prevented his return to Inveraray for another three days. MacIain thus only took the oath of allegiance on 6 January, nearly a week after the deadline had expired. Only his desperate pleading made Ardkinglas relent in his initial refusal to accept his submission.

Dalrymple's Motives

As Paul Hopkins has stressed, however ugly the truth, the Highland chiefs only flocked to take the indemnity once they became seriously alarmed by the army's march against them. The winter campaign itself had its origins in the previous summer. Indeed, only the prospect of Breadalbane succeeding in buying off the Jacobite chiefs had then prevented the army from marching to put down the Highland chiefs still in rebellion. Afterwards, when Breadalbane could not bring them to honour their agreement at Achallader, Sir John Dalrymple became ever more harsh and uncompromising towards them. He had returned with King William from the Low Countries on 19 October, only to find nothing had been achieved. Soon afterwards, he wrote to Breadalbane, referring to the magnanimous attitude of King William to the rebellious Highlanders: 'There is no Prince alive but ours whose success should not have tempted him to harken . . . to his government there, rather than made the Highlanders examples of his justice by extirpating them . . . And certainly, if there do remain any obstinacy . . . by their ruin, he will rid himself of a suspicious crew.'

Sir John Dalrymple had already written to Breadalbane in such terms, and several more letters followed, couched in increasingly vindictive language. Until recently, exactly how Breadalbane replied to Dalrymple was a matter of surmise, since none of his own letters were thought to survive. However, Paul Hopkins has now unearthed several such letters from the crucial period in November 1691, when Breadalbane was still attempting to cajole the Highland chieftains into submission. They show nothing of the bitter hostility to the Jacobite clans, and to the MacDonalds of Glencoe in particular, which is usually attributed to him, especially in the traditions of Clan Donald. Indeed, his replies to Dalrymple's vitriolic tirades were mild enough in comparison, while hinting he had his own scheme for pacifying the Highlands, based on his raising of a local militia. Nowhere did he attempt to work up Dalrymple's anger against the Jacobite chiefs in general, and the MacDonalds of Glencoe in particular.

Indeed, Dalrymple even accepted Breadalbane's good faith in a letter to him in October:

> All the Papist chieftains stand forfaulted [forfeited] by act of Parliament, and it ought to be made effectual. My Lord, you have done very generously, being a Campbell, to have procured so much for

MacDonalds, who are the inveterate enemies of your clan; and both Glengarry and Keppoch are papists, and that's the only papist clan in the Highlands. Who knows but by God's providence they are permitted to fall into this delusion, that they only may be extirpate, which will vindicate their Majesties' justice, and reduce the Highlands without further severity to the rest?

As Paul Hopkins comments, Dalrymple's words are a 'startling mixture of incitement to clan hatred and bigoted mysticism', directed against the Catholic clans in the Highlands.

Collapse of Dalrymple's Policy

Indeed, Dalrymple was now faced with the collapse of his Highland policy, which had depended on the voluntary submission of the Highland chiefs. They in turn were listening to the seductive offers made by Dalrymple's enemies, who hoped to discredit him in the eyes of King William. By backing Breadalbane in his negotiations with the Jacobite chiefs, which had failed so dismally, Dalrymple had even laid himself open to charges of Jacobitism, at least in the eyes of his enemies. Moreover, Dalrymple's bid for political power was about to reach its climax, as he tried to destroy George, fourth Earl of Melville. All might be lost if he did not act resolutely.

If the chiefs would not submit, there was little alternative but to mount a punitive expedition against them, as even Breadalbane was forced to admit. But 'stiff, peremptory and very proud . . . [Dalrymple] would hear no reasoning when he took up a pique', erupting on occasion into unthinking and ruinous violence. Circumstances would direct it against the MacDonalds of Glencoe. Once Melville was ousted from office in December 1691, Dalrymple had no one else to blame for his own failures of policy as he was now the sole Secretary of State for Scotland. Moreover, King William had his own reasons for wanting the Highlands pacified. Ever since declaring war against Louis XIV of France in May 1689, French aggression had forced him on the defensive. Now, intending to launch a continental offensive in the spring of 1692, he could not afford to have troops tied up guarding the Highlands. By the middle of December, he had agreed to a winter campaign.

Plans for a Winter Campaign

Already, Dalrymple had taken the advice of Lieutenant-Colonel James Hamilton, Colonel John Hill's deputy at Fort William. Writing to him in early December, Dalrymple revealed that 'it may be shortly that we have use of your garrison, for the winter time is the only season in which we are sure the Highlanders cannot escape us, nor carry their wives, bairns and cattle to the hills'. Two days later, he wrote again to Hamilton: 'The MacDonalds will fall in[to] this net. That's the only popish clan in the kingdom, and it will be popular to take a severe course with them. Let me hear from you . . . whether you think that this is the proper season to maul them in the cold long nights.' In fact, there is every reason to believe that the MacDonalds of Glencoe were not Catholics but Episcopalians in their religion, as John Prebble had argued.

The winter campaign envisaged a double thrust along the Great Glen from Inverness and Fort William. Nearly all the regular troops in the north-east were to muster at Inverness, including even contingents from Perth. Strengthened by 500 auxiliaries, among whom were Grants, MacKenzies, Frasers, MacIntoshes, MacPhersons, Rosses and Munros, the force would number nearly 2,000 men. Siege cannon and ammunition were to be shipped north to Inverness. They were then to be hauled forty miles along the Great Glen to Invergarry, since Alasdair MacDonald of Glengarry was at first the intended target as the most belligerent of all the rebellious Highlanders.

Another force of 1,100 men was to muster at Fort William, including 600 men from Hill's regiment as its garrison, reinforced by 500 men from Argyll's regiment, and another 200 from Breadalbane's and Atholl's companies. In issuing his orders, Dalrymple bypassed the Privy Council, whose members might well have restrained his actions. He also sent Sir Thomas Livingston back to Edinburgh as commander-in-chief of the army in Scotland, before he could consult King William in London. The troops were given their marching orders on 15 December, even before Major Menzies of Fornooth left London for Edinburgh, carrying the warrant from King James in St Germain.

Dalrymple's Orders to Livingston

London only learnt that the Highland chiefs had started to submit on 9 January 1692. Apart from Alasdair MacIain of Glencoe, only Alasdair MacDonald of Glengarry was then thought to be holding out, along with Sir John MacLean of Duart, Sir Donald MacDonald, third Baronet of Sleat, Alan MacDonald of Clan Ranald, and Sir Kenneth MacKenzie, fourth Earl of Seaforth, who still had not taken the indemnity. Two days later on 11 January, Dalrymple gave Sir Thomas Livingston his orders:

> You are hereby ordered and authorised to march our troops which are now posted at Inverlochy [Fort William] and Inverness, and to act against these Highland rebels who have not taken the benefit of our

indemnity, by fire and sword and all manner of hostility; to burn their houses, seize or destroy their goods or cattle, plenishings or clothes, and to cut off the men.

Chieftains, tacksmen and other leading clansmen should all be allowed to surrender, but then only as prisoners of war, safe from death but not from forfeiture. The common clansmen, if they took the oath of allegiance and surrendered their arms, would escape retribution, provided they took a new tack (or lease) of their lands from the government. Dalrymple had King William authorise the orders to Livingston by putting his name at their head, and countersigning them at their foot. It is often thought Dalrymple did this deliberately to cast blame upon King William for any subsequent atrocity, allowing him to excuse his own actions. In fact, it was apparently just the start of a new policy of authorisation.

Actions of the Privy Council

More sinister was the covering letter that Dalrymple wrote to Livingston. Even as Dalrymple put pen to paper, Archibald Campbell, tenth Earl of Argyll, had learnt that MacIain was not listed among the Highland chiefs who had submitted at Inveraray by 1 January 1692. Colin Campbell of Dressalch, acting as the clerk to Sir Colin Campbell of Ardkinglas, Sheriff-Depute of Argyll, had brought the certificate that MacIain had signed at Inveraray to Edinburgh, but Sir Gilbert Elliot and David Moncrieff as the Clerks to the Privy Council had refused to accept it from him. Colin Campbell then made informal soundings among the Privy Councillors, who advised him that 'it would neither be safe to Ardkinglas, nor profitable to Glencoe, to give in the certificate' without a warrant from King William. The Clerks to the Council promptly expunged MacIain's name from the list, and neither did they present the Privy Council with Hill's letter of explanation which MacIain had given to Ardkinglas at Inveraray, nor Ardkinglas's own letter, addressed directly to the Privy Council.

Indeed, by accepting MacIain's submission after the deadline of 1 January 1692, Ardkinglas had laid himself open to charges of treason in treating with a rebel. But his own feelings were clear enough. Writing to Colonel John Hill, he rejoiced that

> I endeavoured to receive the great lost sheep Glencoe [somewhat exaggerating his importance], and he has undertaken to bring in all his friends and followers as the Privy Council shall order. I am sending to Edinburgh that Glencoe, though he was mistaken in coming to you to take the oath of allegiance, might yet be welcome. Take care that he

and his friends and followers do not suffer till the King and Council's pleasure be known.

Dalrymple was not so accommodating. He finished his letter to Livingston on 11 January with the chilling words: 'Just now, my Lord Argyll tells me that Glencoe has not taken the oaths, at which I rejoice. It's a great work of charity to be exact in rooting out that damnable sept, the worst in all the Highlands.'

Dalrymple's elation ought to have doused by 16 January, when he learnt of Glengarry's proposal to submit, made to Colonel John Hill at Fort William, which had included MacIain under its terms. Moreover, Dalrymple was now aware of the grave difficulties faced by a winter campaign in the Highlands. The shipping of a siege train from London had come to nothing, while the transport of cannon and other necessities from Edinburgh Castle was not yet in place. He now issued 'Additional Instructions' to Sir Thomas Livingston, and again King William authorised them with his double signature. They gave Livingston the authority to 'give Glengarry the assurance of the entire indemnity for life and fortune, upon the delivering of his house and arms, and taking the oath of allegiance'. Indeed, Livingston was even granted the discretion to offer better terms to Glengarry, if he deemed it necessary. But Dalrymple was still determined to make an example: 'If MacIain of Glencoe, and that tribe, can be well separated from the rest, it will be a proper vindication of the public justice to extirpate that sept of thieves.'

Livingston's Orders to Hamilton

Livingston had received his revised instructions from Dalrymple by 23 January, when he wrote to Lieutenant-Colonel James Hamilton at Fort William:

> I understand that the Laird of Glencoe, coming after the prefixed time, was not admitted to take the oath, which is very good news here . . . So Sir, here is a fair occasion for you to show that your garrison serves some use; and seeing that the orders are so positive from Court for me not [to] spare any of them that have not timely come in, as you may [see] by the orders I sent your Colonel [John Hill], I desire you would begin with Glencoe, and spare nothing which belongs to him, but do not trouble the Government with prisoners.

By writing directly to Hamilton, Livingston had bypassed Colonel John Hill as his commanding officer, 'knowing how slow he was in the execution of such things'. Moreover, he had issued the formal orders that allowed the Glencoe Massacre to take place.

In fact, Livingston knew of MacIain's attempts to submit, making him the 'great, unsung villain of the affair', in the words of Paul Hopkins. He neither took the matter up with Dalrymple, nor altered his instructions, although he had sufficient authority to do so. Meanwhile, Dalrymple in London still apparently did not know at the very end of January that MacIain had belatedly submitted to the government, more than three weeks earlier. Although his first sentence might suggest otherwise, he wrote to Livingston on 30 January:

> I am glad that Glencoe did not come in within the time prescribed. I hope what's done there may be in earnest, since the rest are not in the condition to draw together to help. I think to harry their cattle or burn their houses is but to render them desperate, lawless men, to rob their neighbours; but I believe you will be satisfied it were of great advantage to the nation [that] that thieving tribe were rooted out and cut off. It must be done quietly, otherwise they will make shift for both men and cattle.

Role of Colonel John Hill

Dalrymple wrote at the same time to Colonel John Hill in similar terms: 'Pray when any thing concerning Glencoe is resolved, let it be secret and sudden, otherwise the men will shift you, and better not meddle with them than not do it to purpose.' His letter had perhaps not even arrived from London before the massacre was underway, delayed on its journey north by the atrocious weather. Hill was under even greater an obligation than Livingston to prevent what was planned against Glencoe from taking place, knowing it to be a 'nasty, dirty thing'. Indeed, Hill had ignored Livingston's earlier orders to march against the rebels, justifying his lack of action by reporting to him on 14 January that Lochaber was just as peaceful as the streets of London or Edinburgh. Indeed, he told Livingston that he was even then negotiating the submission of Alasdair MacDonald of Glengarry.

Glengarry's original offer to submit had safeguarded MacIain of Glencoe, and indeed Hill now had authority from Dalrymple to administer the oath of allegiance. After lengthy negotiations, Glengarry arrived at Fort William on 4 February to do so. Even at this late stage, Hill should surely have insisted that Alasdair MacIain of Glencoe came under the terms of submission, originally proposed by Glengarry's emissary on 30 December. But he depended on his pay as Governor of Fort William to marry off his daughters, and he evidently feared that he might be ousted by Hamilton as his second-in-command, leaving him destitute. He did nothing.

Quartering upon Glencoe

Meanwhile, Lieutenant-Colonel James Hamilton acted on the orders he had received from Livingston. He determined to use Argyll's regiment, commanded by Major Robert Duncanson, which had marched from Stirling on 25 December. The soldiers had already quartered themselves on Glencoe in early January, where 'they were civilly and kindly entertained', before continuing their march north to Fort William. Openly contemptuous of Hill's leniency, it was perhaps Hamilton who now suggested the strategem that made the Glencoe Massacre notorious in the annals of Highland history, or so Paul Hopkins has suggested. Two companies of Argyll's regiment would be quartered upon Glencoe to disarm any suspicion, and then be ordered to fall upon their hosts, against all the traditional tenets of Highland hospitality, and indeed of civilised behaviour.

Accordingly, Argyll's regiment marched south from Fort William on 1 February 1692 to camp on the north side of the ferry at Ballachulish. Two companies of 120 men, commanded by Captain Robert Campbell of Glenlyon and Captain Thomas Drummond, then continued towards Glencoe. The rest remained at Ballachulish under Major Robert Duncanson. The soldiers advancing towards Glencoe were met by a party of twenty armed men under Alasdair MacIain's elder son Iain. One of Glenlyon's officers showed them an order from Colonel John Hill, authorising the two companies to quarter themselves upon the MacDonalds. Indeed, they were entitled to free quarter under the law, since Alasdair MacIain of Glencoe owed arrears in taxes to the government. Glenlyon and two other officers assured Iain MacIain that they meant no harm, and indeed it seems they knew nothing of what was planned, as Duncanson's orders to Glenlyon would later show. The soldiers were made welcome to Glencoe, and the days passed in courteous entertainment. Reportedly, the weather was unusually mild.

Glenlyon's Company

Tradition has it that the Glencoe Massacre of 13 February 1692 was perpetrated by the Campbells against a sept of Clan Donald as their hereditary enemies. Yet as John Prebble has shown from the muster-rolls of Argyll's regiment, dating from only a few months earlier, few of the common soldiers were Campbells. Indeed, apart from their captain, there were then only nine Campbells in Glenlyon's company, and even fewer in Drummond's company. There were two other officers, and a single corporal. To judge by the names of the rank and file of both companies, Gaelic-speaking Highlanders were even a minority compared with Lowlanders, although there were more in

Glenlyon's company than in Drummond's. The truth seems to be that they were merely regular soldiers of the standing army, who simply obeyed orders in what followed.

The same stricture applies to Captain Robert Campbell of Glenlyon. He is often seen as the villain of the whole affair, 'whose guilt remains as black as ever', at least in the traditions of Clan Donald. But as Paul Hopkins has stressed, Glenlyon did not obviously bear any special animosity towards MacIain of Glencoe, despite the latter's role in the infamous raid against his lands in 1689. Nor was he financially dependent on Sir John Campbell of Glenorchy, first Earl of Breadalbane, as so often thought. Indeed, it was Breadalbane who finally brought Glenlyon to the brink of financial ruin, even though he had brought his downfall upon himself. A drunkard and a gambler, he had fallen prey in the 1670s to the territorial machinations of John Murray, Marquis of Atholl. But it was Breadalbane's advice in December 1691 that finally made Glenlyon spurn Atholl's offer of £30,000 Scots to settle his debts. By then, he had lost his lands of Glenlyon to the Marquis of Atholl, partly with the connivance of Archibald Campbell, tenth Earl of Argyll, forcing him to rely upon his captain's pay in Argyll's regiment as his only source of income.

Chain of Command

Glenlyon received his orders from Major Robert Duncanson at Ballachulish late on 12 February. They had been relayed to him by Lieutenant-Colonel James Hamilton, who had received his own orders from Colonel John Hill at Fort William as follows: 'You are with four hundred of my regiment, and the four hundred of my Lord Argyll's regiment, under the command of Major Duncanson, to march straight to Glencoe, and there put into due execution the orders you have received from the Commander-in-Chief.' By such oblique wording, Hill perhaps hoped to evade responsibility for his own part in the Massacre.

Hill had delayed issuing such an order until he had received a reply to his own report of 14 January. By stressing that peace was now restored to Lochaber, he evidently hoped that Livingston would countermand his earlier orders. Indeed, he had even mentioned that Argyll's regiment and the Independent Companies had quartered themselves upon 'rebel' lands without any trouble. But it was Dalrymple, not Livingston, who wrote back on 30 January, saying, 'Let it be secret and sudden', even if there is no evidence to show that his letter had arrived at Fort William by 12 February. Moreover, Hill had reported on 14 January that any attack on Glencoe must wait until the negotiations were complete for the surrender of Invergarry. But

Glengarry had come to terms on 12 February, when he agreed to surrender Invergarry, so that Hill now had no excuse left to delay the attack upon Glencoe. All his procrastination had achieved was a delay which made the Glencoe Massacre appear even worse in retrospect.

Lieutenant-Colonel Hamilton now issued his own orders to Duncanson camped at Ballachulish:

> Pursuant to the Commander-in-Chief and my Colonel's orders to me for putting in execution the service against the rebels of Glencoe, wherein you with that party of the Earl of Argyll's regiment now under your command are to be concerned. You are therefore to order your affairs so that you be at the several posts assigned to you by seven of the clock tomorrow morning, being Saturday, and fall in action with them, at which time I will endeavour to be with the party from this place at the post appointed them. It will be necessary the avenues [that is, the passes] minded by Lieutenant Campbell, on the south side [of Glencoe], be secured, that the old fox and none of his cubs get away. The orders are that none be spared, nor the government troubled with prisoners, which is all I have to say to you until then.

Evidently, Duncanson was already party to the plan of attack. He not only held a commission in Argyll's regiment as a lifelong follower of the family, but he also acted as Procurator-Fiscal in Argyll's courts at Inveraray. He was surely turning a blind eye to the illegality of what was proposed.

Glenlyon's Orders

Duncanson now wrote out his own orders to Glenlyon:

> You are hereby ordered to fall upon the rebels, the MacDonalds of Glencoe, and to put all to the sword under seventy. You are to have a special care that the old fox and his sons do upon no account escape your hands. You are to secure all the avenues that no man escape. This you are to put in execution at five of the clock precisely; and by that time, or very shortly after it, I'll strive to be at you with a stronger party. If I do not come to you by five, you are not to tarry for me, but to fall on. This is by the King's special command, for the good and safety of the country, that these miscreants be cut off root and branch. See that this be put in execution without feud or favour, else you may expect to be dealt with as one not true to King nor Government, nor a man fit to carry Commission in the King's service. Expecting you will not fail in the fulfilling hereof, as you love yourself.

The language used is so heavy with threats against Glenlyon should he disobey Duncanson's orders that he surely knew nothing of what was planned until then. He was threatened with the loss of his commission, on which he depended for his very livelihood, and perhaps he even feared being charged with treason. Glenlyon did not have the strength of character to refuse his orders, unlike two of his officers, who broke their swords rather than take part in the massacre. They were arrested, and afterwards sent as prisoners to Glasgow. Moreover, if we are to believe the sworn testimony of James Campbell, a sentinel in Glenlyon's company, he 'knew nothing of the design of killing the Glencoe men till the morning that the slaughter was committed, at which time the companies were drawn out and got orders from Glenlyon and our other officers to shoot and kill all the countrymen we met with'. On learning of their orders, tradition has it that several soldiers warned their hosts of the danger facing them, so allowing them to escape the massacre.

Glenlyon on the other hand apparently had no qualms in concealing the true nature of his orders. When questioned by Iain MacIain as he mustered his own men before dawn, he simply replied that he was ordered with Drummond to march against some of Glengarry's men. It is said that Glenlyon even assured the chief's elder son Iain that, had he intended any ill to Glencoe, he would surely have warned his own niece, who was married to Iain's brother Alasdair Og. Only afterwards was Glenlyon ridden with guilt at what he had done, angrily justifying himself with maudlin self-pity in the taverns of Edinburgh that he had only followed the King's orders. The soldiers under his command at Glencoe were more revealing when they said afterwards: 'MacIain hangs about Glenlyon night and day. You may see Glencoe in his face.'

The Glencoe Massacre

It was still dark at 5 o'clock and a blizzard was raging when the massacre began. Among the very first victims was Alasdair MacIain of Glencoe. He was surprised while still asleep in his house at Polvieg at the foot of the glen by a party of soldiers under Lieutenant Lindsay and Ensign Lundie. Greeted courteously by the old chieftain on entering his house, they shot him in the back at point-blank range as he struggled to dress, and then murdered two of his servants. His wife was stripped naked, and the rings taken from her fingers. Afterwards, Lindsay's party started up the glen to catch MacIain's sons. However, warned by their servants, they escaped into the hills. Fleeing up the slopes of Meall Mhor, they began to rally the survivors. Another party under a sergeant went to Achnacone, where it surprised Iain MacDonald of

Achtriachtan, shooting him dead along with four others. Although wounded, his brother Angus MacDonald of Achnacone escaped, as did his three companions. By now, the sound of musket-fire had alerted the other settlements in the glen, allowing nearly all their inhabitants to escape.

Meanwhile, Glenlyon saw to the execution of nine men at Inverrigan, where he had quartered himself. Sworn testimony suggests that they were bound and gagged, presumably to prevent them from raising the alarm before 5 o'clock. According to the Glencoe bard, Glenlyon stood aside watching as they were shot on his orders. Afterwards, he gave them the *coup de grâce* with a bayonet. Among the dead was his erstwhile host, MacDonald of Inverrigan, who was found to have a protection from Colonel John Hill at Fort William in his pocket. Yet Glenlyon attempted to spare a youth and a boy, who were only then killed on Drummond's orders. But even at Inverrigan, several men escaped, while the soldiers killed a sixty-year-old woman and a child. The houses were all put to the flames, causing the death of eighty-year-old Archibald MacDonald at Leacantuim, who was burnt alive.

Only after the slaughter was finished did Major Robert Duncanson appear on the scene with his own forces. On receiving his own orders from Lieutenant-Colonel James Hamilton on the previous day, he had crossed the ferry at Ballachulish with 300 men. He then returned the ferry-boats to the northern shore of Loch Leven as instructed by Hamilton, placing a guard over them. It seems unlikely this would have taken him all night, despite the treacherous nature of the tidal race at the mouth of Loch Leven, or even the deteriorating weather, so delaying his arrival in Glencoe. Moreover, his orders to Glenlyon specified 5 o'clock for the start of the massacre, whereas his own orders from Hamilton gave 7 o'clock. It seems he deliberately avoided arriving in Glencoe while the massacre was still underway. By advancing the time to 5 o'clock, he made sure that Glenlyon would instead shoulder any blame for the atrocity.

After sending his orders to Duncanson on 12 February, Hamilton had waited until darkness fell before marching out of Fort William with several companies of Hill's regiment. Had he left any earlier, spies keeping watch on the garrison from the hillsides would no doubt have observed his movements, allowing the alert to be raised. He marched up the valley of the River Kiachnish behind Fort William towards Kinlochleven, following the later line of the military road. But after only a few miles, his forces were forced to bivouac as the blizzard struck in all its fury. He only reached Kinlochleven long after the alarm was raised on the morning of 13 February. Most of the inhabitants had already fled into the hills, apart from one old man, who was killed by a search party.

It is often thought that Hamilton then crossed towards the head of Glencoe by way of the Devil's Staircase. However, as Paul Hopkins comments, there is no evidence that he attempted by this means to prevent the escape of any survivors up Glencoe towards the Moor of Rannoch. Neither were the 'avenues' sealed off, as Hamilton had ordered. In fact, Duncanson's orders to Glenlyon did not even mention that they consisted of the valleys to the south of Glencoe, so he may not even have known what was meant. Nearly all the survivors escaped over these passes into Appin. But they had

> nothing left them, and their houses being burnt, and not one house nearer than six miles; and to get thither they were to pass over mountains, wreaths of snow, in a vehement storm . . . poor stripped children and women, some with child, and some giving suck, wrestling against a storm in mountains and heaps of snow, and at length overcome, and give over, and fall down and die miserably.

MacIain's widow was among those who died of exposure, but how many others died with her was never revealed by the clan.

All the government forces returned to Fort William on the same day as the massacre, driving before them 400 cows, as well as sheep and goats, or so Colonel John Hill reported to the Government. Later at the enquiry in 1695, the MacDonalds of Glencoe put their losses at 1500 cows and 500 horses. According to Hill, thirty-eight MacDonalds were killed, including their chieftain. But given that Glencoe was home to 200 or so families, perhaps amounting to 1,000 men, women and children, the casualties were far lighter than the government might have expected. Both MacIain's sons escaped, and the thirty-eight dead did not even match the 100 or so fighting men who would normally have obeyed MacIain's call to arms. Hill admitted as much in writing to Dalrymple, taking credit for the massacre by saying that he 'valued himself on it as his deed, and regretted the storm that hindered all to be cut off'. Yet he evidently had second thoughts, urging for the next six months that the Glencoe men might be allowed to submit. They eventually did so in August 1692, when Sir Colin Campbell of Ardkinglas gave security for their good behaviour, acting on behalf of Archibald Campbell, tenth Earl of Argyll.

Aftermath of the Massacre

By then, nearly all the other Highland chieftains and their kinsmen still in rebellion against King William had also submitted, among whom were Robert Stewart of Appin, Alan MacDonald of Clan Ranald, Alastair MacDonald of Glengarry, and Sir Donald MacDonald, third Baronet of Sleat. Not long afterwards, the castles of Duart, Cairnaburgh, Tioram, Eilean Donnan, Invergarry, Inverness, Ruthven, Blair, and Finlarig were occupied by garrisons from Hill's regiment at Fort William. As James Johnston of Warriston, newly appointed as Joint Secretary of State for Scotland to balance the power of Dalrymple, commented: 'Thus it is evident [that] severity is the way to deal with them though the manner here has been odd.' Dalrymple for his part remained quite unmoved on first hearing of the massacre, simply saying: 'All I regret is, that any of the sept got away . . . there is necessity to prosecute them to the utmost.' Indeed, when Colonel John Hill urged mercy upon the survivors, Dalrymple replied that it was unfortunate that the massacre 'was neither so full nor so fair' in its execution, 'so necessary [was it] to rid the country of thieving'.

Indeed, when the full horror of the massacre was revealed, Dalrymple still showed no remorse, merely saying: 'It's truth that the affair of Glencoe was very ill executed, but 'tis strange to me that means so much regret for such a sept of thieves.' He wrote to Hill saying that his Majesty was only willing to give remissions to such 'irreclaimable thieves' for their past behaviour if they agreed to go abroad to Ireland or the Plantations. However, he did allow Hill 'if you think fit to take Caution from them to live honestly and peacefully anywhere except Glencoe, but that quarter is so advantageous to their thieving trade, that his Majesty does not allow any of them to return to Glencoe . . . If after all we come to slack and yield, the works that's well begun will come to ill effect.'

Reaction to the Massacre

It was not long before the news of the Glencoe Massacre reached London, where John Campbell, first Earl of Breadalbane, first heard a report from his agent Colin Campbell of Carwhin on 27 February 1692. Shocked and dismayed, and fearful of retaliation against his own territories, he protested at once against the 'precipitate action at Glencoe . . . [which was] contrary to what I have ventured my life and fortune to have completed in the Highlands, and that is peace'. But King William was about to embark for the Low Countries, and Breadalbane's protestations at Court made little impression. Indeed, hardly anyone was prepared to believe his account of the massacre, and especially that the MacDonalds of Glencoe had been slaughtered in cold blood by government troops after spending the previous fortnight enjoying their hospitality. Dalrymple's secrecy had paid off for the time being.

Meanwhile, Argyll's regiment had marched south from Fort William to Edinburgh, where Jacobite spies learnt of the massacre from Robert Campbell of Glenlyon. Indeed, he openly showed his orders from Major Robert

Duncanson to anyone who cared to read them, and copies soon found their way around all the coffee-houses and taverns of the Scottish capital. Soon afterwards, the news had reached Paris, and a brief but fairly accurate report of the massacre appeared in the French official *Gazette* of 12 April. It only omitted to mention what was perhaps the most reprehensible aspect of the whole affair in the quartering of government troops upon their intended victims.

However, not until September 1692 did the full story of the Glencoe Massacre become widely known, when Sir James Montgomerie of Skelmorlie published his Jacobite pamphlet *Great Britain's Just Complaint*. But he lacked credibility, since he had been involved in the Parliamentary intrigues that had followed the 'Glorious Revolution' of 1689 in Scotland. It was instead the Reverend Charles Leslie, an Anglican cleric in London with Jacobite sympathies, and the son of the Bishop of Raphoe, who published the first devastating account of the massacre, early in 1693. He had much earlier learnt what had happened from his informants in Edinburgh, after receiving copies of Duncanson's and Hamilton's orders. These he incorporated into 'A Letter from a Gentleman in Edinburgh', which laid the ultimate blame for the Glencoe Massacre upon the orders countersigned by King William himself.

By now, incredulity had given way to outrage. Certain that her husband was innocent of such dishonourable conduct, Queen Mary pressed Secretary Johnston for an official inquiry. It was put secretly in train, 'to enquire thoroughly into the business of Glencoe and then to resolve what in prudence is to be done for the vindicating the honour of our government'. Parliament in Edinburgh threatened to withhold any supply of money for waging the war against France unless an inquiry was ordered, but it came to nothing. Yet Secretary Johnston was slowly piecing together the evidence that would bring down Sir John Dalrymple of Stair as Joint Secretary of State for Scotland, while protecting the reputation of King William.

Commission of Enquiry

When the Scots Parliament next met in 1695, it demanded a full and independent enquiry into the massacre, only to be informed that King William had appointed his own commission 'whereby the honour and justice of the nation might be vindicated'. Lord John Murray, eldest son of the second Earl and Marquis of Atholl, was the moving spirit behind the Commission of Enquiry, determined to destroy the influence of John Campbell, first Earl of Breadalbane, and Sir John Dalrymple of Stair. Indeed, Breadalbane was charged with treason when the Commission received evidence of the 'Private

Articles' he had supposedly signed at Achallader. Held captive in Edinburgh
Castle, it was not until December 1695 that he finally received a remission
from King William for a crime he had not committed.

Meanwhile, the Commission of Enquiry had examined the chief partici-
pants in the tragedy, among whom were Sir Thomas Livingston, Colonel
John Hill, and Sir Colin Campbell of Ardkinglas, as well as the two Clerks to
the Privy Council. Lieutenant-Colonel James Hamilton was summoned from
Ireland to appear before the enquiry, and he answered the call, but Captain
Robert Campbell of Glenlyon, Major Robert Duncanson and Captain Thomas
Drummond were all on active service in the Low Countries, and could not
appear. Only James Campbell, a common soldier in Glenlyon's company,
gave evidence, as he was then stationed at Stirling Castle. However, protection was given to Iain and Alasdair MacIain, sons of the murdered chief of
Glencoe, and eight of their followers to appear, which they duly did.

The evidence given to the Commission was therefore only a partial account
of the massacre. Most importantly, Colonel John Hill failed to mention that
Livingston as commander-in-chief of the army in Scotland already knew of
Alasdair MacIain's submission when he issued his fatal orders of 23 January
1692 to Lieutenant-Colonel Hamilton. Even so, the Commission knew of
this order from Hamilton's evidence, which included copies of all the rele-
vant orders he had received from Livingston. It chose to ignore such a damaging piece of evidence in order to protect Livingston as the commander-in-
chief of the King's forces in Scotland. Instead, it accepted his excuse that he
did not realise that troops were to be quartered upon Glencoe as completely vindicating him from any blame whatsoever.

When the Commission of Enquiry reported to Parliament on 24 June
1695, it caused a sensation. Naturally enough, it shielded King William from
all responsibility, arguing with a degree of sophistry that the instructions he
had signed and countersigned for Dalrymple did not really mean what they
said in the matter of 'extirpation'. Neither did it pronounce judgement
upon the officers and men responsible for the massacre. Parliament took a
more robust attitude, voting that since the King's instructions had allowed
for mercy to all who submitted, even after the deadline of 1 January 1692,
the killings were murder under the law. It then proceeded to cross-examine
the chief witnesses. Sir Thomas Livingston and Colonel John Hill had
appeared before Parliament, only to be judged innocent of any wrongdoing
after rigorous questioning. Lieutenant-Colonel James Hamilton fled to
Flanders rather than face such a damning interrogation. By 10 July,
Parliament had drawn up its own *Address to the King touching the Murder of
the Glencoe Men*.

Address to the King

The document was far more critical than the anodyne report drawn up by the Commission of Enquiry. Even so, it still exonerated King William from any responsibility, and excused Sir Thomas Livingston and Colonel John Hill for their part in 'the slaughter of Glencoe men under trust'. Instead, it laid the blame squarely upon the shoulders of Sir John Dalrymple of Stair, whose letters and orders were 'the only warrant and cause of this barbarous murder'. Utterly discredited, he was soon afterwards dismissed from his position as Joint Secretary of State for Scotland. Demands were made to King William that Captains Robert Campbell of Glenlyon, Robert Duncanson, and Thomas Drummond, and their immediate subordinates, should be prosecuted for murder. But although King William was willing to send them back to Scotland, it could not be done. Argyll's regiment had surrendered to the French at Dixemunde, and they were all now in enemy hands.

In Retrospect

As Paul Hopkins has demonstrated, the political circumstances behind the Glencoe Massacre are extraordinarily complex. Apart from John Campbell of Glenorchy, first Earl of Breadalbane, and King James's exiled minister John Drummond, first Earl of Melfort, who persuaded the King to release his followers from their oath of allegiance, few of the major figures involved can escape some degree of censure. Even the Jacobite chiefs played their part in bringing destruction upon Glencoe by their utter folly of playing Breadalbane off against his enemies, who cynically offered them better terms, when they should have gladly accepted the settlement made with him at Achallader. According to Sir Ewan Cameron of Lochiel, they learnt of the Glencoe Massacre with 'inexpressible surprise and amazement'. Thereafter, they 'resolved to trust their safety to their swords, seeing they could depend no more upon Articles, Oaths or Proclamations'.

Chapter Fourteen

AN UNEASY PEACE

The Glencoe Massacre marked the very end of the Highland War. Even so, hostilities might well have flared up again had a French attempt at invasion succeeded a few months later. Doubtless, the Jacobite chiefs would happily have abandoned their solemn oaths of allegiance to King William without a qualm. Indeed, Alan MacDonald, Captain of Clan Ranald, and Sir John MacLean of Duart appeared soon afterwards at the court of King James at St Germain. Major-Generals Thomas Buchan and Alexander Cannon had landed at Le Havre with their officers in mid-April 1692, after receiving passes to leave Scotland. Before their departure, they had even been entertained by their opposite numbers to dinner in Edinburgh as a courtesy due to their military rank. On arriving in France, they found that King James and his first minister John Drummond, first Earl of Melfort, had persuaded Louis XIV to mount a large-scale invasion across the English Channel as a diversionary tactic.

Already, James VII had joined his Jacobite forces stationed around Cherbourg in Normandy. They consisted mostly of Irish troops, strengthened by a French contingent. Major-General Thomas Buchan was ordered to march north from Cherbourg with his officers to Dunkirk, where most of the exiled Scots had gathered, ready to set sail for Scotland. They planned to land at Dunnottar Castle, just south of Stonehaven, or farther north at Slains Castle in Buchan. But the whole enterprise foundered when the French navy was decisively defeated in a running battle over several days with the Anglo-Dutch fleet. It ended with the destruction of fifteen French men-of-war off Cherbourg and Cap de la Hague. France never again regained control of the high seas, thus effectively isolating King James on the far side of the Channel for the rest of his life as the 'King across the Water'.

Jacobite Plot against King William

Yet the reluctance of Louis XIV to support King James directly in any more adventures to regain his throne did not greatly benefit King William. The death of his consort Queen Mary at the very end of 1694 removed any real legitimacy to his rule as the son-in-law of King James. Indeed, widespread discontent had mounted in England over the 'indisguised rule of a foreigner', who seemed incapable of winning the war with France, or even of competent generalship. King James began to receive protestations of loyalty from some very unlikely sources. The time thus seemed ripe for yet another attempt to remove King William from the throne.

Early in 1696, a plot was even hatched in London for his assassination as the prelude to a Jacobite rising in England. If it proved successful, an invasion would follow from France. There can be little doubt the plotters were deadly serious, apparently able to command 2,000 horse, but they were betrayed to the government by a traitor in their ranks. King William took full advantage of his revelations, proclaiming from Kensington Palace that 'wicked and traitorous persons, [have] entered into a horrid and detestable conspiracy, to assassinate and murder his Majesty's sacred person'. There was an immediate surge of popular support for the beleaguered King.

Then in 1697 came the Treaty of Ryswyck, which ended the Nine Years' War with France. Louis XIV was forced to recognise William of Orange as the rightful king of Great Britain, ruling over the country 'by the grace of God'. So ended any hope for the time being that France might help King James or his successors to regain his throne. Curiously enough, James had already thrown away any chance of the Stuart dynasty returning to rule over the three kingdoms of England, Scotland and Ireland in the person of his only son James Edward Stuart. King William had let it be known that he was prepared to recognise James's son as his lawful heir, provided he was allowed to rule in peace until his own death. King James spurned such a proposal amid strong criticism from his own family, fearful that his young son would be brought up as a Protestant.

When King James again refused to consider such a proposal after the death in 1700 of Princess Anne's last surviving son, the English Parliament passed the Act of Settlement of 1701. It guaranteed the succession to the Electress of Hanover and her issue should King William or Princess Anne die without any heirs, as looked increasingly likely. Moreover, it required the sovereign to be an Anglican. No such act was passed by Parliament in Scotland. Offended that it had not even been consulted in such a matter of constitutional importance, it passed the Act of Security in 1703, which left the succession open upon the death of Queen Anne.

Whatever King William's standing in England, it was far worse in Scotland. His attempts at religious toleration after 1689 found no favour with the strict Presbyterians of the Scottish Lowlands, who had brought him to power, nor with the Episcopalians north of the Tay, whom he had failed to protect from the 'rabbling of the curates' in 1688, and who still regarded their oath of allegiance to King James as sacrosanct. William's reputation was further damaged by his entanglement with Dalrymple in the Glencoe Massacre, which even strict Presbyterians found abhorrent. King William recognised as much when he 'expressed his horror at the Glencoe business, [saying] that it had been very near his heart, [and] that it had brought reproach upon him, not only over Scotland and England, but all the world over'. Then, attempting to restore his reputation with the Scots, he put in train the policy which led directly to the Darien disaster. Indeed, legislation enabling the formation of a trading company, and allowing it to establish a colony overseas, was approved in the very same session of the Scots Parliament which established a Commission of Enquiry into the Glencoe Massacre in 1695. Perhaps a quarter of the liquid assets of Scotland were invested in this scheme for a Scots colony on the Darien peninsula of Central America. Two disastrous expeditions were mounted, the first almost completely overwhelmed by the combined assault of the hostile native people and of fever, and the second forced into submission by the Spanish.

'Seven Ill Years'

The failure of the Darien scheme made King William and his government deeply unpopular in Scotland. But the seething discontent was further aggravated by the seven years of dearth which only ended with his death in 1702. Tradition long afterwards in Glenlyon and Argyll still recalled the King's demise 'almost as the breaking of an evil spell; the cows began to yield plentiful milk again, and the sun's rays once more gave warmth'. The harvest had first failed in 1695, after long years of plenty, and then in 1696 and 1698, when a series of wet summers and long winters made famine endemic throughout the country. Indeed, untold thousands starved to death, and the suffering was still a vivid memory among the people nearly 100 years later, when the First Statistical Account of Scotland was compiled. The Highlands in particular were badly affected, and meal had even to be imported from Ireland to feed the Hanoverian garrison at Fort William.

The misery of the common people was made much worse during these years of famine by a massive increase in cattle-raiding and robbery, which the newly-revived Highland Justiciary struggled to contain. Its task was made much more difficult by the incorporation into the regular army of the five Independent Companies that had been raised during the course of 1691 and 1692. While the garrison at Fort William remained under the command of Colonel John Hill until 1698, various detachments of the regular army were posted throughout the Highlands south of the Great Glen to protect the Lowlands from Highland reivers, or cattle raiders. But the Justiciary was itself corrupt, more intent on exacting heavy damages to benefit its own members than convicting and punishing the law-breakers themselves, even if many were hanged.

Yet this disorder hardly ever involved entire clans being caught up in feuds with one another, as had happened in the sixteenth century. Although the skirmish at Mulroy in 1688 is described as the last of the clan battles, it did not end the long-lasting feud of the MacIntoshes of Clan Chattan with the MacDonalds of Keppoch. After the end of the Highland War, Coll MacDonald of Keppoch returned to live on his estates under the protection of Colonel John Hill at Fort William. Then, after Hill was replaced by Brigadier Maitland, the 1688 commission of fire and sword was renewed against Keppoch. It gave Lachlan MacIntosh of Torcastle official sanction to invade his lands with a sizeable party of clansmen, who however were soon evicted by Coll MacDonald and his own clansmen, reinforced by the MacDonalds of Glengarry. Coll defied the government for two years, until an agreement was eventually forged in 1700 between the two protagonists, which brought their ancient feud to a conclusion. It gave Keppoch a lease of the disputed lands for the next nineteen years, which then passed to his descendants. However, he had to wait until 1703 until he finally obtained a pardon for the loss of life at the battle of Mulroy.

Simon Fraser, Lord Lovat

The era of clan feuds would most likely have ended once and for all in this agreement if the maverick figure of Simon Fraser of Beaufort had not then appeared on the scene. He was the grandson of the seventh Lord Fraser of Lovat, which gave his own father a claim to the title when Hugh Fraser, ninth Lord Lovat, died in 1696. He left his nine-year-old daughter Amelia Fraser of Lovat to succeed him, born of his marriage with Lady Amelia Murray, daughter of John Murray, second Earl and first Marquis of Atholl.

Simon Fraser now embarked on a long and nefarious career of duplicity and double-dealing, which was perhaps made possible by his extraordinary capacity for self-delusion. He first attempted to kidnap the young heiress of Lovat, perhaps intending to marry her, but the plot foundered, and Amelia Fraser was taken to safety with her mother's family at Dunkeld. It was then decided that she should marry the eldest son of William Fraser, second Lord Saltoun, when she came of age. However, when her prospective father-in-law came north in October 1697 to discuss the marriage, he was seized by Simon Fraser and his accomplices. Threatened with hanging, he only obtained his freedom by repudiating his son's proposed marriage with the young heiress.

Meanwhile, Simon Fraser had kidnapped her mother, whom he now determined to marry himself, so giving him control over the Lovat estates as the husband of Lovat's widow, Lady Amelia Murray. Against her heart-rending protests, an armed body of Frasers burst into her room, and forced her into marriage, which was then consummated by Simon Fraser in an act of rape. Despite his wrongdoing, however, troops ordered north from Atholl by the Privy Council found their efforts thwarted by the widespread support given to Simon Fraser by his clansmen. Indeed, eight months of long-drawn-out campaigning to capture him ended ignominiously after yet another expedition marched north from Atholl under Lord James Murray.

Only 300 strong, they invaded the Fraser heartland of Stratherrick on 15 June 1698, only to find themselves confronted next morning by Simon Fraser at the head of his own forces. Fifty men mounted a frontal attack on the Atholl encampment, while he directed a flanking movement with the main body of his forces. The tactic succeeded, and the Atholl forces started to flee in a confused rout towards the narrow defile of Aultnagorrie, only to find their escape cut off. Rather than stand and fight, they sued for peace. Humiliated, the Atholl men left the field to Simon Fraser after what was a bloodless victory.

Prosecutions against Simon Fraser

Their prestige shattered, the only course left to the Atholl family was a private prosecution against Simon Fraser, whom they charged with treason, rebellion, rape and kidnapping. Although Lady Amelia Murray would not testify against him, he was found guilty, and his estates forfeited. Yet he still had powerful friends in high places. Archibald Campbell, tenth Earl of Argyll, interceded on his behalf with King William, who eventually granted him a pardon on 22 August 1700. Then, John Murray, second Earl and first Marquis of Atholl, mounted another prosecution against him for the rape and 'hamesucken' (or domestic attack) on Lady Amelia Murray. Simon Fraser appeared openly in Edinburgh, only to flee south beyond the jurisdiction of the Scottish courts just before the trial opened.

The final blow came with the death of King William on 8 March 1702, and the accession of Queen Anne. Although Simon Fraser tried to ingratiate himself with King William's successor, he failed miserably, since Lord John Murray, who succeeded his father as the third Earl and second Marquis of Atholl in 1703, was close to the new Queen. Indeed, any such expectations were utterly extinguished upon Simon Fraser's arrival in London, where he learnt that Amelia Fraser, the young heiress of Lovat, had married Alexander

MacKenzie of Frazerdale. He was the nephew of Sir George MacKenzie of Tarbat, who was himself appointed as Secretary of State for Scotland in November 1702, and afterwards ennobled as the first Earl of Cromartie in 1703. Many of Simon's erstwhile friends in the Highlands promptly changed sides as the balance of power shifted decisively in favour of the Murrays, Earls of Atholl.

Later Career of Simon Fraser

Disappointed in London, Simon Fraser reluctantly turned instead to the Jacobite Court at St Germain, where James VII had died the previous year, leaving his thirteen-year-old son James Edward Stuart to succeed him as the 'Old Pretender'. Simon Fraser now played the role of a double agent to such effect that the French government placed him in preventive detention. He languished in prison for nearly a decade before making a dramatic escape to lead the Fraser resistance to the Jacobite cause during the 1715 rebellion. After its suppression, he was pardoned for all his crimes by the Hanoverian government of George I, and eventually restored to his estates as Simon Fraser, eleventh Lord Lovat.

By then, Simon Fraser had abandoned the use of force in his drive for power and influence in the Highlands. Instead, he now engaged his Machiavellian talents in the corrupt and bitter intrigues of local politics. Indeed, as Bruce Lenman has remarked, political infighting had taken the place of the bloody feuds once waged between the Highland clans, and indeed the anachronistic and power-hungry figure of Simon Fraser was a prime exemplar of such a radical change. But while the Highland magnates and their minions jostled for supremacy amongst themselves, the Campbells, Dukes of Argyll after 1701, still remained supreme, just as they had done a century earlier.

The Protestant Succession

Even though the chiefs of the Highland clans had abandoned the use of force in feuding with one another, they could still call upon their clansmen to rise in arms, as indeed happened during the 1715 and 1745 rebellions in support of the Stuart dynasty. After William of Orange died in 1702, he was succeeded by Queen Anne as the elder half-sister of James Edward Stuart, the 'Old Pretender'. The last Stuart monarch to rule over Great Britain, her reign ended in 1714 with the accession of George I, Elector of Hanover, under the 1701 Act of Settlement. The hereditary right of the Stuart dynasty to rule over Great Britain was rejected in favour of a Protestant succession.

The next half-century saw a bitter rift between the Whig and Tory parties in England. The right of George I to the throne was upheld by the Whigs, who enjoyed a monopoly of power until 1760. Opposing them were the Tories, but their adherence to the Church of England and its doctrines made them wary of offering their whole-hearted support to the 'Old Pretender'. Only in Scotland were the Jacobite clans of the Scottish Highlands, supported by nearly all the country lying to the north of the River Tay, prepared to take up arms in support of James Edward Stuart. What they shared in common was a deep-seated aversion to the Presbyterian regime that had finally triumphed after 1689 over the Episcopalian Church in the Lowlands of Scotland, south of the River Tay.

Divisions within Clan Society

Yet despite the wide support given to the Stuart cause by the Jacobite clans, deep divisions had already opened up within Highland society by the end of the seventeenth century. Not only were the Jacobite and Whig clans separated from one another across a religious and political divide, but the very nature of clanship had begun to dissolve under economic and social pressures. The Statutes of Iona at the start of the century had ushered in an era when the clan chiefs and their leading gentry fell increasingly under the influence of Lowland society. This was only partly a consequence of the annual visits made by the chiefs to appear before the Privy Council in Edinburgh, interrupted as they were between 1638 and 1660. Just as significant was the requirement laid upon them to educate their eldest sons, or daughters if they had no sons, who were sent away to Lowland schools in order to learn English. This was compounded by a steady decline in the traditional practice of fostering the chief's children on his clansmen, so that they were no longer brought up within the clan.

But while the clan chiefs became ever more cosmopolitan in their outlook, and economic necessity forced them to extract increasing amounts of revenue from their estates, their clansmen were left unaffected by such influences. Another hundred years would pass before the chiefs of the Highland clans finally abandoned any sense of patriarchal responsibility to their clansmen, who still retained their traditional customs and values, rooted in the past. Meanwhile, the chiefs of the Jacobite clans were just as committed as their clansmen to restoring the Stuart dynasty. It was only in the aftermath of the Jacobite defeat at Culloden that social and economic changes began in earnest in the Scottish Highlands. Even then, it was more than fifty years before they finally came to fruition in the Highland Clearances at the turn of the nineteenth century.

BIBLIOGRAPHY

The political and ecclesiastical history of Scotland has received much attention for the period under review, and it is only possible to mention the more important of the secondary sources used in writing the present book. The historical background is well-covered by such scholarly works as G. Donaldson, *Scotland: James V to James VII* (Edinburgh, 1965), and W. Ferguson, *Scotland: 1689 to the Present* (Edinburgh, 1968). More recent but less detailed accounts are given by R. Mitchison, *Lordship to Patronage: Scotland 1603-1745* (Edinburgh, 1983), and by M. Lynch, *Scotland: A New History* (London, 1992). The first three books give very detailed bibliographies, although they obviously do not take account of the more recent work. The political background to Anglo-Scottish relations after the Union of the Crowns in 1603 is discussed by W. Ferguson, *Scotland's Relations with England to 1707* (Edinburgh, 1977) and K. M. Brown, *Kingdom or Province: Scotland and the Regal Union 1603-1715* (London, 1992).

The nature of Highland society, and how it evolved during the seventeenth century (and afterwards) under the impact of external events, is discussed very fully by A. I. MacInnes, *Clanship, Commerce and the House of Stuart 1603-1788* (East Linton, 1996), drawing on a number of his earlier articles. See also J. M. Hill, *Celtic Warfare 1595-1763* (Edinburgh, 1986) for an account of Highland warfare, and the tactics used in the more important battles, and R. A. MacLeod, *The Battle of Auldearn, 9 May 1645* in L. MacLean (ed.), *The Seventeenth Century in the Highlands* (Inverness, 1986).

The revolutionary years in Scotland after the signing of the National Covenant in 1638 are covered by D. Stevenson, *The Scottish Revolution, 1637-1644: The Triumph of the Covenanters* (New York, 1973), and *Revolution and Counter-Revolution in Scotland 1644-1651* (London, 1977), while the Irish dimension is discussed by the same author in his *Scottish Covenanters and Irish Confederates* (Belfast, 1981). The role played in these events by the Highland clans, and especially the MacDonalds of Antrim under Alasdair MacDonald, is fully explored by D. Stevenson, *Alasdair macColla and the Highland Problem in the Seventeenth Century* (Edinburgh, 1980), which also covers the period up to the Revolution of 1689. This work supplements the many biographies of James Graham, Marquis of Montrose, among which E. J. Cowan, *Montrose: For Covenant and King* (London, 1977) can be recommended as being the most objective study of this inherently romantic figure. The part played by the Highland clans in Glencairn's Rebellion is best covered by F. D. Dow, *Cromwellian*

Scotland 1650–1660 (Edinburgh, 1979). See also J. D. Grainger, *Cromwell against the Scots: The Last Anglo-Scottish War 1650–1652* (East Lothian, 1997).

The post-Restoration history of the Highlands is dissected in great detail by P. Hopkins, *Glencoe and the End of the Highland War* (Edinburgh, 1986), which covers the period up to the Union of 1707, although concentrating on the 1689 Revolution and its immediate aftermath; see also J. R. Elder, *The Highland Host of 1678* (Aberdeen, 1914). Various works on Jacobitism deal with this period as an introduction to the events of the eighteenth century, including C. Petrie, *The Jacobite Movement* (3rd Edition, London, 1959) and B. Lenman, *The Jacobite Risings in Britain 1689–1749* (London, 1980) and *The Jacobite Clans of the Great Glen 1650–1784* (London, 1984). The central figure of this period is John Graham of Claverhouse, Viscount Dundee, who has attracted much romantic interest, just like Montrose before him. See D. Stevenson, *Montrose and Dundee*, in L. MacLean (ed.), *The Seventeenth Century in the Highlands* (Inverness, 1986) for a comparison between the two men. M. Linklater & C. Hesketh, *For King and Conscience: John Graham of Claverhouse, Viscount Dundee 1648–1689* (London, 1989) supplements the earlier biography by C. S. Terry under the same title (London, 1905).

The work by P. Hopkins already cited provides the most detailed and objective account of the Glencoe Massacre of 1692, placing it in its historical context. See also the article by the same author *Glencoe: An English Historian on a Very Scottish Subject* in L. MacLean (ed.), *The Seventeenth Century in the Highlands* (Inverness, 1986), which provides a useful summary. Among the popular accounts, the vigorous but emotive study by J. Prebble, *Glencoe: The Story of the Massacre* (Harmondsworth, 1968) cannot be ignored for its useful summary of the documentary evidence, but D. J. MacDonald, *Slaughter under Trust* (London, 1965) gives a more balanced account.

INDEX